1993

THE CINDERELLA COMPLEX
Women's Hidden Fear of Independence

by Colette Dowling

SUMMIT BOOKS
New York

Acknowledgments

I'd like to thank Lowell Miller and my children, Gabrielle, Conor, and Rachel, for understanding—and accepting—the closed door to my study. During my final year of work on this book the door was often closed until midnight. Complaints from my loved ones were few and far between, and they were never unfair.

Early in the research I was exhilarated by my work in two particular libraries and decided that too often libraries get overlooked in writers' acknowledgments. Therefore, I want to express my thanks to the Princeton University Library and the New York Academy of Medicine Library. The Princeton University Library has open stacks (open even to the public), which is a joy to the serious researcher. While the stacks are not open to the public at the New York Academy of Medicine Library, its librarians are competent, fast, and unfailingly courteous to any and all who come to them for help.

The women I interviewed were wonderfully open and eager to help. Theirs, I think, is the most important "material" in this book. Information I found in libraries and by interviewing social scientists provided the armature for *The Cinderella Complex*; the women's stories provided its flesh and blood.

My ongoing relationship with my own psychoanalyst, Steven Breskin, is undoubtedly central to the development of my own independence as well as to my urgent wish to communicate what I have learned to other women. He was the first adult in my life—including teachers, employers, and mates—who did not support my dependency.

Lowell Miller was the second such adult in my life. (It is interesting, now, to look back on the fact that it was not a woman or women who refused to support my dependent ways; it was two men.)

Paul Bresnick, of Summit, took pains with the manuscript in its final stages, and through his efforts the book was made better.

In addition to being the sort of literary agent few writers are lucky enough to have, Ellen Levine has been a continuing inspiration to me through her own growing independence.

Finally, I want to thank my daughter Gabrielle, who began typing the manuscript when she was sixteen, finished typing it—three drafts later—at seventeen, and who was so sensitive to the material, and so intelligent, she was able, by draft three, to make valuable editorial suggestions.

For my mother and father

Contents

Contents

The Telltale Dream . . . Wrenching Away from the Dependency Trap . . . Springing Free.

THE
CINDERELLA
COMPLEX

CHAPTER I

The Wish to Be Saved

I am lying alone on the third floor of our house with a bad bout of the flu, trying to keep my illness from the others. The room feels large and cold, and as the hours pass, strangely inhospitable. I begin to remember myself as a little girl, small, vulnerable, helpless. By the time night falls I am utterly miserable, not so sick with flu as with anxiety. "What am I doing here, so solitary, so unattached, so . . . floating?" I ask myself. How strange to be so disturbed, cut off from family, from my busy, demanding life . . . disconnected . . .

A break occurs in this stream of thought, and I recognize: I am *always* alone. Here, without warning, is the truth I spend so much energy avoiding. I hate being alone. I'd like to live, marsupialized, within the skin of another. More than air and energy and life itself, what I want is to be safe, warm, taken care of. This, I'm startled to find, is nothing new. It has been there, a part of me, for a long time.

Since that day spent in bed I've learned that there are other women like me, thousands upon thousands of us who grew up in a certain way and who have not been able to face up to the adult reality that we, alone, are responsible for ourselves. We may pay lip service to this idea, but inside, we do not accept it. Everything about the way we were raised told us we would be *part* of someone else—that we would be protected, supported, buoyed up by wedded happiness until the day we died.

One by one, of course, we discovered—each in our own way—the lie in the promise. But it was not until the Seventies that a cultural shift occurred, and women were looked at, thought about, and treated differently than ever before. Different things were expected of us. Now we were being told that our old girlhood dreams were weak and ignoble, and that there were better things to want: money, power, and that most elusive of conditions, freedom. The ability to choose what it was we would *do* with our lives, and how we would think, and what we would deem important. Freedom is better than security, we were told; security cripples.

But freedom, we soon found out, frightens. It presents us with possibilities we may not feel equipped to deal with: promotions, responsibility, the chance to travel alone, without men to lead the way, the chance to make friends on our own. All kinds of opportunities opened up to women very fast, but with that freedom came new demands: that we grow up and stop hiding behind the patronage of someone we choose to think of as "stronger"; that we begin making decisions based on our own values—not our husbands', or parents', or some teacher's. Freedom demands that we become authentic, true to ourselves. And this is where it gets difficult, suddenly; when we can no longer get by as a "good wife," or a "good daughter," or a "good student." Likely as not, when we begin the process of separating from our authority figures to stand on our own two feet, we discover that the values we thought were our own are not. They belong to others—vivid persons from a vivid, all-encompassing past. Eventually a moment of truth arrives: "I don't really *have* any convictions. I don't really *know* what I believe."

This can be a frightening time. Everything we once felt so sure of seems to crumble like the soft loam of a landslide, leaving us unsure of everything—and terrified. This dizzying loss of old and outmoded support structures—beliefs we don't even *believe* anymore—can mark the beginning of true freedom. But the fact that it's frightening can send us scurrying into retreat—back to where it's safe, familiar, known.

Why, when we have the chance to move ahead, do we tend to retreat? Because women are not used to confronting fear and going beyond it. We've been encouraged to avoid anything that scares us, taught from the time we were very young to do only those things which allow us to feel comfortable and secure. *In fact we were not trained for freedom at all, but for its categorical opposite—dependency.*

Childhood is where the problem begins. Childhood, when we were safe, when everything was taken care of and Mommy and Daddy could be counted on whenever we needed them. Nighttime was not nightmares, or insomnia, or the haunting, obsessive litany of what we'd done wrong that day, or might have done better; it was lying in bed listening to the wind caress the trees until sleep came. There is, I have learned, a connection between our feminine urge toward domesticity and those lulling reveries about childhood which seem to lie just beneath the surface of consciousness. It has to do with dependency: the need to lean on someone—the need, going back to infancy, to be nurtured and cared for and kept from harm's way. Those needs stay with us into adulthood, clamoring for fulfillment right alongside our need to be self-sufficient. Up to a point, dependency needs are quite normal, for men as well as for women. But women, as we shall see, have been encouraged since they were children to be dependent to an unhealthy degree. Any woman who looks within knows that she was never trained to feel comfortable with the idea of taking care of herself, standing up for herself, asserting herself. At best she may have played the game of independence, inwardly envying the boys (and later the men) because they seemed so *naturally* self-sufficient.

It is not nature that bestows this self-sufficiency on men; it's training. Males are educated for independence from the day they are born. Just as systematically, females are taught that they have an out —that someday, in some way, they are going to be saved. That is the fairy tale, the life-message we have introjected as if with mother's milk. We may venture out on our own for a while. We may go away to school, work, travel; we may even make good money, but underneath it all there is a *finite* quality to our feelings about independence. Only hang on long enough, the childhood story goes, and someday someone will come along to rescue you from the anxiety of authentic living. (The only savior the *boy* learns about is himself.)

I should tell you right now that my introduction to the subject of women's dependency came through personal experience, and *that,* only recently. For a long time I had fooled myself and everyone else with a sophisticated brand of pseudo independence—a facade I'd been building for years to hide my own (frightening) wish to be taken care of. The disguise was so convincing I might have gone on believing in it indefinitely if something hadn't happened that produced a disturbing crack in the thin veneer of my self-sufficiency.

It happened when I was thirty-five. A series of events led me to the discovery of feelings I had never known I had, hidden feelings of incompetence so threatening to my security I'd do virtually anything to manipulate someone else into taking over when things got rough —when the demands of life began to feel suspiciously like real, consequential, grown-up demands and not just a precocious girl's forays into a world where games can get you by. Several years out of a marriage, with three young children of whom I was the sole support, I was about to enter a period of remarkable growth. Oddly, its painfulness was redoubled by the fact that I had fallen in love.

The Collapse of Ambition

In 1975, I left New York and what had been a solitary four-year struggle to make ends meet as a single parent, and came with my children to live in a small rural village in the Hudson Valley, ninety miles north of Manhattan. I had met a man who seemed a perfect companion: stable, intelligent, marvelously funny. We'd found ourselves a big, inviting house to rent, with land and gardens and fruit trees. In my new euphoria I believed that writing for a living would be no more difficult in the hamlet of Rhinebeck than it had been in the metropolis of Manhattan. *What I hadn't anticipated—what I'd had no way of foreseeing—was the startling collapse of ambition that would occur as soon as I began sharing my home with a man again.*

Without any conscious decision or even recognition of the fact, my life changed dramatically. I used to spend several hours a day writing, developing a career I'd begun ten years earlier. In Rhinebeck, my time seemed to be taken up in homemaking—*blissful* homemaking. After years of throwing together frozen TV dinners because I'd been too busy to do more, I started cooking again. Within six months of our move to the country I gained ten pounds. "Healthy," I told myself, strangely pleased with the change. "We are all more relaxed." I took to wearing plaid shirts and rather large overalls. I was always lingering a bit—tending a flower pot, building a fire, looking out a window. Time seemed to fly. The gorgeous days of fall slipped into winter and I wore boots and a down jacket and chopped wood. At night I slept dreamlessly, though I often found it hard to get up in the morning. There was nothing compelling me to rise.

My new retreat into housewifery should have been more disconcerting than it was—a sign. After all, I was capable of supporting myself; had, in fact, been doing so for four years. Ah, but it had been four years of peril; four years of feeling I was pitted against challenge, day after day. The children's father was too ill to be able to help with their support, so I was accustomed to paying the bills. But I had been scared most of the time—scared of the inexplicably rising costs, scared of the landlord, scared that I would not be able to hang in there and keep us all afloat month after month, year after year. The fact that I profoundly doubted my own competence seemed neither strange nor unusual to me. Didn't most "single mothers" feel this way?

So the move to the country that glorious, winesap fall had felt like a tremendous reprieve from what I had thought of, rather vaguely, as "my struggle." Fortune had brought me back to another kind of place, an inner space not unlike the one I had inhabited as a child—a world of cherry pies and bed quilts and freshly ironed summer dresses. Now I had land and flowers, a big house with plenty of rooms, small, comfy window seats, nooks and crannies. Feeling safe for the first time in years, I set about concocting the tranquil domicile that lingers as a kind of "cover memory" of the most positive aspects of one's childhood. I made a nest, insulating it with the softest bits of fluff and cotton I could find.

And then I hid in it.

At night I prepared big meals and spread them proudly on the groaning board of a real dining room. During the days, I laundered, raked, and mulched. At night, playing helpmate, I would type Lowell's manuscripts for him. Oddly, though I'd been writing professionally for ten years, it felt as if typing for someone else was what I ought to be doing. It felt . . . *right* (by which, I now know, I meant comfortable and secure). For months it went like that. Lowell would be writing and making phone calls and conducting business at his big desk in front of the fire in the living room. I would be filling my time stapling decorator sheets to the walls of my daughter's bedroom. Every so often I'd go to my desk and try my hand at some work, riffling through papers, thinking in a distracted, preoccupied way. Frustrated, occasionally, because I seemed to have lost my touch for getting writing assignments, I thought, "My luck will change."

It was not a question of luck at all. Without my being aware of it on a conscious level, my idea of myself had shifted drastically. So had my expectations of Lowell. In my mind he had become the provider. Me? I was resting up from those years of having struggled, half against my will, to be responsible for myself. What liberated woman would ever have imagined this? The moment the opportunity to lean on someone presented itself I stopped moving forward—came, in fact, to a dead halt. I no longer made decisions, never went anywhere, didn't even see friends. In six months I had not met one deadline, or gone through the friction involved in working out a contract with a publisher. Without so much as a fare-thee-well I had slipped back into woman's traditional role of helper. Putterer. Amanuensis. Typist of someone else's dreams.

The Flight from Stress

As Simone de Beauvoir observed so astutely over a quarter of a century ago, women accept the submissive role "to avoid the strain involved in undertaking an authentic existence." This flight-from-stress had become my hidden goal. I had slipped back—*lounged* back, really, as into a large tub of tepid water—because it was easier. Because tending flower beds and organizing shopping and being a good—and provided-for—"partner" is less anxiety-provoking than being out there in the adult world fending for oneself.

Lowell, however, was not what you would call a "traditional male," for he did not support this regression of mine. Unhappy with what looked, increasingly, as if it might develop into a permanent inequity (he would pay the bills, I would make the beds), he finally confronted me: I was bringing no money into the household, he said. Financially, he was providing everything—supporting me and my three kids as well as himself—and I didn't even seem to be *aware* of the inequity. It hurt him, he said, that I seemed content to sit back and take advantage of his willingness to help out.

The suggestion that I was not living up to my end of the bargain was utterly enraging. No man had ever made this suggestion before. Didn't he appreciate all that I was doing for him, the lovely *home* that I was making, the wonderful cakes and pies? Didn't he notice that when friends came to visit for the weekend it was *I* who changed the sheets and cleaned the guest bathroom?

It was true that in our domestic arrangement I was the one who was doing most of the "shit work." It was also true that I had arrogated that role to myself, never even bringing it up for discussion. Inwardly, I *wanted* to be doing the shit work. Shit work is infinitely safe. In exchange for doing it you can exact an unconscionable return—the woman's pound of flesh.

When Lowell and I decided to move out of New York City and share a house in the country, our agreement had been that each of us would continue to be self-supporting. How easy it had been to let that slide! I'd been going through the motions of proposing ideas for magazine articles and books, but I was neither emotionally nor intellectually engaged in what I was doing. It's amazing to me now, when I look back on it, that I didn't actually experience the *need* to be working. Instead, I was enjoying the luxury of being a wife. And Lowell was saying, "It isn't fair." And I was thinking, "*What* isn't fair? Isn't this the way it's supposed to be?"

An inner transformation had occurred. When I was alone and the need to provide for myself and the children had been clear and unambiguous, I had managed to pursue my career and at least *behave* independently; once Lowell moved in, however, I regressed. It wasn't long before I was thinking and feeling and acting just as dependent as I had been during the nine years of my marriage. That recognition was the real kicker. Here I'd left my marriage because I had begun to hate my own feelings of dependency. My life had felt stifled and restrictive and so I'd burst free. Now I was acting it out all over again —only with gardens and woodsmoke and a big old house to sweeten the deal.

The economics of the situation was crucial to what was going on. Because I'd dropped on Lowell's shoulders the responsibility for paying all our bills, I was serenely oblivious of how much anxiety can be involved in earning a living. It's difficult for me to admit this now, but my attitude toward Lowell had been exploitative. I didn't *want* the stress involved in being responsible for my own welfare. On a gut level I also had this idea that it was appropriate for Lowell to work harder and take more risks simply because he was a man. I believed this, at least in part, because it made my life easier to believe it. That's where the exploitative part comes in. (I also felt that there was something not entirely "feminine" about a real, heave-ho commitment to work—as if I would become something less than womanly if I were to really get out there and dig and haul in the common market of the adult economy. Eventually, this small, basically unexamined suspicion would turn out to play a surprising role in my struggles with independence.)

Once a month Lowell would take out his checkbook and mail off payments for the rent, electricity, water, and fuel. He also maintained the car. (For that matter, he also *drove* the car; I was phobic about driving and couldn't/wouldn't learn how.) To show my Girl Scout cooperation with Lowell's efforts I bought nothing at all that was personal—no clothing, no makeup, no bits of bric-a-brac for the house. I prided myself on making decorative arrangements of old objects I found in the cellar. My distance from having anything to do with money allowed me to remain cut off in a very fundamental way. "I'd *like* to work," I kept insisting to Lowell. "If someone would just give me an assignment I'd be *happy* to write. Is it *my* fault if my ideas for pieces haven't worked out?"

"What if you keep on like this?" he finally asked, after a year had gone by. "What then?"

The "What then?" was chilling. To me it seemed proof that his care was not very deep, or else why would he be pushing me like that? Why would he be saying, in effect, "I don't *want* to take care of you"?

The fact that I wasn't doing any work of my own began to corrode my self-esteem. It took only three or four months of being a *hausfrau*, that year, for the fact of my dependency to become blatantly apparent. My blissful domesticity seemed to vanish overnight, and depression set in like ice on a winter lake. I felt, for one thing, that I had very few rights. Without even being aware of it I had begun asking Lowell's *permission* for things. Would he mind if I stayed late in Manhattan to visit a friend? Did he think we could go out to the movies on Friday night?

Inevitably, deference developed: I started to feel intimidated by the man who was supporting me. It was then that I began finding fault with him, carping and criticizing him for the most ridiculous things. It was a sure sign of how powerless I felt.[1] I resented Lowell's greater ease with people, the smoothness with which he could swing back and forth in a give-and-take, whether socially or in business. He seemed to have so much confidence. I found myself hating him for it.

While Lowell was forging ahead, with success appearing to await him at every turn, I was feeling depressed and anxious and having trouble sleeping at night. I found myself craving sex—or more precisely, craving the contact sex provided—for I'd begun to have doubts about my sexual desirability, along with everything else. If anything, that period could be described as one in which my entire self-image was in jeopardy. I had lost confidence in my abilities as a writer, as a person able to make her way in the world, and—inevitably—as a lover.

Perhaps most symptomatic of all, I no longer had the perspective that permits one to see the humor in things. A vicious cycle had set in; I'd lost respect for myself and couldn't seem to set things straight. I was cowering and thought the only way I could stand up straight was if someone *lifted* me up. I wanted Lowell to recognize the bind I was in and empathize. I wanted him to see that all the facts of my life had militated against the possibility of my ever really standing alone. I believed this deeply; I felt as if I had been crippled in a way that would affect me for the rest of my life.

"Look at how I was raised," I'd say. "No one ever *expected* me to have to earn a living year after year, so how could I ever expect it of myself?"

"No good," he'd reply. "You earned a living fine for all those years you were alone. Now that you're living with me, you're paralyzed. There's something wrong with that."

The worst part of all this was that intellectually he and I were committed to the same idea. We *both* believed women ought to be responsible for themselves. How had I regressed so rapidly? What had happened to me?

A great many things, I was to learn. Many of the difficulties I was having had gotten a firm start in childhood. Yet I couldn't leave it at that. Somehow, through all the pain and confusion, I recognized that I had a hand in keeping things the way they were, that there were certain distortions in the way I was seeing things, and that *I was actively maintaining those distortions.*

Certainly my relationship with Lowell—with him the provider and me the protected—was distorted. So was my relationship with myself. For some reason I was seeing myself as less strong than Lowell, less competent. *That* was a major distortion, and consequent upon it was another: Lowell "should" take care of me. Yes, that is the twisted morality of the weak (or those who persist in seeing themselves as such). It is the "burden" of the strong to drag us along; if they don't, we keep telling them, in so many ways, we won't survive.

Once I recognized that I was *angry* at the idea of having to resume responsibility for my life, that I was angry at Lowell for "making" me—I felt ashamed and profoundly isolated. How could it be that I was so frightened of independence? So far as feminism was concerned, I was back in the Ice Age. *Whom else did I know, whom had I ever met, who preferred—as I seemed to prefer—being dependent to being independent?*

At those times in my life when I have been most frightened and alone, I have felt the urge to write. This time was no exception. Maybe if I described the experience I would find that there were others out there like me. The idea that I might be an anomaly, some kind of helpless, dependent misfit, alone in the world, was horrifying.

Not until I'd gone through the process of writing about these feelings did I summon the nerve to discuss them with anyone. I had never heard anyone else talk about such an experience. A sympathetic editor I knew disappointed me when I described the article I'd written and he didn't seem to get what I was talking about. I took a big breath and plunged in again, for in truth, if this guy didn't get it, I didn't know what editor would. As I began recounting to him what had happened to me since I'd moved to the country, and why I wanted to write about it, the feeling came over me again. I knew something, I had learned something, and I was not going to allow it to become diminished the moment someone else didn't *see*. I told the man that what I had experienced and learned was *important*. It was important for women in particular to hear about the problems I had been wrestling with. My experience exposed something real and something crippling—a psychological phenomenon with which the women's movement had not yet come to grips: the piece I wanted him to publish described what it is women *get* from maintaining their dependent positions in life—the goodies; what psychiatrists call the "secondary gains."

"I think I'm beginning to see what you're talking about," the editor said.

Other Women, Same Conflicts

A month later, *New York* magazine published my essay as a cover story with the title "Beyond Liberation: Confessions of a Dependent Woman." The mail that came flooding in was a revelation. I've received mail from readers over the years, but never, it seemed, had I struck a chord like this one. "You are not alone," they would say, before plunging, with palpable relief, into their own personal experiences.

Each day the mailman would arrive with a new batch of letters and I would take them out back to a little gazebo behind the house to read them and cry. The letters were from women all over the country—women in their early twenties, women in their late fifties, professional women, would-be professional women, ex-professional women. All were suffering from the same anxieties, struggling toward their independence with graduate work, good jobs, better salaries—and yet, underneath, resentment. Resentment, anger, and a terrible, painful confusion, a sense of, *"Is this what it's really supposed to feel like?"*

"After years working on a newspaper I decided to quit and try free-lancing," a woman from Santa Monica wrote. "My husband's income was there to fall back on, wasn't it?" A good move, at least potentially, but one that stirred up terrific conflict toward the man she was inwardly leaning on in order to be able to make her move in the first place. Since that time, she wrote, "I've vacillated between total guilt about my reliance on him and internal fury that he would question that right."[2]

The conflict between wanting to stand alone and wanting to hang on to someone "just in case" (the ace-up-the-sleeve motivation some people have for going to church on Sunday) creates a chronic, energy-sapping ambivalence. At thirty-four, a woman who described herself as having "bailed out of two marriages," raised two children,

and then gone back to law school found she was still hopelessly
enmeshed "in this neurotic double bind of hating and fearing both
dependence and independence simultaneously." After working for
the government for a brief time, she decided to set up her own law
practice and went into business with a male partner who'd had no
more experience than she. The difference in the way each handled
the new responsibility was, she noted, remarkable. "From the beginning there was simply never any question in his mind that he would
do whatever had to be done. No such clarity for me. Whenever I
have to face a new situation I still weigh charging ahead against running and hiding behind some man who'll protect me. What an easy
trap to fall into, and how lazy and dependent I become whenever
there's someone around I can use in this way."

The wish to be saved. We may not always recognize it as clearly as
this woman did, but it exists within us all, emerging when we least
expect it, permeating our dreams, dampening our ambitions. It's possible that woman's wish to be saved goes back to the days of cave living, when man's greater physical strength was needed to protect
mothers and children from the wild. But such a wish is no longer appropriate or constructive. We do not *need* to be saved.

Women today are caught in the crossfire between old and radically new social ideas, but the truth is, we cannot fall back on the
old "role" anymore. It's not functional; it's not a true option. We
may *think* it is; we may *want* it to be; but it isn't. The prince has
vanished. The caveman has grown smaller and weaker. In fact, in
terms of what is required for survival in the modern world, he is really no stronger, or smarter, or more courageous than we are.

He *is*, however, more experienced.

Facing Up: The Crumbling of False Autonomy

These omens have existed for a long time, licking beneath the surface of things like the fires of volcanic change. Social transformation
doesn't occur overnight. The "role" of women was in the process of
change long before women's liberation had a name. The fact that
things for women were no longer secure, that the road ahead was not
at all clear may have frightened us, as we were growing up, more

than we knew. Something was happening, but neither we nor our parents knew what it was. Unwittingly, most parents were less than successful in raising their daughters in the Forties and Fifties because they hadn't an inkling of what they were raising their daughters *for*. Certainly, they weren't raising them for independence.

Like a lot of girls, by the time I reached high school I'd developed a deceptive sort of feistiness—what a psychiatrist would quickly recognize as a "counterphobic facade": a shell one constructs to hide fear and insecurity. Something was sabotaging my confidence, some inner confusion about who I was, and what I wanted to do with my life, and what girls were about in general. But all of this went unrecognized. I was flip to my teachers, sarcastic to the boys. In college I learned to argue with sophistication, to debate. Years later, after the Human Development Movement came along, I became the star of my encounter group—tough, confrontational, almost swaggering in my "honesty." A black ex-con in our group, a man who'd grown up in the streets and spent seventeen years in jail, told me that even *he* was afraid of me during our encounter group's sessions. Ah, what power; what thrilling autonomy.

When the time came for this "autonomy" to crumble, people who knew me were surprised. "But you've always been so strong," they said, "so together."

When, after my marriage broke up, I became phobic—barely able to walk down the street for attacks of anxiety and vertigo—the sudden change from my old apparent strength confused me as well. *Wasn't* I tough? *Wasn't* I "together"? *Hadn't* I kept my family intact, almost single-handedly, for years?

Looking back, it seems clear to me now that there were signs all along the way of a potentially devastating lack of congruence between my inner self and my outer self. The outer self was "strong" and "independent" (especially as compared with how women were *supposed* to be). The inner self was stricken with doubt; self-effacing. There had been a peculiar episode in college, something I'd put behind me as quickly as possible. One Sunday, during high Mass, I was suddenly impelled to run from the chapel. The pomp and incense and remote formality of the ritual made me sweat with unprecedented anxiety and nausea: my first "panic attack." What was happening to me? I wondered, hanging on to the pew in front of me for support as waves of dizziness flooded over me.

It seemed to take forever before I got up the nerve to leave the chapel. The leaving, I think now, was symbolic of a greater leaving, a premonition that the rituals of Catholicism would not always be there for me to fall back on. Would there ever be *anything* to fall back on?

It was an issue I chose not to examine for many years. The first man in my life, my husband, couldn't take care of me; not emotionally, at least. His own psychological problems interfered with his ability to contribute to a stable relationship, much less provide me with the kind of inner security I yearned for—and believed would come from someone else.

The second man in my life, Lowell, *wouldn't* take care of me (or, rather, he wouldn't act out the traditional role of pretending to). He was very clear about wanting a woman who would take care of herself, and I was very clear about wanting *him*. The fact that I couldn't fit him into my old, preconceived ideas about what a man "ought to do" created a psychological impasse which led, a long way down the road, to my changing some destructive attitudes.

What lay ahead in the immediate future was the work of putting together the first crude essentials of a belief in myself. It seems odd not to have grown up with this, but I didn't. It seems strange that a privileged girl in a privileged society with a college professor for a father and a perfectly nice woman for a mother should develop so sharp and deep a vein of self-contempt; but that, nevertheless, is how I grew up. Doubting my intelligence. Doubting, as well, my sexual desirability. And that, you see, was the damning double bind: to have no confidence in my ability to make it in this world on my own, the *new* way, and to be equally doubtful of my ability to succeed in woman's *old* way, which is to seduce a man into being her patron and protector. Uncomprehending—stricken by the kind of gender confusion that assails so many contemporary women—I never knew where I stood. Through all those years of doing the "right" things, of going to college, of working on the staff of a magazine, marrying, stopping work, having children, rearing them, and beginning, slowly, to work again, at odd hours, during the children's naps—through all of that I remained fundamentally in conflict. While the relatives nodded and brought cakes, approving my apparently smooth acceptance of my "role" in the world, during all those years of a peculiar kind of Method acting known only to women, I hid from who I was.

Getting to the Bottom of It

So, as the response to the *New York* article made clear, there were others like me: women who felt dependent, frustrated, angry. Women who yearned for independence but were frightened by what it might mean. Fear was actually paralyzing them in their efforts to break loose. *The question was, why was no one talking about this? How many women might be suffering in silent confusion? Is an inner fear of independence epidemic among women?*

I wanted facts and I wanted theories. I wanted to hear women themselves talk about their lives now that we are supposedly free to be free. I felt there was something happening that wasn't being talked about, or written about; something all the articles and surveys missed.

The psychological need to avoid independence—the "wish to be saved"—seemed to me an important issue, quite probably the most important issue facing women today. We were brought up to depend on a man and to feel naked and frightened without one. We were taught to believe that as women we cannot stand alone, that we are too fragile, too delicate, needful of protection. So that now, in these enlightened days, when our intellects tell us to stand on our own two feet, unresolved emotional issues drag us down. At the same time that we yearn to be fetterless and free, we also yearn to be taken care of.

Women's leanings toward dependence are, for the most part, deeply buried. Dependency is frightening. It makes us anxious because it has its roots in infancy, when we were indeed helpless. We do what we can to hide these needs from ourselves. Especially now, with the new, socially encouraged thrust toward independence, we find it tempting to keep that other part of ourselves cut off, damped down.[3]

That part, buried and denied, is the troublemaker. It crops up in fantasies and dreams. It sometimes takes the form of phobias. It affects the way women think, and act, and speak—and not just *some* women, but virtually *all* women. Hidden dependency needs are causing problems for the protected housewife who has to ask her husband for permission to buy a dress, and for the career woman with the six-figure income who's unable to go to sleep at night when her lover's out of town. Alexandra Symonds, a New York psychiatrist who has studied dependency, says it's a problem that affects most of the women she's ever met. Even those women who appear to be the most outwardly successful, she believes, tend to "subordinate themselves to others, become dependent on them, and quite unwittingly devote their major energies to the search for love, for help, for protection against that which is seen as difficult, or challenging, or hostile in the world."[4]

The Cinderella Complex

We have only one real shot at "liberation," and that is to emancipate ourselves from within. *It is the thesis of this book that personal, psychological dependency—the deep wish to be taken care of by others—is the chief force holding women down today. I call this "The Cinderella Complex"—a network of largely repressed attitudes and fears that keeps women in a kind of half-light, retreating from the full use of their minds and creativity. Like Cinderella, women today are still waiting for something external to transform their lives.*

Using my own personal experience as a jumping-off point, I have woven the psychological and psychoanalytic theory that informs this book into the stories of women themselves. (Where noted, names and certain details have been changed.) In the pages that follow you will find single women, married women, women with live-in lovers. Some have careers, some have never ventured from their homes, some *have* ventured but eventually crept back again. There are urban sophisticates and wood-chopping country women; widows, divorcées, and women who want a divorce but haven't got the nerve. There are women who love their men but fear for the death of their own souls. Many of the women I talked to were educated, some were not; but virtually all of them were functioning well below their native capabilities, living in a kind of gender limbo of their own making. Waiting.

Quite a few of the women I interviewed in the course of researching this book are oblivious of "the problem." Their heads tell them that all they want—or have ever wanted—is freedom. Emotionally, though, they show signs of suffering from deep inner conflict.

Others struggle intermittently with glimpses of what it is that's making them anxious and often depressed.

Still others, inspiringly, take the plunge, fully recognizing their deep desire to be protected and taken care of—and are then able to generate new strength, along with a realistic sense of who they are and what they are actually capable of accomplishing. These women become what one therapist calls *courageously vulnerable*. Instead of continuing a life of repression and denial, they face up to the truths of their inner selves, triumphing, finally, over the fears that have kept them hovering by the hearth. These are the women who have truly sprung free. From them we have much to learn.

CHAPTER **II**

Backing Down: Women's Retreat from Challenge

Sometimes it is easier to meet an external challenge, a crisis or a tragedy, than to rise to the challenge that comes from within—the mandate to take risks, to grow.

I had always considered myself a fighter, someone who if called to battle would slog through its muddiest parts undaunted. There had been times that required courage and fortitude, and I had risen to them. Soon after my marriage broke up it became clear that the job of supporting the children would fall to me. My husband became emotionally ill, suffering from manic episodes that ended in hospitalization. For nine years, until he died of an untreated ulcer, he was hospitalized about once a year. In between these episodes, maintained on lithium, he would remain relatively stable. His illness was so debilitating, however, that although he had a keen intellect he was unable to manage any but the most untaxing jobs—working as a bartender, a dishwasher, and finally a messenger during the last five years of his life. I made two decisions, the consequences of which were sometimes difficult. I would not abandon him during those times when his illness became severe, and I would not prevent the children from visiting him except for the times when he was acutely manic and delusional.

Manic-depressive disease is slippery and elusive. The episodes of mania seem to occur in cycles, but the onset of any given episode is unpredictable. Ed would often come flying into our apartment at the peak of one of his manic episodes, convinced he was on the verge of winning some great national election. Then, having had no sleep for weeks, his motor revving beyond all endurance, he would reel out onto the streets, soon to go crashing down with depression and paranoia. I visited him in the wards of hospitals that echoed with loneliness and despair. I learned, if I ever learned anything, that there are things in this world over which we have no control.

At the same time, there was a secret, hidden part of me that felt sorry for myself. To have gone so quickly—in one short year—from being a "wife," protected and supported, to being a "single mother" of three, alone and unprotected and quite unsure of my ability to support us all, was utterly terrifying. Writing was my only skill, tenuously arrived at, barely even believed in, in 1971. I was challenged, at first, and fascinated by the reality of having to pay the rent every month. There was tremendous support for what I was doing. Within a year, half of the women I knew best had left their husbands and were going it alone in big, bulky rent-controlled apartments just like mine, with children just like mine and concerns just like mine. We became very close. We saw each other every day and talked on the phone every night. We were without doubt a support network, and God knows how any of us would have managed without it.

But we were also hiding. We seemed to be more interested in maintaining our lives exactly as they had been before the father-figure left than in rising to the challenge of making something new. It's remarkable how long I was able to exist without really *deciding* anything. I didn't want to be alone, to experience myself as being alone, so I continued to share my responsibilities as I had always done. None of us really wanted to make decisions on our own. We consulted all the time—particularly on things having to do with the kids. We lent money to one another and met on street corners in the early New York mornings. Sometimes we would stand right out on the street and put our heads on one another's shoulders and cry. We were shameless in the expression of the weakness we felt within, but we also found our new lives exhilarating. We drank wine late into the night, and smoked pot, and began dating again like girls. I had no idea what kind of man interested me or was good for me. I met and went out with men like a teen-ager: this one was funny-looking, the next one was overbearing and earnest, the one after that was sexy but too pushy. Going out with men terrified me. I felt like a four-teen-year-old locked inside the body of a woman of thirty-three. I began setting my hair, tweezing my eyebrows, and worrying about my breath.

We were growing up—that was it. Voluptuous, smart-assed, with a slick veneer of sophistication that only living in Manhattan can give you, we were really pubescent girls with spinach caught in our braces. Having no men at home, no husbands, revealed us for what we were: frightened, insecure, amazingly underdeveloped both mentally and psychologically. We were glad to be sprung from the cage, but inwardly we shrank back from the new freedom to manage our own lives. Before us lay only dark, uncleared paths leading into the jungle.

Symptomatic of my unwillingness to really commit myself to the world of adults was my peculiar attitude toward money. I needed more but felt helpless to do anything about it. As a writer I lived from month to month, hoping for some magical "break," hoping the brass ring would swing within reach and I would be able to grab it. During those first years on my own I never evaluated the financial realities of my work life, never considered going back to school, never developed a plan that might stabilize my situation. I kept my head firmly stuck in the sand, eyes shut tight, hoping "things would work out." Certain stark realities impinged upon me because the monthly bills had to be paid, but I responded to this with a frightened passivity. I was not making gains in the direction of taking charge of my life; I was simply avoiding the gallows.

At the same time, I was quite convinced I wasn't interested in marrying again. Married, I hadn't had the strength to fight off those overwhelming dependency needs; alone, I was forced to. In a way, the instinct was correct. Although the underlying dependency was still there, lying dormant beneath the frantic struggle of my life as a single woman, at least I wasn't *acting* on it all the time, reinforcing my helplessness with every passing day as I had done when I was a wife.

On the other hand, a secret, unconscious part of me was waiting to be bailed out again. Like an adolescent, I enjoyed my newfound freedom, but when anything disturbing happened I longed for the protection of the old days. Inwardly, I had established a moratorium on growth. Out of fear, I lived within certain rigid boundaries that prevented me from learning, from expanding my mind, from finding out what I might actually be capable of doing.

Psychologically, things were more complicated than my simply feeling inferior and timid. I wavered between grandiose notions of my ability and the most degrading feelings of incompetence. While I felt this bind viscerally, I couldn't imagine how I might get out of it. "Woman is loser," as Janis Joplin cried. I became quite fascinated with the new view of women as oppressed. Unfortunately, the trendier aspects of the feminist movement meshed with and reinforced my own personal paralysis. I used feminism as a rationalization for staying right where I was. Instead of concentrating on my own development, I focused on "them." "They" were keeping me down. Women couldn't get it together because men wouldn't *let* them, period.

A peculiar thing happened. My writing got better and my career began to lift off the ground. This frightened me too, and I was unable to get behind myself and push. Instead of feeling good about the writing breakthrough I began to feel that I was not very smart, only clever and manipulative. I saw myself as "getting by" as a journalist. A splash here, a splash there, but one day I'd be exposed for the fraud I knew I was.

At this point it should have begun dawning on me that there was something I *got* out of maintaining so negative a view of myself. I didn't really *want* to succeed; not all the way, not so the world would know, once and for all, that I didn't really *need* anyone to take care of me. "I can take care of myself." To utter those words, and *mean* them, would be like putting a pox on myself. Gone would be the ace-in-the-hole. "I can take care of myself!" What monumental hubris. What tempting of the fates and the gods. Once you admit *that*, you've as much as thrown in the towel, giving up all residual claims to helplessness.

The game, then, was "I can take care of myself . . . *sort of.*" Unfortunately, though, you can't stay on the fence and progress at the same time. My life became narrower rather than broader. I learned the slickest ways of avoiding. I spent virtually all my spare time with other people—and quite a lot of time that wasn't spare. I told myself I needed this, after the long, friendless years of my marriage. Probably I did need it, but I also used people to avoid developing my own personal consciousness. I became a social butterfly, the queen of West End Avenue. I worked very late at night and slept very late in the morning. Even the writing became a kind of safety valve. With it, I would bore right to the center of the volcano, release a little steam, and then drop off to sleep, ignoring once more the cause of the destructive fire raging within.

Women don't know it, because just supporting ourselves seems so radical an effort, but hanging in is not, in and of itself, a noble occupation. It is marking time, treading water. Ultimately, "hanging in" is a retreat from challenge. Women need to do more. We need to find out what it is we're afraid of, and go beyond.

The Girl-Child Lives On

It's very hard for me to do anything alone.

I've always felt that my place was *behind* somebody. I had an older brother who was perfect. In a lot of ways I was quite content growing up in his shadow. It felt safe there.

I often have a sense of illegitimacy because of not being married and not having children, even though I know it's the cool and groovy thing to do, especially here in San Francisco. But it wasn't the way I grew up, and it isn't what I want to be. I never really felt that I wanted to be independent.

These admissions of dependency were taken from a tape-recorded interview with a successful psychotherapist, a single, thirty-two-year-old woman with a doctorate in psychology. She is a feminist with a practice in California, and as her statements show, she's confused about her own role in the world—her inner need to be safely "behind" someone in sharp contradiction to her ambition to succeed, to be out in front, to be on her own.

"Any time life gets too hard, the possibility of giving up to be protected by a man is still there for women; it takes the edge off the will to survive independently," writes Judith Coburn in *Mademoiselle*.

"The times in my life when I've let the bills pile up, the car fall apart, the logistics of a trip snarl, I'm broadcasting: see, I can't do this myself, I need someone to save me."[1]

Another woman, a talented songwriter who thinks of herself as a "militant feminist," is trying to figure out why she can't seem to generate the energy to go out and take on the music industry. "Maybe I just want a man to take care of me," she says.

Listen to women talk today and you soon discover that the "new woman" isn't really new at all; she's mutant. She lives in a kind of never-never land, seesawing between two sets of values, the old and the new. Emotionally, she has not made peace with either; nor has she found a way to integrate the two. "All doors are open," says Anne Fleming Taylor, writing in Vogue, but the question is deciding which door to enter. "If we mother well, can we work? If we work well, can we love? Shall we compete out there or not? Can we stay at home and not feel guilty, useless, and strangely hurt?"[2]

Inwardly confused and anxious, women back off from living full out, at the frontier edges of their capabilities. A travel agent I met last summer said, "We're not yet able to stand on our two feet and say, 'Yes! I can do this. I'm competent.' Women are still afraid."

Why are women so fearful? The answer to that question lies at the root of The Cinderella Complex. Experience has something to do with it. If you don't go out and do you'll remain forever fearful of the workings of the world. But many women achieve a certain amount of success in their careers and professions and still remain inwardly insecure. In fact, as we shall see in later chapters, it's remarkable how many women these days retain a hidden core of self-doubt while performing on the outside as if they were towers of confidence. Current research in psychology has established that core doubt is characteristic of women today. "We found that the qualities of passivity, dependence, and most of all lack of self-esteem are the variables that repeatedly differentiate women from men," reports psychologist Judith Bardwick, of studies done at the University of Michigan.[3]

Few women need studies to convince them. Lack of confidence seems to follow us from childhood, an intensity so palpable it sometimes feels as if it exists on its own. Miriam Schapiro, a New York painter, says she's spent her whole life with the feeling that an unprotected child lives inside her, a "fragile, unarmored creature, timid and self-doubting." Only when she paints, she says, is the child within "able to grow more assertive, alive . . . and freer in her movements."[4]

No matter how fiercely we try to live like adults—flexible, powerful and free—that girl-child hangs on, whispering her frightened warnings in our ear. The effects of such insecurity are widespread, and they result in a disturbing social phenomenon: women in general tend to function well below the level of their native abilities. *For reasons that are both cultural and psychological—a system that doesn't really expect a great deal from us, in combination with our own personal fears of standing up and facing the world—women are keeping themselves down.*

The Famous Female "Achievement Gap"

Consider, to begin with, the history of our economic progress over the past twenty years. In spite of the consciousness-raising of the Sixties and Seventies, women are worse off today than they were in the days of crinolines and waist cinches. We earn less money (compared with men) than we did two decades ago. In 1956, the income figure for females constituted 63 percent of the money earned by males. Now we earn less than 60 percent of what men earn. Women's-studies courses and political action notwithstanding, most of us still enter the work force with low-salaried jobs and creep upward—or sideways—like crabs on a string. Two-thirds of women who work earn less than $10,000 a year.[5] We barely make enough, *ever*, to be able to do much more than pay the baby-sitter, let alone earn what it would take to make our futures secure. Capital gains, profit sharing, fancy retirement plans—these are entrepreneurial luxuries, *male* luxuries. *Half of women working are in jobs with no pensions.* We constitute—apparently willingly—an army of underpaid drones so massive and so fixed in character that social scientists have seized upon a new name for us: "The Eighty Percent." "Eighty" refers to the percentage of women workers who occupy menial or semiskilled jobs paying rotten salaries—women who, economically at least, are scrambling around at the bottom of the basket of crabs.

Until recently, people who work with statistics bandied the expression "women in the labor force" as if we were an army of Amazons about to take over the land. The notion of women's burgeoning strength and mobility has been in the air for at least a quarter of a century. But as sociologists are finally beginning to recognize, "For every successful woman professional there's another woman whose 'labor force participation' consists of running a punch press eight hours of every working day, and another whose work amounts to making beds and cleaning rooms, and another who spends her day typing letters and filing correspondence in the large, impersonal offices of America's bureaucracies." (That statement was made by James Wright of the University of Massachusetts, who concluded, from information provided by six large national surveys, that the level of satisfaction of women who work outside the home is no greater than that of women who work inside the home.[6] It's easy to see how working women might show up statistically as being less than thrilled with their jobs when 80 percent of them are leaving the comforts of home to take work cleaning out offices and/or file systems for low pay and no pension.)

On the surface it may appear as if the problem is no different for women than it is for men: precious few people of either gender will ever rise to the top of the economy. But the story—for women—*is* different. Studies have shown consistently that while IQ bears a fairly close relationship to accomplishment among men, it bears essentially no relationship at all to accomplishment among women. This shocking discrepancy was first brought to light by the Stanford Gifted Child Study. More than 600 children with IQ's above 135 (this represents the upper 1 percent of the population) were identified in the California schools. Their progress was followed into adulthood. The adult occupations of the women, whose childhood IQ's were in the same range as the men's, were for the most part undistinguished. In fact, *two-thirds of the women with genius-level IQ's of 170 or above were occupied as housewives or office workers.*[7]

The waste of women's talent is a brain drain that affects the entire country. Psychiatrists have begun to look closely at the problem. Struck by the number of achievement-conflicted women who've come to her for help in recent years, Dr. Alexandra Symonds noted that talented women are often loath to move ahead to positions of real self-sufficiency. They balk at or become unduly anxious about promotions. Many gravitate toward mentors, preferring to work as the brilliant but unrecognized backup for men in power—refusing both the credit and the responsibility for their own contributions. In therapy, they cling to their backwardness. "Each step toward healthy self-assertion is consciously or unconsciously resisted," says Symonds. "Some women clearly state that they like being taken care of and have no wish to change this position. Others come . . . with the apparent intent of developing further but when confronted at the crossroads of actual change, with the inevitable choices toward separation and self-emergence, panic."[8]

In her Manhattan practice Dr. Symonds treats many successful, upwardly reaching women; among them she has found the problem of self-constraint to be widespread. In relation to their innate abilities, too many women seem incapacitated, unable to realize their full potential.

Why? What is it that holds these women back?

Fear, says Dr. Symonds. Women do not want to experience the anxiety that's intrinsic to the growth process. It has to do with the way they've been reared. As children, females are not taught to be assertive and independent; indeed, they are taught to be nonassertive and dependent. The fact that the signals have been switched and women are now "allowed" to be independent has thrown them into inner turmoil. Around this "core of dependency" that was bred into women as children there develops, says Symonds, "a whole constellation of character traits which are interrelated and which reinforce each other." These traits take years to develop. "As with any established character pattern, [they] cannot be given up without anxiety."

So it is the giving up of an entire character pattern—or the prospect of having to do so—that makes women today feel so torn. The dependent pattern has been touted as appropriately "feminine" by the most influential of psychoanalysts. The following passage from Helene Deutsch's classical text *The Psychology of Women* may have a queer, dated quality (it was published in 1944), but make no mistake: it reflects the same ideas our mothers and fathers had as their daughters were growing up. Consequently, Deutsch's notion of woman as "the ideal life-companion" belongs to the very fiber of our being.

Deutsch assured the world that women are likely to be happiest when they are subordinating themselves to their men.

They seem to be easily influenceable and adapt themselves to their companions and understand them. They are the loveliest and most unaggressive of helpmates and they want to remain in that role; they do not insist on their own rights—quite to the contrary.

On the subject of women's capacity for being original and productive, Deutsch sounded like the Mistress of Novices in a convent:

. . . they are always willing to renounce their own achievements without feeling that they are sacrificing anything, and they rejoice in the achievement of their companions. . . . They have an extraordinary need of support when engaged in any activity directed outward.

Enlightened psychiatrists these days recognize the contortionist's act that was required of women in an age when they were expected to stifle their own healthiest impulses. As Symonds observes, women weren't *born* "ideal"; they had to work at it. "To be able to renounce your own achievements without feeling that you were sacrificing requires constant effort. To be lovely and unaggressive, a woman spends a lifetime keeping hostile or resentful impulses down. Even healthy self-assertion is often sacrificed since it may be mistaken for hostility. Therefore, [women] often repress their initiative, give up their aspirations, and unfortunately end up excessively dependent with a deep sense of insecurity and uncertainty about their abilities and their worth."[9]

Bearing in mind the enormous change that's taken place in what society considers to be "appropriate" female behavior, let's return to the subject of women's current attitudes toward work and money. (These attitudes, as we'll see, are vital to what social scientists call the "female achievement gap.")

Certain newly emergent (or newly recognized) trends begin to make clear that women have not simply been *kept* economically dependent; they themselves do a good deal to contribute to the situation. Between 1960 and 1976, for example, the number of women who graduated from college increased by almost 400 percent.[10] And yet over half the eleventh-grade girls in the country are still cautiously saying they want jobs from among only three categories: clerical and secretarial, educational and social services, and nursing.[11]

"Sex discrimination in the marketplace is a fact, but a more cogent reason for the lack of women's work productivity is their unwillingness to assume a long-term professional commitment," writes Judith Bardwick in *The Psychology of Women: A Study of Biocultural Conflicts*. Gathering information from the National Manpower Council, the President's Commission on the Status of Women and the Radcliffe Committee on Graduate Education, Bardwick concludes: "Academically talented girls are less likely to enter college and complete the undergraduate degree than equally bright young men; they are less likely to take advanced degrees; they are less likely to use the Ph.D.'s they do take; they are less productive than men even if they do take the Ph.D., remain unmarried, and continue to work full time."

Women are continuing to *choose* low-paying careers. In 1976, 49 percent of all bachelor's degrees, 72 percent of all master's, and 53 percent of all doctorates awarded to women were in six traditionally "female" and poorly paid fields.[12] "If women continue to cling to traditional, female-intensive professions," says Pearl Kramer, chief economist for the Long Island Regional Planning Board, "the gap between what they earn and what their male counterparts earn will continue indefinitely."[13]

This is the famous female "achievement gap." It's been known for a long time that women are not achieving what they're capable of achieving. *What hasn't been recognized is the role women themselves play in maintaining this gap.* Women are not just being excluded from power (although that has been systematic). We are also actively *avoiding* it. "See how independent we've become!" we exult, noting how many women have left their homes to go to work. But root beneath the surface of those deceiving Census Bureau statistics and you'll find that many women these days don't really *want* to be working. They feel taxed by it; even, sometimes, abused. In their heart of hearts they still believe that women shouldn't really *have* to make a living. Leaving the warmth and security of their kitchens to enter the work force, many are motivated not by a sense of responsibility for themselves or fairness to their husbands so much as by a sense of crisis. Inflation has gone berserk, and Charlie isn't making enough to keep up.

Or there *is* no Charlie. Charlie has remarried, or died, or simply split in the dead of night to dally in the arms of younger, less burdensome women. Widowed or divorced, the leftover wives have little or no money for supporting themselves and the kids. Under these circumstances, the feeling about "going back to work" is not so constructive and joyful as we might like to imagine. There may be initial exhilaration, like the joy an adolescent feels upon receiving a first paycheck, but the thrill of emancipation is soon supplanted by a horrifying suspicion: *This could go on forever.*

Signs of a Backlash

There is indication that some women, at least, are not just digging in their feet, but are involved in a *reaction* to their new freedom—a moving backward. A *Wall Street Journal* study found manufacturers complaining that they can't get their female employees to enter advancement programs that companies have designed especially for them. "We have to drag them kicking and screaming," a General Motors executive said. (A male labor-relations director concluded, with less irritation but equal smugness, "It's social conditioning. Women have never aspired to those jobs before. It's hard to convince them to aspire now.") [14]

Some wives are quitting their jobs, saying the work creates more stress and anxiety than they're capable of handling. "It's as if they feel The Great American Dream slipping through their busy fingers," said *Better Homes and Gardens*, reporting on a new survey of 300,000 readers' reactions to work.[15] Mostly married, with children, these women tend to displace their anxiety about their own development onto the safer issue of "being needed more at home." In truth, they had lost the sense of "being needed" that was so important to their inner psychic organization, and had projected that loss onto their families, becoming convinced that the families felt "let down" by their absence. Floundering and anxious, some of these wives said they'd persuaded their husbands to move to smaller homes and less desirable neighborhoods because they wanted to quit work and "rededicate themselves" to the family—a decision they said provided them with feelings of "extreme relief."[16]

There is also the "have-another-child" syndrome—a socially approved way of getting to stay in (or retreat back into) the home. According to Ruth Moulton, a feminist psychiatrist on the teaching staff at Columbia University, even highly talented women will become pregnant to avoid anxiety about their blossoming careers.[17] Characteristic, she says, is the case of an artist she knows who conceived "accidentally" twice, five years apart; each time she had been presented with an opportunity to put together a one-woman show of her work, and each time she had "chosen" pregnancy instead. The result was that her shows were put off until she was past fifty, "vastly decreasing," writes Moulton, "the time left for development and acknowledgment of her talent."[18]

Looking over the roster of her patients in recent years, Dr. Moulton discovered she could easily count twenty women between the ages of forty and sixty who had used pregnancy as an escape from the outside world. "In at least half of these cases," she noted, "a third or fourth child was conceived just at a point when the older children were in grammar or high school and the mother was freer to devote more energy to outside work."

"Compulsive child rearing" is what Moulton calls this syndrome, by which she means mothering not for its intrinsic gratification but because it provides a substitute for action in the world. (Indeed, women "are using pregnancy as a vehicle to get out of" the Army, M. Kathleen Carpenter was quoted as conceding in a 1977 report, "Evaluation of Women in the Army.")

The phenomenon of "pregnancy-to-avoid-stress" certainly has no positive influence on that most revered of institutions, American family life. A destructive cycle is perpetuated when women have children as a way of avoiding the anxiety that attends personal development. They become resentful of the narrow, self-limiting role they have chosen as an out, and sometimes they become phobic and hypochondriacal. Perhaps most important of all, *they do not raise independent children*. Says Moulton, the dependent woman's dependency on her own children "interferes with the independent growth and individuation of all concerned."

One strong idea being put forth these days (it seems to appeal to everyone—feminists, nonfeminists, men) is that women should above all be given choice. They should be able to *choose*, for example, whether or not they work, whether or not they earn a full-time income, whether or not they stay home and "devote themselves" to their families. No one should push women around, telling us we "have to" or "can't" do this or that. To suggest that women are copping out by staying home is just as arbitrary, feminists tell us, as insisting that women stay home when they want to go to work. Staying home with the children, cleaning the house, nurturing the husband so that *he* can cope with the anxieties involved in going out and winning the bread—these are supposedly important social contributions of which any woman can feel justifiably proud. But this "right to choose" whether or not we provide for ourselves has contributed mightily to the female achievement gap. Because they have the social option to stay home, women can—and often do—back off from assuming responsibility for themselves.

The truth is that many women who don't "have to" work, because their husbands are willing and able to support them, *don't*. The rising number of working women is notably correlated with the increase in deteriorating marriages. Forty-two percent of all women who work are heads of households.[19] *What is surprising in this day and age is that of the women who are married and living with their husbands, half still prefer to stay home by the hearth.*[20]

There is something wrong with this. You begin seeing it—begin making the connection—once you look at the economic plight of older women in this country. While everyone's talking about choice, we might more profitably ask ourselves, "Who takes care of women once they get old?" The answer is, of course, no one. By the time women's hair has turned gray, the old "women-and-children-first" support system has long since fallen away. Reality hits hard when the men die off. The latest government figures show fifty-six to be the average age of widowhood in the United States. Over one out of two women can expect to be a widow by the age of sixty-five. And even those women who spend their adult lives working are not protected in old age: one out of four of them will be poor—much poorer than men the same age. In 1977, the median income of all older females was $3,087, or $59 a week, compared with a median income for older males of almost twice that. (The chief reason women who've worked fare so badly in old age is that Social Security is tied into the wage system, and women, as has already been noted, earn only 60 percent of what men earn.)[21]

This, then, is the bitter truth on which younger women—still romantic, still in love, still cushioned by the dream that women can safely allow others to take care of them—turn their backs. The myth is that security, for women, lies in remaining forever and permanently attached, coiled within and stuck to "the family" like mollusks within their shells. But by the time these same women grow older, they are horribly disenfranchised, snapped off from the main economy before they know what hit them. *The devastation of old age is the most poignant outcome of The Cinderella Complex, if not the most destructive. It is tantamount to a kind of sickness, this blind spot we maintain—the inability (or refusal) to see the connection between the false security we connect with being wives and the loneliness and poverty of older, often widowed women.* We want so desperately to believe that someone else will take care of us. We want so desperately to believe that we do not have to be responsible for our own welfare.

Confusion in Atlanta

The myth is particularly prevalent among women of the middle class. Wearing rose-colored glasses, they continue to seek work as a kind of experiment, a form, almost, of play. They languish in part-time jobs; jobs that will "broaden their horizons," or allow them to "get out of the house and meet people." There is a certain kind of young, upper-middle-class wife who is not at all sure what to do with the opportunities before her, who has more or less decided to sit pretty for as long as she is able because any brightly beckoning future holds more fear for her than fascination. I had occasion to meet a group of such wives at a small dinner party in Atlanta, Georgia.

They were small-boned, polished women in their early thirties, attractive and lively. Their husbands were successful men—stockbrokers, a bureaucrat in the State Department, a psychology professor at a local university. One of the women, whom I'll call Paley, still fit the image of a sassy Southern Rebel girl. Another, Helen, had recently emigrated south from Cambridge. Lynann had lived happily in Atlanta for all her thirty-odd years. These women spoke of feeling a certain degree of frustration in their lives—the children were in school, or close to it—but their thinking about work was lethargic. They spoke of getting jobs that were easy—jobs offering short hours and good money. Bridge, they said, had become boring (although they still belonged to their bridge clubs).

So far, Paley was the only one of these women who'd actually gone out and nailed down a job. "I work in a little health-food restaurant down the street from our house," she said. "It's only a few days a week for a couple of hours, but with tips I make more per hour than my husband!"

The others laughed. In Paley's life money had never really been an issue. She came from a small Georgia town where everyone knew everyone and everyone was loaded. Now she lived in Atlanta, still as "wild" as she had been in her college days at old Georgia State.

After dinner, the tune seemed to change. The women left the men sitting in the Chippendale-style dining room and clustered together at one end of the living room, where they spoke, now, about the eventlessness of their lives. Self-consciously they joked about how all they ever discussed was "floor wax and ring-around-the-collar." These could have been the same women Betty Friedan discovered twenty years ago in her study of Smith College graduates going nuts in the suburbs of the Northeast. Only this was not 1960; it was 1980. And these women were not yet going nuts with frustration. If anything, they were too comfortable—country-club lunches, soft cars, plenty of parties, and only the residue of their old college days to remind them that they had once had a different view of themselves; had felt free, *swinging*; had once imagined themselves *doing* things.

The cushiness of their married lives made it difficult for these women to accept having to start out on the first rung of the ladder. "Working *for* someone isn't for me," blurted Lynann, who said she'd gotten far enough in her job thinking to recognize that she didn't want to work as an underling. "I want in at top-management level. *I* want to be the one who's doin' the bossin'." (Again, a laugh from the women.)

Would she consider going to graduate school and getting an M.B.A. in order to make her dream come true? Well, no, not really. She was interested in this "little course" she'd heard about, one that would provide "certain tools and ways of presenting myself so I'll *look* as if I'm smart." (More laughter.)

Paley was not blind to the social setup in which they were entrenched. "The point of pride, for a lot of women in Atlanta, is still how much money your husband makes and how well he takes care of you," she said. "The important things are: What kind of car can he buy for you? Do you have help with the children, the house? Can you afford to go on trips?"

Still, there was that problem of eventlessness. What did they *do* to fill the empty hours when they weren't shopping, or chauffeuring the children? They read romances. Jokingly, now (for they knew better), they began rating the authors of the currently popular romance novels for their literary merit. Everyone jumped into the game.

"How much time do you actually spend reading romances?" I asked.

Paley—all frizzed hair, painted nails, sling-back pumps, and probably bright as hell—told me, "I read and read and read. I go several hours at a sitting, easy. I get so engrossed my little girl could walk out the front door and I wouldn't know. When she cries, there are times I don't hear her."

These are the protected ones: young, attractive, sassy—and safe. They presume financial dependence to be their right, as women. In exchange they devote themselves to homemaking, happily priding themselves on their ability to clean, to organize, to rear children, to entertain. But inwardly, without being conscious of it, they have set up an agenda: they avoid, almost ritualistically, any recognition of how precarious their lives are. They do not think about what would happen if their marriages were to break up. Divorce happens, of course. They see it around them, and its female victims, they think, are quite courageous in the ways they have of trying to pull together the snapped threads of their lives. But for women who sit pretty, divorce is not really something you imagine *happening*. It is for others; for women who are . . . well, not quite so fortunate.

Like cancer. Or death.

Depression Across the Country

Stemming directly from the confusion of wives such as those in Atlanta is a relatively new cultural phenomenon—the "displaced homemaker." A vast subculture of women who've been widowed or left by their husbands and who have never developed the skills with which to support themselves, displaced homemakers constitute an emotionally disabled class of 25 million women.[22] Told society would reward them for being good wives and mothers and keeping the home fires burning, these women have truly been "caught in the middle," uprooted by the seismic shift in marital mores. They believe themselves incompetent, any talents they may have had years ago, when they got out of school, having long since atrophied. Their *muscles* are unused; their minds. These are the women who have spent their lives believing the Cinderella myth that men would always be there to support them. *Statistics from a Center for Displaced Homemakers in Maryland show what a cruel dream it is. Only 17 percent of the women served by the center received any income at all from former husbands. One-third were living in poverty.*[23] *And these women are not old. They range in age from thirty to fifty-five.*

In more or less supporting divorce—and at the same time supporting the new idea of the working mother—society has shattered the security of women like these. As a result, according to Milo Smith, a founder of the organization called Displaced Homemakers and head of the center in Oakland, California, the women she's trying to help are angry. They don't like the idea that everything, suddenly, has changed. They resent having to leave their homes, learn skills, and go to work.

They are also depressed. "Suicide is our biggest problem," Ms. Smith told me. "We've had four suicide attempts this year, right at this center."

The day I visited that particular center (there are dozens more around the country), the women arriving to get help were neatly coiffed, wearing bright red lipstick. A number, overweight, wore long muumuus. While waiting for interviews they were given coffee and sympathetic receptions by staff members who were also displaced homemakers. Like ex-jailmates, the ex-supported were trying to help one another. Newcomers were bright-eyed and seemed eager to please. Insecurity shone in their eyes like fever.

"A lot of them are a mess when they first come in," said Ms. Smith, a woman in her sixties who began this work because some years back she herself had been a skill-less, frightened widow. "They're like legalized junkies, Valium junkies who were made that way by their doctors."

Bereaved from the day their husbands departed, stricken with a sense of loss not just of their husbands, but of a way of life that provided them with their sense of identity, these women went to their family physicians needing more than any doctor could give them—and got pills. The despair of displaced homemakers is palpable. Society doesn't know what to do with them—and they, having lost the *raison d'être* for which they were born and bred—don't know what to do with themselves. Their self-esteem seems to vanish overnight. Pointing to the Center's foyer, Milo Smith told me, "Virtually every woman who's walked in that door has internalized the idea that she's now ugly, and old, and fat, and useless."

Worse, they feel as if this newly tarnished self-image is something that's been done to them, and it makes them vengeful. "These women waste their energies turning everything into a negative effort to get even," says Ms. Smith. "They are terribly rigid and inflexible. It's all part of the depressive picture. You try to send them out to *do* something for themselves and they come back with excuses. The typical displaced homemaker can come up with fifty reasons to your one why she's unable to do something you suggest might be helpful for her. It all comes from fear."

"The depressed woman is someone who has lost," says Maggie Scarf, reporting on the "frightening amount of depression" showing up in many new studies of women, the upward surge of suicide attempts among women (especially younger women), and the inordinate amount of pill popping for emotional pain. A study conducted by the National Institute of Mental Health completed in the early Seventies says a third of all women between the ages of thirty and forty-four use prescription drugs to treat their moods. Eighty-five percent of these report never having seen a psychiatrist.[24]

Just what is it the depressed woman has lost? "Something on which she vitally depended," says Scarf. "What I have seen emerge with an almost amazing regularity is that the 'loss' in question is the loss of a crucially important and often self-defining emotional relationship."

Women look to others to provide definition—a sense of who they are. They see themselves in the eyes of the other to such an extent that if something *happens* to the other—if he dies, or leaves, or even *changes* significantly—they cannot see themselves anymore. As one woman who had lost her lover of three years said (speaking, I have no doubt, for millions): "It begins to feel as if I don't exist."

How the Cinderella Complex Affects Women's Work

This need for, and attachment to, "the other" inhibits in all kinds of ways women's capacity to work productively—to be original, zestful, and committed. The myth that our salvation lies in attachment carries with it the hidden corollary that we will not be *required* to work forever. When suddenly something happens that makes working a necessity, many become inflamed with a fierce inner rage. To *have* to work is a sign, somehow, that they have failed as women.

Or it is a sign that the dream itself is a sham.

"I might as well have been working on the assembly line in a hairpin factory for all the pleasure I was getting from my job," a museum curator recalled. She was thirty-one, unmarried, and holding a glamorous job in the art world of Washington, D.C., when suddenly everything that had once seemed so exciting turned drab and lusterless. Something happened to her on the day she hit thirty-one, for that day was her particular inner deadline, the time she had set for her deliverance from independence. "Too late," a voice inside had announced. "You shouldn't *have* to be working anymore. Women your age should have the option *not* to work; they should be able to stay home and paint, or do charity work, or rear children."

She felt as if she had already missed some golden opportunity; ridiculous, perhaps, but it made her angry and she became deadened. She found that she was doing her work each day mechanically, as if by rote. She had lost the excitement of experiencing—and working with—her own creativity. Several years later she would tell me: "I felt futile, as if I was battling an endless series of chores that were nothing but obligations. It cut down my effectiveness by half, I'd say. Why get a particular job done when another outrageous demand will instantly appear in its place?"

A college-educated woman I know works as a housekeeper, cleaning people's apartments in New York, because, she says, "I don't want to have the feeling that I'm working at something permanent, that I've chosen something which says, 'Okay, this is the kind of work you're going to do, this is how you're going to take care of yourself.'"

This woman is twenty-four and unusually intelligent. In addition to her housekeeping, she works as a free-lance, writing direct-mail advertising copy—brilliantly. Her boss thinks she's terrific, and she is —except for the fact that every two months or so she screws up and starts missing deadlines. She gets "blocked." She can't write a thing. It happens whenever she begins to earn slightly more money than she actually needs for paying the rent and utility bills for her tiny one-room apartment in Greenwich Village. "If I'm not on the verge of having Con Edison turn off my electricity I feel as if my life isn't *real,*" she says. "To have to work just to hang on from month to month is one thing. To have to work because that's what grown-ups *do,* that's going to be your *life* . . . I can't face that. It's completely neurotic and infantile, but *deep down I don't want to have to take care of myself; I want someone else to do it.*"

There are any number of red flags signaling that women are suffering functional problems as a result of their distorted attitudes toward work. Some stay on year after year in jobs that bore them witless. Some protest the "competitiveness of the male world of work," saying they "refuse" to participate in it. Yet these are often the very women who envy men for being able to do things which they themselves feel unable to do, or which they find inordinately difficult. Negotiating, for example. Initiating their own projects. Asking for, and getting, more money.[25] In short, taking an active role in relation to their own well-being. There's a whole network of psychological problems whose symptoms stay comfortably buried until women go after a job or try to enter a profession. Then, suddenly, the blitz.

Test anxiety, for example, is notoriously higher in women than in men.[26] If testing is required to enter a profession, change careers, or rise to a significantly higher level at a given job, it can throw a devastating monkey wrench into a woman's plans. (Some women are terrified of *any* type of test, whether for college entrance, or getting a driver's license, or qualifying as a broker in the real estate business.)

Public speaking is harder for women, too. In a survey of 200 postgraduate students at Columbia, one professor found that 50 percent of the women were unable to speak in public, as compared with 20 percent of the men. For some, the anxiety was so overwhelming it produced attacks of dizziness and fainting.[27]

Communication in general is difficult for women whose self-esteem is low and who harbor an inner wish to be taken care of. Some women get confused, forget what they wanted to say, can't find the right word, can't look people in the eye. Or they blush, or stutter, or find their voices getting quavery. Or they have trouble sustaining the line of an argument the moment someone disagrees with them. They may become flustered and tearful—especially if it's a man doing the disagreeing.

A number of women I talked to described the experience of having their feeling of connection, their sense of knowing what they know, their *authority*, diminish the moment the conversational pendulum swings away from them and in the direction of the man.

All these problems are actually forms of performance anxiety, and performance anxiety is connected to other, more general fears which have to do with feeling inadequate and defenseless in the world: the fear of retaliation from someone with whom one disagrees; the fear of being criticized for doing something wrong; the fear of saying "no"; the fear of stating one's needs clearly and directly, without manipulating. These are the kinds of fears that affect women in particular, because we were brought up to believe that taking care of ourselves, *asserting* ourselves, is unfeminine. We wish—intensely—to feel attractive to men: nonthreatening, sweet, "feminine." This wish crimps the joy and productiveness with which women could be leading their lives.

To say nothing of making us behave like ninnies.

The "Look" and Language of Daddy's Little Girl

At a meeting in Beverly Hills of the American Academy of Psychoanalysis, Alexandra Symonds told an amazed audience of her colleagues: "It is not appropriate for an executive in a bank to break down in tears when her superior criticizes something she's done. It is not acceptable for a senior editor earning $30,000 a year to act cute and seductive when her plan is rejected; or for a college professor to sulk because she has been given a poor schedule, hoping the Dean will notice and change it. These are behavior patterns suitable for 'Daddy's little girl' rather than a liberated woman acting autonomously."[28]

Dr. Symonds did not just invent a bunch of high-salaried Daddy's girls to make a point. These "successful" professionals were among the patients who had come to her for help—"superwomen" in deep conflict over their inner feelings of dependency.

As women climb the business and professional ladder, certain affectations and mannerisms give the lie to the confidence they are trying to exude. In fact, women who inwardly have not given up the claim to being "Daddy's little girl" can throw off some very confusing messages to colleagues and people with whom they do business. Not unlike the current "dress for success" look—halfway between born-again angelicism and the latest Scavullo cover for *Cosmopolitan* —there is often something schizoid in the presentation of inwardly dependent career women. They *seem* so tough—until they begin winking and dimpling and in general behaving helpless and seductive.

It's an act that's not always appreciated by the men with whom these women do business. A financial reporter, a Wall Street broker, and an advertising executive recently sat down with me to offer their impressions of the way women look and act and sound when they do business. Here are some excerpts from the conversation:

REPORTER: A few months ago I interviewed a woman with a big position on the New York Stock Exchange. She was wearing a little white silk blouse, lots of makeup, long, painted fingernails, and gold earrings that dangled and jangled. I could hardly look at her she had so much *on*, such a presentation. As she talked she would shift into and out of different styles. For a while she'd be very serious and confident-sounding. Then she'd back off that for a second and kind of giggle, and give a little shoulder, or a little nod.

BROKER: I see that in women I work with too. You get this schizy feeling, as if you don't know what person they're going to slip into next. You begin looking for signs, wondering when the Big Switch is going to happen again.

REPORTER: This woman's diction was super slow. She was very careful with her words, hyperconscious of how she was speaking, how she was coming across. Then she did this thing I've seen a lot of women in good jobs do. They finish their sentences by softening their words and nodding a little as they soften.

ADMAN: Yeah, I've heard that. It's a kind of gauzy brag; they end their sentences with a gauzy swagger. They're shrouding what they have to brag about because they don't want to seem to be really "selling" it.

REPORTER: It's as if women are afraid to actually get behind the *force* of a statement. They'll be talking and talking and really working up some force, and then suddenly it's as if they *see* themselves getting forceful and they have to back off. I think they're afraid of power.

BROKER: It's very common to have this drop and hushing of the voice with a nod.

ADMAN: The nod's intended to get you to agree.

BROKER: Yeah.

ADMAN: I've noticed that women in business never really swing, conversationally. You'll never hear them say, "Are you *crazy?*" or something like that. Very often you'll find that men in business really let their personalities fly and soar. That's how they *do* business. They don't worry about being who they think they should be. They get *into* it. Women are polite and formalistic. They want the rules right out there in front. They remind me of the girls who used to be first in the class in sixth grade.

BROKER: It's why women are so good for jobs like customer relations. People can come in there and rant and rave and scream at them and they just sit back behind their blusher and base, just sort of sit back. In a way, women are really once removed. The costumes and the makeup and the *femininity* stand in the way.

REPORTER: There's a prototype in adolescence in which the girl goes along for the ride in the fella's car. That idea seems to follow throughout life. The woman goes along for the ride in the man's world. When the woman gets in the man's car, which is his institutions, the woman goes along for the ride. She doesn't try to get into the driver's seat, do things her own way, make changes. She doesn't ever try to seek power. That dependency is a real "go-along" quality. "Go-along" Jane.

Women do not feel comfortable being straightforward; asking directly for what they want; selling what they believe in, especially when it means overriding the opinions of others. There lurks—some-times at the oddest moments—the temptation to slip into the in-genue role, or the seductive role, or the itty-bitty-little-girl role. It takes only a glance or a gesture to do it—"giving a little nod, or a little shoulder," as the reporter said.

In *Women, Money and Power*, the psychologist Phyllis Chesler suggests that women do all this deliberately (if not always con-sciously) to keep themselves riding comfortably in the back seat. "Women of all classes, within the home and in public, use a basic body language to communicate deference, inconsequentiality, help-lessness . . . a stance which is supposed to put others at their ease, and men 'on top.' "

There are other ways women have of keeping men—or, for that matter, anyone other than themselves—"on top." A fresh outburst of scholarly work on women's speech and language patterns indicates that fear and insecurity shape the way we talk—our diction or choice of words, our intonation, our general tone of hesitancy, even the pitch (which some women make high and girlish in an appeal for help). The following characteristics were found by linguist Robin Lakoff to be *consistent* in women's speech:

- Use of "empty" adjectives (marvelous, divine, terribly, etc.) that connote little meaning and have a fluffing effect. People whose speech is larded with empty adjectives are generally not taken seriously.
- Use of tag sentences after a declarative statement. ("It's really hot today, don't you think?")
- Use of a dipping or questioning intonation at the end of a statement, which renders it less forceful.
- Use of hedging or modifying phrases ("like," "sort of," "I guess"), which give speech a tentative, uncommitted quality.
- Use of "hypercorrect" speech and excessively polite speech (not making contractions, for example, or being overly cau-tious about slang).

Lakoff's findings—highly controversial at first—set off a flurry of research by scholars around the country.[29] Much of what they found reinforced Lakoff's observations: women do indeed use tentative styles of speech. Sally Genet, at Cornell, coined the term "diffident declarative," to describe our wobbly tendency to back off from strong, unmodified assertions.

By talking the way we talk, women are definitely making something happen—or not happen—in terms of our effectiveness in dealing with others. "Speech may not only *reflect* power differences," notes Mary Brown Parlee, staff psychologist of *Psychology Today.* "It may help to *create* them."[30]

In other words, career women who rely on the "diffident declarative" may not be entering the boardrooms of the Fortune 500 for a long time to come.

There is a new crisis in femininity, a conflict over what is and what is not "feminine," preventing a lot of women from functioning in a happy, well-integrated way. For years, femininity has been associated—indeed, *identified*—with dependency. Women, succumbing to what I call "Gender Panic," fear that independent behavior is nonfeminine (see Chapter VI). We may not actually think of it as *masculine*, but at the same time we do not *feel* that it is feminine. Vividly expressing this new Gender Panic, a young stockbroker told me: "I think that someone—it could be a man or a woman—will teach me to be like a man, make money in the market like a man, be as confident and resourceful as a man. When that's accomplished, I'll become like a woman again. I'll get pregnant and stay home with the baby for six years or so. Then I'll go back to being a man."

The terrible confusion women are experiencing about femininity is strongly related to our choosing not to live like our mothers. Psychiatrists have begun to discover that the more confined and dependent our mothers, the more anxious we'll be about pushing off in directions that are different. "The self-effacing, silently suffering mother—even if she *tells* her daughter, 'Don't get caught like me; amount to something'—may still feel resentful and threatened by the fact that her daughter doesn't emulate the same role model," says Alexandra Symonds.[31]

Having a resentful mother tends to produce one of three characteristic patterns in daughters. The first is chronic, low-grade depression—an undercurrent of sadness or depression that seems ever-present. This, says Dr. Symonds, is typical of the woman who'll get heavily involved in her work and give a lot to others, but be emotionally malnourished herself.

The second syndrome likely to show up in women who've turned their backs on Mother's way is insecurity in the area of feminine identity (the kind of gender confusion expressed by the young stockbroker). "I've been struck by the panic, even terror that these women feel at aspects of their personalities they consider masculine," remarks Dr. Symonds, noting that women who strive to live independently are still—to this day—flying in the face of what the culture expects of them.

Third is the core of hidden dependency such women spend years denying, often hiding behind remarkably convincing facades of self-sufficiency. The pseudo-independent woman may work full time, take care of a family, cook and bake without processed foods, and in general show a compulsive need to be "super" both at home and on the job. She may also weep in her sleep at night when her husband's away from home.

There is a strong tendency, these days, for a woman to try to solve her problems by changing things on the outside—by getting married (or unmarried), by changing jobs, moving, by joining a union or fighting for women's rights. But the fact is that if she's hamstrung by unresolved dependency conflicts, her life will never change as a result of her finding the "right" man, or the "right" job, or the "right" lifestyle. Her work in the fight for women's rights might alleviate her sense of personal isolation. But none of these external changes will untangle the confused and self-destructive attitudes lying within.

Women who want to start feeling better about themselves must begin by facing what's going on inside. After talking with psychotherapists and psychiatrists in different parts of the country, interviewing women, and simply observing the lives of women around me, I've come to this conclusion: *the first thing women have to recognize is the degree to which fear rules their lives.*

Fear, irrational and capricious—fear that has no relation to capabilities or even to reality—is epidemic among women today. Fear of being independent (that could mean we'd end up alone and uncared for); fear of being dependent (that could mean we'd be swallowed by some dominating "other"); fear of being competent and *good* at what we do (that could mean we'd have to keep *on* being good at what we do); fear of being incompetent (that could mean we'd have to keep on feeling shlumpy, depressed, and *second-class*).

The fear bind is present in every stage of a woman's life, from the time she becomes pubescent, and desirous of attracting men (maybe she won't get a man; on the other hand, maybe she *will*, and then she'll be trapped and limited for the rest of her life). Fear is palpable in displaced homemakers whose husbands abandon them, and in widows who find themselves unable to cope once their husbands die. It's there in women trying to get started in professions, in women who want out of their marriages but are afraid to take the step, in women who've *gotten* out but find themselves utterly paralyzed at the prospect of being on their own.

Perhaps most poignantly of all, it's there in women who've traveled all the way up the professional ladder—and who *thought* they had this problem beat—only to find that at Point X in their careers, the level at which true independent action could no longer be avoided if they wanted to go all the way, they are suddenly overwhelmed by anxiety and can go no further. *Phobia has so thoroughly infiltrated the feminine experience it is like a secret plague. It has been built up over long years by social conditioning and is all the more insidious for being so thoroughly acculturated we do not even recognize what has happened to us.*

Women will not become free until they stop being afraid. We will not begin to experience real change in our lives, real emancipation, until we begin the process—almost a de-brainwashing—of working through the anxieties that prevent us from feeling competent and whole.

CHAPTER **III**

The Feminine Response

In high school I became a problem for the nuns, who found in me a paradoxical personality. I was both a discipline problem and a leader. I behaved with a kind of breathless daring, contemptuous of those strange, black-garbed creatures and also intimidated by them. By the time I was a sophomore I was president of my class and getting into trouble for wisecracking behind the teachers' backs at every opportunity. Being a smart aleck was an impulse I couldn't seem to resist. Even now, to recall those days brings back the delicious feeling of defying a system I thought stupid, and mentors I couldn't respect.

My confusion was genuine. Inside my smart-aleck exterior was a little girl—not a young girl on the verge of womanhood, but a *little* girl, frightened and confused about everything, a girl disturbed most of all by the fact that no one seemed to know how to take care of her. While my parents more or less assumed that I was in safe hands, the nuns seemed to be making a worse botch of my education with every passing year. I was being forced to grow up too fast. I had entered high school at the age of twelve and gone off to college when I was sixteen. Everyone marveled at my precocity, but no one seemed to know what I needed emotionally, least of all me. I was a burgeoning counterphobic—tough on the outside, frightened on the inside, and trying desperately, at all costs, to hide my fear.

I left college at twenty. Not two hours after graduation I was in the airport in Washington, D.C., ready to take off for a new life. My future had been neatly sealed (or so I imagined) by a stroke of fortune. Having entered a *Mademoiselle* magazine contest for college students, I suddenly found myself a winner. Nineteen other young women and I—"guest editors"—were being whisked off to spend a month working on the magazine's College Issue. What would happen after this thrilling month? Who knew? Who cared? For people as special as we, the world obviously had its plans.

Fifteen years later, when Sylvia Plath published a lacerating account of her own depressing Guest Editor experience in *The Bell Jar*, I found it so disturbing I couldn't, at that time, finish the book. But when I was going through the same tinselly introduction to the "glamorous" world of magazine publishing I was oblivious of what was happening to me underneath. Emotionally, *none* of us really knew what was happening. Bright, talented young women who came of age in the Fifties were moving toward the edge of a precipice. We didn't know how our lives would change, how pulled apart we'd be by the deep shifts taking place in the culture. Much would be expected of us, things that women in general had never before been expected to deliver. Things for which we had never been prepared.

When the monthlong Guest Editor period was over, I was offered a routine staff job. I'd never spent much time thinking about work or planning what I'd do with my life. Expecting, somehow, to be "taken care of" once again, I accepted the job offer and set up housekeeping in an apartment on New York's Upper East Side with three friends from college.

After a year or two, as I wearied of doing the same thing day after day, the glamour of the job began to wane, and the strain of earning barely enough money to survive had gotten on my nerves. I told myself I was better off than my roommates, girls whose parents always interfered in their lives, begging to pay their dental bills and buy them clothes. On a salary of $50 a week, I lived a poor, proud, and utterly confused life. It did not occur to me to try for a change—a new job, different roommates, perhaps even a *male* roommate.

By year three, questions began hounding me and I was drinking too much on weekends. What am I doing here? Will life just go *on* like this? Will something eventually *happen* to me? Will I meet someone? Will I marry?

Finally, something did happen. Four years after I'd set down on the LaGuardia landing strip, with the lights of New York twinkling in greeting, I became phobic.

It happened without warning. For over three years I'd been working in the same, futureless job as a researcher. I had never mustered the nerve to try writing an article, though my pride was wounded and I thought I really ought to be "*doing something.*" (Clipping articles from college newspapers and going out to interview someone once a month or so was hardly "*doing something.*") I know now that what I really wanted was to be rescued, transported on fairy wings to a new life, one in which I was confident, creative, compelling, and most of all, secure. The endless grind of being a single New York working girl with no man and no prospects was lowering my self-esteem with every passing day. I wasn't consciously "looking for a man." On the other hand, I wasn't trying to create a life. I had no idea of how I might fill a future that loomed before me—huge, demanding, and potentially obliterative.

Here it was—The Cinderella Complex. It used to hit girls of sixteen or seventeen, preventing them, often, from going to college, hastening them into early marriages. Now it tends to hit women after college—after they've been out in the world awhile. When the first thrill of freedom subsides and anxiety rises to take its place, they begin to be tugged by that old yearning for safety: the wish to be saved.

Not all women suffer the accompanying fear in its acute, or phobic state. For most it's a diffuse, amorphous thing, a gradual flaking around the edges. I, it turned out, was vulnerable to the acute version. At times when the wish to be saved hit me the hardest—in my last year of college, say, and after I'd been working for a few years and had no plan for my life, and after my marriage broke up—I became phobic.

One afternoon, while doing some research at the Brooklyn Museum, I was hit with a wave of vertigo so stunning I had to sit with my head between my knees. Never having felt faint or dizzy in my life, I found the experience terrifying. For six months I lived in fear that another of those attacks might overtake me, and I wasn't disappointed. The vertigo would flush up into my brain when I stepped on the bus to go to work in the morning, or when I entered a department store, or went down into the subway. Masses of people would swim past, giving me the strangest feeling of being unanchored. What would happen if I fainted in the middle of a crowd, or out in the street somewhere? For six months these bizarre symptoms took precedence over everything else. It was as if they constituted a metaphor for an unarticulated but central question: *Who will catch me if I fall?*

In fleeing college for New York, I'd thought I was escaping the stifling oppression of the Catholic girls' school environment in which I'd grown up. The trouble was, I didn't believe in my ability to carve a place for myself in the world. As time passed and the days were filled with the same unchallenging rituals my self-image began to crumble, its old supports replaced by a feeling of rootlessness. The reality of my relationship with my parents, my religion, my entire background was buried in a past whose influence over me I kept trying to ignore. Much as I had rebelled against the safety and restrictions of my childhood—the nuns, the rules, the weekly treks to the confessional, my father's bluntly unerring instinct to jump into the breach whenever I might have worked something out for myself, my mother's silent support of him—much as I wanted nothing more to do with any of this, at the same time I depended on it, *all* of it. I had grown up with the Church making my decisions in matters of morals and my parents telling me how to decide the secular issues of my life. If, on occasion, things got confused, I would let the Church make the practical decisions and my father the moral ones. Apparently it made no difference who decided what for me, just so long as *someone* did.

In September of that fourth year in New York, the panic attacks disappeared as mysteriously as they'd arrived. For several months I lived with an extreme sense of caution, afraid that if I should look over my shoulder, the "thing"—the terrible palpitations of fear—would still be there. At one point I had gone to a doctor, who assured me there was nothing physically wrong. Now that the debilitating symptoms were gone, I thanked God for my reprieve. I buried the experience, choosing to think of it as an unusual interlude, rather than see it as a sign that something was fundamentally amiss. I had never heard anyone describe an experience such as the one I had been through, which made it seem all the more horrible and threatening. *It is characteristic of the dependent personality to ignore signs of problems, to examine as little as possible, to "endure."*

("Maybe things will change," said Cinderella, endlessly sweeping the ashes from the hearth.)

In April I met someone. He was Catholic and an intellectual. He had lived in Paris for three years, studying at the Sorbonne on the GI bill. Now he worked as a reporter for a television trade magazine, wrote poetry, and baked his own *Dobostorte*. I found him fascinating. Almost immediately, I decided to put my fate in his hands.

Within a month I was pregnant, and shortly thereafter, married. It was one of the last decisions my father helped me make. I didn't ask for his intervention; on the other hand, I didn't reject it. My father told me that under the circumstances, the only moral course of action was to marry. "You made your decision in the very act of conception," he said.

I was not really involved with the morality of things. To be moral, one must be authentic. I had no true idea of right from wrong, only a catechetical one. I had lived my life conveniently following rules set for me by others. Now, as before, I followed. I fell into marriage as into a featherbed, not to know my street fears and night terrors for another ten years.

Early Signs

Psychiatrists who work with phobic women have discovered certain similarities in their backgrounds. They tend to reveal, early in their lives, the need to appear self-reliant and in control of their feelings. As children they work hard to develop the skills and qualities that will give them the illusion of strength and invulnerability. As adults, they will often pursue the kinds of jobs that reinforce an image of self-sufficiency. Much of what prephobic girls try to accomplish in their lives is perfectly normal—indeed, admirable—in and of itself. It becomes neurotic as the drive to achieve develops into a compulsion—they cannot *not* achieve.

The *raison d'être*, for such a young woman, is the building of a fortress behind which she can hide her core of insecurity and fear. "You always acted as if no one could tell you anything," the mother of a friend of mine likes to remind her to this day. "From the time you were fourteen or fifteen, you made it very clear there was nothing I could do or say that would be helpful to you in any way."

What was unfortunate was that the mother took at face value her daughter's self-confident swagger. She was intimidated by it, perplexed, wondering how it was that her child had suddenly turned into such a know-it-all. But in broadcasting the message "I *don't need anyone; I can take care of myself,*" her teen-age daughter was exhibiting a clear-cut symptom. Her bossy self-assurance was a performance, an attempt to overcompensate for a deep-seated lack of confidence.

It is not uncommon for prephobics to exhibit a daredevil quality as teen-agers. They may be physically active, taking risks and being aggressive in sports, or they may be defiant with those who have authority over them. Whatever the particular style, says Alexandra Symonds, who has studied phobias in women, the message is the same: *I don't need anybody; I can take care of myself.* Step by step, year by year, an elaborate counterphobic facade develops. The particulars may change from one person to the next, but the overall characterological picture remains the same: domineering, bossy, self-assured. There may be an attractive vibrancy laid over that cold core, a compelling energy that comes, in part, from the counterphobic's efforts to master her immediate environment. Often, for example, counterphobics are good talkers—charged by a need to articulate and define. In company their presence can be quite commanding. Who would ever guess that that dashing congressional aide in the green silk dress who's the center of the party—bowling everyone over with her anecdotes and her aggressive décolletage—is a phobic in disguise, unsure of her intelligence, her "attractiveness," the size of her breasts.

Counterphobic women have trouble relating positively to men. They have an inner need to feel superior, to be "in charge." In love relationships they find themselves complaining about the men with whom they chose to get involved. After the honeymoon's over, they begin to act cold and rejecting. Their men are dumbfounded, feeling strangely guilty without knowing what they've done wrong. What they've done wrong is *believe* in the assured image projected by women who are basically frightened. Taken at face value, these women never get to lean on their men, which—secretly—is what they have always really wanted. A system of mixed messages prevails, with the women acting bold and sassy and independent as a cover-up for their basic feelings of insecurity and helplessness. The men don't understand that they've been taken in by a false mask of self-sufficiency. They may even have wanted what their *women* want: a strong, independent "other" to lean on. Terrible clashes ensue as the truth of the women's needs emerges and the men are either unwilling or unable to fulfill them. This was the dynamic in the first love relationship of a young California woman I'll call Jill.

Jill's father was a feisty, highly successful lawyer. Her mother, though socially retiring, had a pleasant career as a free-lance magazine illustrator. Jill, a first child, had always felt caught between her conflicting images of male and female: female being mousy, but well taken care of; male being lively and outgoing, but alone and unprotected in dealing with the world. When she was twenty, Jill began to act out the conflict building inside her. She started living with a carpenter, an intelligent but uneducated young man who wasn't clear about what he wanted to do with his life. Soon Jill was feeling unhappy, frustrated, and down on the poor guy. She went into therapy, and complained of being unable to decide whether she wanted to become a psychologist, a lawyer, a potter, or a musician. Though she opened a pottery shop eventually, career conflict was the least of her problems.

For one thing, Jill was sexually insecure, the sort of person who needed to be the main attraction at a party, a woman who lived with the underlying fear that her boyfriend might meet—and leave her for —someone more attractive. Also symptomatic were Jill's complaints about money. She wanted a larger house and was confused as to whose responsibility this was—hers or her boyfriend's. Inwardly she harbored a grudge against him for not making enough to buy the kind of house she wanted. She was oblivious, though, to the depth of her grudge, because it clashed so sharply with her feminist ideals.

"It's interesting," Jill's therapist recalls, "that Jill always gave the impression of being terrifically responsible. She came to her therapy sessions on time; she ended them herself rather than waiting compliantly for me to end them. She seemed efficient and in charge of things. Then, somewhere between her second and third years of therapy, everything cracked open."

Quite without warning, one morning, Jill began to hyperventilate, to feel dizzy, to have heart palpitations—to experience the whole panoply of anxiety symptoms. She was afraid to go out of the house. Her "sudden" insecurity manifested itself in all sorts of ways. For example, she would call her therapist at home on Saturday night to say she was going to be late for her session the following Thursday. "I can always be called at home in an emergency," said her therapist, "but this was no emergency. Suddenly this super-responsible person was treating me like her mother. I was supposed to be there whenever she wanted me, on command. Eventually we discovered that the earlier counterdependent behavior had been a big defensive maneuver on Jill's part. She'd pulled it off so successfully that after two years I was thinking, 'Why is this woman still with me?' She seemed, you know, so *competent*.

"Now Jill has begun to express her anger. It turns out she's furious because for two years she felt dissatisfied with me and *I* never said anything to her about it. I told her the question was: Why had she never talked to *me* about it? Now, suddenly, she's afraid to go out and do things on her own. She's afraid to take a vacation because she can't let go of the rigid structure in her life. With her facade gone we're finding that she's still very dependent on her parents, and *that*'s what all that counterdependent behavior was covering up. Her dependency is coming out in the form of anger at her boyfriend as well as me. She's mad as hell at him because he's not going to become a lawyer and take proper care of her. And *I'm* not going to be her mother."

Jill had superimposed the image of her strong, dynamic father onto her lover, wanting him to bring home the bacon as well as the social stimulation, just as her father had always done. Money, excitement, stimulating political friends—all of this had been provided for both Jill and her mother by "Daddy." By comparison with her father, the man Jill was living with just wasn't cutting the mustard. "He's a nice, soft, sweet guy, very well liked by her parents," said the therapist, "but it's clear that Jill is dissatisfied with him. In college she went with another man who wasn't sure of what he wanted to be, and they split up because Jill couldn't tolerate his ambivalence. She can't feel strong unless her man feels strong."

Jill doesn't want to be like her mother, cloistered and passive. Her main identification is with her father. But she certainly doesn't want to have to *be* that powerful, all-providing figure in her own life. That's what the *man* should do for her. When he doesn't, she feels let down and furious. "Jill is the sort of woman who's very sexual at the beginning of a relationship but after a while the excitement goes out the window because she's so angry," says her therapist.

Touching the Fear

Jill's phobic symptoms arrived at precisely that moment in her life when she realized that she was never going to get what she really wanted, which was to have someone else do her risk-taking for her. "I see her, now, at the edge of having to make really crucial, maturing decisions," her therapist says, "having to relinquish the internalized father who would make her life all right. She may have to go back to school to learn something that'll be more intellectually satisfying for her than her little pottery shop—something, also, that will support her in the manner in which she really wants to be supported. At twenty-seven, she may have to decide to do these things for herself, and not expect her mate to provide everything for her. She's just beginning to come to grips with all this, and what's coming out is pure fear. She's panicked."

That pure fear, if she can bring herself to see it through, can actually lead Jill to a freer, more relaxed, more satisfying life. Before the "crack," she was doing everything in her power to avoid experiencing that fear. Mostly she tried duplicating the same protected environment she'd had as a child, manipulating her lover in the hope that she could get him to act like her daddy. In part it was her boyfriend's refusal to play the role of Jill's father that precipitated her crisis with dependency. Painful and frightening though this crisis may be, she has the chance now to break free of her old habits and grow up. She saw—actually, she *experienced*—her own counterphobic facade, and was willing to try to go it alone, without the shell, unguarded, unprotected, vulnerable.

Not so fortunate are those women whose counterphobic patterns go unrecognized. They are likely to spend their lives constructing an increasingly impenetrable defense. These are the women who'd do anything, *deprive* themselves of anything—love, satisfaction, happiness—in order never to have to experience what Jill went through: the panic, the confusion, the anger.

Counterphobic women pick certain image-enhancing jobs—jobs about which many more overtly inhibited women might say, "Oh, I could never do *that:* I'd be too afraid." Which is, of course, the point. Feeling helpless and frightened is so threatening to these women that they devote all their energies to constructing a life—and a style—calculated to throw everyone (themselves included) off the track. They may become racing-car drivers. Or actresses. Or prostitutes. (Jane Fonda played a typical counterphobic personality in *Klute.*)

Or, like Abigail Fletcher, they might yearn to track down criminals. Just as there are degrees of phobia, so too are there degrees to which a basically fearful person develops a counterphobic personality. In Abigail's case, the style, the swagger, the cynicism, was developing into a hardened shell. She *believed* in her own image of strength, except for those times when a boyfriend would leave her to marry and have babies with someone else. Then Abigail would feel miserable and defeated for weeks, maybe even months, but eventually she would pick herself up, and dust herself off, and her vindictiveness and recrimination would return, redoubled. Occasionally, just to prove how utterly dispensable men were, she would have an affair with a woman.

It was all there, that "toughness," honed to the sharpness of a hound's tooth, by the time Abigail had become a young mother of eighteen. That happened in 1976. She got pregnant to get away from her parents—insecure people who, by indulging and overprotecting their pretty daughter, had made her feel stifled and scared. To deny those helpless feelings she had become a tough little version of the Jewish American Princess. She believed with all her tight little heart that she should have the finest things in life. She also suspected—deeply, bitterly—that no one would ever turn up to provide those things for her. Certainly they had not been provided by that pothead husband of hers, the man she married at seventeen and left, a year later, after bearing his daughter.

Hiding the Fear: The Counterphobic Style

Abigail's story will give you a glimpse of the counterphobic defense, a pseudo-independent style which pretends self-sufficiency when underneath one is timid, unsure, and too fearful of losing identity even to be able to fall in love.

Though the details of this story are unique to Abigail Fletcher (her name has been fictionalized), the pseudo-independent style may be recognizable to many. It is the style of the sheerly terrified, the woman so swamped by feelings of gender-vulnerability she would almost rather be a man.

The ad in the Sunday *Globe* said, "INVESTIGATOR, MALE OR FEMALE," and was placed by the personnel department of a specialty store in the Quincy Market area of downtown Boston. That "INVESTIGATOR" caught her attention. Abigail Fletcher needed a job pretty bad, and with her year at B.U. and her good looks she could probably find work as a receptionist somewhere, but who wanted to sit next to a rubber plant all day acting friendly? One way or another Abigail had managed to avoid that boring office scene, and she had no intention of getting sucked into it now. Lately, she'd been working on a film deal with her boyfriend, pretty high-powered stuff, and while it had fallen through temporarily and she needed money, she wasn't trading her sharp wits for a desk in a typing pool—no way. She had a good nose and a big mouth (as she put it), by which she meant quite plainly that she liked rooting into other people's business and could talk good and tough when the occasion called for it. Abigail liked to imagine herself as an investigator on the side of law and justice. She used to fantasize about going to work for the Department of Consumer Affairs. She could see herself in her suede aviator's jacket and Jordache jeans, her long chestnut hair with the Farrah Fawcett wings, confronting Boston's butchers about the fat quotient in their chopped chuck.

"WILL TRAIN," the newspaper ad had said. It was for a job on the security staff of Towne & Country, a big, fancy specialty store. Abigail decided this was it: the time had come to act. She was small, but tough enough for the job; rather well built if she did say so herself, thanks in part to jujitsu lessons she'd taken once in the basement of a Buddhist church, and thanks in part to the genes of her dear, sweet mama. Yes, old Abigail Fletcher could definitely play the part.

In the personnel office of Towne & Country, Abigail was amused. She could see this guy named Hollis turning on to her right away. He interviewed her for an hour. Once he finished with the essentials

("You take drugs?" "Sure, I smoke pot." "Ever steal anything from a former employer?" "Nope." "Take any other kinds of drugs?" "Nope." "Have any outstanding debts?" "Yeah, four hundred dollars with Checking Plus"), he whined a bit about the inadequacies of his present staff and then explained the training program.

"You're on," Mr. Hollis told her on the phone the next day. "Welcome to the Towne & Country Security Force."

Abigail chuckled when she discovered that one of the guys she'd be training with was this cat named Mario from her old jujitsu class. A real crybaby, she called him. When they used to work out together and she'd try to kick him he'd instinctively buckle his knees to protect his nuts, and he always ended up getting it in the shins. "Old Scaredy-Nuts," she called him.

Abigail noticed a difference between herself and the male trainees: *they* got lessons in karate and come-along techniques. (A come-along is when you get a shoplifter's arm twisted up behind the back so the person will come along to the Security Office without any trouble.) Abigail had confronted Hollis right off: "When am *I* going to get to take these courses?" But he had smiled his oily, fake-paternal smile and said, "When you get your first apprehension."

"Hell," thought Abigail. "I already *have* my Green Belt, which is more than Old Scaredy-Nuts can say."

Abigail started showing up for work in jeans and sneakers. The sense of intrigue and action appealed to her from the beginning. She was taught how to "burn out," which means following suspects so closely you scare them out of the store before they're able to take anything. She learned how to "go-for-a-throw," which is attempting to force someone you *think* but aren't sure has taken something to sneak off and throw the merchandise on a table or back into a dressing room.

Abigail was a quick study. She learned the highways and byways, the main traffic thoroughfares, the positions of the mirrors and crash alarms. In the beginning she spent a lot of time crawling around on the lint-carpeted floors of dressing rooms. It was the part of the job she liked best, as well as the one most likely to produce results. You carried a little pillbox full of pins in your pocket at all times, and when the spirit moved you, you ducked into an empty dressing room and pinned the curtains shut so you could snoop in privacy. Then you flattened yourself on the floor and peeped through the baseboard air vent to see what you could see. It was fun to watch the women posing and preening and sucking in their flabby guts. Every so often you'd see one of them rip off the tags and start stuffing things into a shopping bag, or handbag, or into her underwear and panty hose. "Crotch workers," these last were called, and they were usually pros.

The pros could be damned scary. Often they were big and black (a combination Abigail had dreaded since her high school days on the South Side) and expert at "making you out." One day this absolute Amazon caught Abigail tailing her, turned, sidled up to her, and said in this hoarse, whiskey whisper, "If you want to know how to follow, do it up *close* and don't use the mirrors."

"Don't talk to *me*, man," Abigail shot back, but her knees had turned to water.

When, after two weeks in training, Abigail made her first "apprehension," the experience was shocking. The woman she nabbed was neither black nor Puerto Rican, as Abigail had anticipated, nor shabbily dressed. She was little Mrs. Hansen, with a graying bun pinned neatly to the nape of her neck and looking sick with fear.

Unnerved, Abigail had to take Mrs. Hansen to Mr. Hollis's office. The contents of the woman's shopping bags were spread out on Mr. Hollis's big mahogany desk for all to see. Mrs. Hansen had no drugs. As for weapons, all she could produce was a packet of needles and thread of the sort fastidious women carry for emergency clothing repairs. The packet was confiscated.

Once the confrontation was over, Abigail (who, oddly, identified with the woman), experienced a sharp drop in her adrenaline rate. The whole scene was depressing as hell. The rest of her job she performed by rote. Security required her to accompany the woman onto the elevator and down to the first floor. Mrs. Hansen kept a clutch on her packages, her head bowed. Abigail took her past the Plexiglas-walled wig boutique, gloves and hosiery, through the heady barrier of patchouli hanging over the perfume counters, as far as the front door. There, without looking back, Mrs. Hansen left Abigail and scurried like a frightened animal into the crowds on Market Street.

Feeling guilty and sick at heart, Abigail struggled, as always, to regain her cool. No point in getting down about this. It was just a *job*. What was that crazy woman who didn't need it shoplifting for anyhow? Abigail knew what she'd do. Once she got off that lousy

subway she'd take a nice hot soak in the tub. Then she'd put her kid
to bed, put on some Stones, and do up a couple of lines.

The next day, strangely enough, Abigail scored again—a double
score, in fact: two young black kids, fifteen and sixteen. This time
she did her job efficiently, remorselessly. She was on a streak. Strong,
invulnerable, she felt herself riding on some strange kind of high.
Taking charge of your life was *easy* once you set your mind to it, she
thought. Her work life was down pat. Her love life was all right too.
Men were drawn to her like bees to honey. In a few years she would
have her own security business and get the hell off the South Side.

There was only one flaw in her plan. What Abigail didn't know—
what she could not foresee—was that she would never be able to fall
deeply, irrevocably in love. Not unless something happened to break
through to her hidden core. She would have a series of boyfriends,
men who were attracted at first by her glossy self-assurance but who
later were repelled by this weird, clutching quality she had. A man
would hardly have begun seeing her when she was all of a sudden
wanting to bake pies for him and model her new underwear. That
ought to be all right, the man would tell himself. But it wasn't. This
Abigail waxed hot and cold. You felt she was spinning a web to en-
snare you. In bed she was good, but somehow, when all was said and
done, *not there*. A tough nut. A narcissist. A little like a whore.

The striking thing about the counterphobic personality is its effectiveness as a defense. Women who are counterphobic rarely experience fear, so they have no idea of the degree to which it dominates
their lives.

Phobia, in women, can be related to fear of abandoning sexual re-
straints and feeling helpless and vulnerable. This fear sometimes
expresses itself in fantasies of prostitution and domination. Abigail
liked to think of herself as a sex pistol, a love-'em-and leave-'em
woman who never lacked for gifts and fancy escorts, but who never
tied herself down. This fantasy was an elaborate cover-up for a terrible, deep loneliness—loneliness that came from her inability to let go
and merge with another human being. To merge was too frightening. It made her feel as if she could lose the boundaries of her own
personality.

Such fears trace back to profound infantile loneliness. The need
for love that goes unfulfilled in childhood can lead to a passive and

potentially destructive wish to give oneself up to anyone. Abigail had been catered to by her parents, but she had never felt supported in the way in which she needed to be supported. And she had never felt that her parents truly cared for her: if they had, wouldn't they have nurtured her need to grow?

So Abigail protected her frightening inner need. But she also had aggressive wishes to be free of this need—free of *men*, whose strength she so needed and envied—and she let out her aggression toward the men on the job. She scorned Mr. Hollis, "Old Scaredy-Nuts," and anyone else who did not arouse her romantic interest.[1] Her true awe of men in general was expressed in her "male" language—indeed, in her whole "tough" style. It would be nice to be strong (the way men are strong); *safe* (the way men are safe); not easily exploitable. Not vulnerable and unsure.

The way women are.

The Feminine Response

Fearfulness has long been considered a natural component of femininity. The idea of being afraid of mice, of the dark, of being alone—these things have been considered ordinary fears for women, but not for men. *Psychologists and social scientists have finally begun to take the position that phobia, or irrational fear, is no more "normal" or healthy in women than it is in men.*

And yet, it *is* more widespread among women. Struck by the numbers of phobic female patients showing up in her practice in New York City, Alexandra Symonds says that while they appear to be afraid of being controlled by others, these women are actually afraid to take charge of their own lives. They fear setting a personal direction. They fear movement, discovery, change—anything that's unfamiliar and unknown. Most disabling of all, they're afraid of normal aggression and assertiveness.[2]

Women experience far more fear than they ought to. Because it goes hand in hand with dependency, the phobic response has to be ferreted out and identified. Women avoid much in life simply to accommodate fear. Vivian Gold, a psychologist practicing in San Francisco, says that women come to see her with every conceivable kind of fear. "They are phobic about going out, phobic about becoming involved with someone, phobic about taking the initiative in their relationships—all sorts of things."

Partly because some degree of fear and avoidance is considered *appropriate* in women, and partly because it's a painful thing to have to deal with, the depth of the fear gripping Dr. Gold's female patients is not always apparent at the outset. "Often it doesn't come out in treatment for over a year," she says. "They prefer, in the beginning, to talk about having trouble with their marriages, or making certain career decisions. It's not until much later that you discover they're utterly terrified of being alone. Sometimes they can't tolerate spending even one night by themselves."

"Many women's phobias can be traced back to having had overprotective parents," says Ruth Moulton, "parents who'd frighten their daughters by laying their own anxiety trips on them. They'd tell their daughters that they shouldn't see strange men, that they should get home early at night, that if they weren't careful they'd get raped." (There are reasons, of course, why girls are taught to be wary, but the crippling effects of all the childhood threats and warnings indicate that mass education in self-defense would be a more constructive course for young women than teaching them that they need to be continuously watchful and afraid if they want to survive.)

The life of the woman who is phobic tends to be lived in smaller and smaller concentric circles. Bit by bit friends are given up; activities. The woman who loved sports in school becomes utterly sedentary as a matron. Skiing is too risky. ("You could break a leg," she tells herself, believing she's being quite sensible.) Swatting a tennis ball is out (too aggressive). Travel may become a problem. Planes are scary. The pilots are lushes, she'll tell you, quoting the latest statistics on plane crashes. Anyone in her right *mind* would be afraid to fly. (It does not, of course, occur to the phobic woman that flying is a symbol of separation from the prince: whomever it is she relies on to take care of her.)

Sometimes the phobic response forces women to avoid activities so apparently innocuous you'd never guess that fear was at the bottom of it. A number of women I talked to reported that as their children came along, they stopped reading. "I just never seemed to have the time anymore" was the usual explanation. "Then it became a kind of habit. My husband would sit around reading all the time, but not me; the children were grown and gone and somehow I never got into the reading habit again. I would knit or watch television instead."

These women avoided reading because to read is to take a trip—a trip away from home and husband, a trip alone. Reading was one of many "dropped" activities which phobic women experienced as simply disappearing from their lives. It went without being questioned.[3]

Less acute forms of phobia are far more common—and they are also harder to identify as irrational. Women's retreat into the home, for example. It's easy to use the domestic alternative as protection against the vicissitudes of a world that is scary. "Too many people make me too excited," says the writer Anne Fleming, explaining why she prefers to stay at home. "The thought of sitting in a newspaper city room full of clicking typewriters appalls me. I don't want to hear the fear of others trying to survive in a professional circus. I certainly don't want anyone to see *my* fear."

A woman I knew who'd supported herself until, at age thirty-three, she married (at which point she dropped her job like someone who'd been handed a lifetime sinecure) was now thinking about going back to work and taking up a new profession. She was also considering leaving her husband—an idea she'd had in the back of her mind for several years but which apparently terrified her. "At night I lie in bed and stare at the ceiling," she told me. "I have this fear that the ceiling is going to crack open and swallow me up."

The anticipation of being on her own again is terrifying to this woman. Walking down streets, she sometimes has the sensation that tall buildings are going to topple over on her.

While marriage seems to bring on phobia in some women, divorce triggers it in others. "I discovered that I had a whole group of women patients who'd become very frightened and isolated after a divorce which *they* initiated," Ruth Moulton told me. These women, she says, suffer from "a compulsive need for a man." In fact virtually all her women patients who were troubled by phobia shared the same illusion: "*If only there was a man in the house—even if he was asleep, drunk, or sick—it was better than being alone.*"

The Flight from Independence

By the time she reaches marrying age, many an excessively dependent young woman finds the pretense of strength difficult if not impossible to maintain. She may have been a big achiever in adolescence but now she yearns to drop the mask and indulge her dependence. Without being conscious of it she looks for a situation in which she can give up her facade of self-sufficiency and ease back into that warm, cradled state reminiscent of childhood that's so seductive to women—a home. What more ideal situation than housewifery for allowing an erstwhile "achiever" to drop out with grace? Her sudden infatuation with homemaking often comes as a surprise.

No one, certainly, was more surprised than Carolyn Burckhardt at the great flush of comforting domesticity that arose in her on that blissful day on which she became Mrs. Helmut Anderson. "This was a side of myself that I never knew existed," she told me twelve years later, recollecting the time (she'd been in her early twenties) when she "decided" to have a few children before proceeding with her career in music. Now in her late thirties, Carolyn (her name and her husband's have been changed) was trying to put things together again. All her youthful plans had fallen apart, crumbling under the weight of an oppressive marriage. It was a situation over which she felt she had no control.

As a young woman Carolyn had been a first-rate contralto, one of the youngest singers ever to be asked to join the Santa Fe Opera Company. As a hard-driving, high-achieving girl in Shaker Heights, Ohio, she had grown up riding in hunts, showing horses, and—ultimately—training, training, training what had turned out to be a remarkable young voice. Everyone who knew her was amazed by her discipline, her maturity, her striking goal-directedness. "Carolyn always knew what she wanted from the time she was a little girl," her mother used to tell her country-club cronies. They would nod, inwardly envious because while *their* daughters were busy creating small, wavy "dips" of hair over their foreheads and starching their crinolines, Carolyn was clearly engaged in something, well . . . *meaningful*.

The girl worked feverishly, whether mucking out stalls in her old jeans and work shirt or smartly taking jumps in her jodhpurs and black velvet riding cap. Then, in late adolescence, she gave up her involvement with horses and began practicing her singing two, three, and four hours a day. In the spring of her senior year at college Carolyn went to Santa Fe to audition for the opera company, and to the thrill and delight of her family, she was accepted. In June they packed her off, bag and baggage, to enter the world of music. Who would have expected that only six months later, when her mama whisked her off to New York for a week of operagoing, she would meet and fall in love with the elegant Helmut Anderson?

On balance, Carolyn could probably have joined an opera company in New York, but when Helmut asked her to marry him she wanted to make things easier for her husband by "staying home for a while." Helmut, at twenty-four, was just finishing his Ph.D. thesis. He needed the peace and quiet of a well-organized household while he wrote.

He needed, in short, a wife.

The Secretly Phobic Wife

Without ever really giving it much thought (Who *did* give much thought to these things? she sighed contentedly), Carolyn got pregnant right away, and then again eight months after the first child was born. Young, energetic, madly in love, and with a whole history of achievement to fall back on, Carolyn had imagined it would be easy to resume her career once the children were in nursery school. Meanwhile she'd play housewife, mother, and amanuensis, a role—and this had come as a shock—which she adored. "I had never played house as a little girl," she told me. "Past the age of six or so, dolls didn't interest me in the least. But when Helmut and I got married I found myself thrilled with being at home, thrilled with *making* a home, thrilled with the whole idea of being a wife. It caught me by surprise. It was as if something within me had taken a quarter-turn, and suddenly everything was in its right place."

Helmut, who immediately got a university job within commuting distance of Brooklyn, presided over one room in their apartment—

the dining room. Being the best room in the place, the one with the most light and ventilation, it quickly became his study.

It was a room Helmut enjoyed presiding over. Through its glass doors he could observe his little family going pleasantly about its business. Carolyn saw to it that the children played quietly whenever Helmut was at home. "Shh, Daddy's working," the kids heard, day in and day out, from the time they were very small. The arrangement was inconvenient in some ways, but Carolyn thought it a small price to pay for having the rest of the large, rambling Brooklyn Heights apartment all to herself. *Except, of course, for when Helmut emerged from his study, at which point the apartment became all his.*

It was one of those ugly little realities we so often choose to ignore: Carolyn had no stake, no real purchase on anything. Everything "they" owned was Helmut's. The dog was Helmut's; the lease to the apartment was Helmut's; the very food on their table—even the escape route from all this, the monthly commutation ticket to New Haven—was Helmut's.

By the time she had come to a recognition of all this, Carolyn was almost thirty. She woke up one morning (it seemed that way, as if she had just awakened) to the fact that Helmut was a Have and she, who had spent her whole childhood having, had somehow been relegated to the humiliating status of Have Not. Helmut had only to growl from behind the glass doors of his study and the rest of them tiptoed and whispered. The kids fought (endlessly, it seemed), and she would come flying out from the kitchen to hush them. When one child was sick and the other not, she hired a baby-sitter to take the healthy one to school. Helmut wouldn't help out with these things. On his two weekdays at home, he wrote—period; *regardless* of what was going on around him. By mid-February of every winter, when the virus season had taken its toll, Helmut would be yowling about the amount of money going out to baby-sitters. It was 1978, and Helmut was teaching at one of the most prestigious universities in the Northeast—the women students there had absolutely bowled over the administration with their demands for policy changes—but in Helmut's home, policy remained inescapably the same: *he*, Helmut, was the bright luminary in the constellation of the family. Carolyn was the wobbling satellite.

Somehow, eight years had slipped by. The opera, by then, had become a vague afterimage in Carolyn's imagination, too bright to be seen in any clarity or detail and too brief to impinge upon her consciousness for more than a moment. She had been a child then, a girl filled with dreams and no sense of the real world. A girl with this crazy, childish idea that life could be lived center stage.

Carolyn was no singer anymore. She was thin and taut, her hair no longer thick as it had once been. The velvet skin of girlhood had begun to lose its luster. "But *sweetie!*" her mother exclaimed, long distance, when Carolyn tried to talk to her. "I don't understand. Helmut's doing so *well*. Associate Professor at his age is nothing to sneeze at. Soon you'll have more money and things will get easier."

Carolyn could not tell her mother that money was not the solution. Carolyn could not find the words to articulate that she was neither girl nor woman anymore; that, living in the timeless limbo of service to another, she was a creature utterly without autonomy. What she dreamt about—but only in sleep—was the possibility of being in control. She dreamt of being a surgeon, one whose operating-room team responded to her so adroitly she had only to ask for the instruments with her eyes.

When Timothy, their youngest, entered first grade, Carolyn began to talk of "doing something." "Helmut, I really think I've got to do something," she'd begin.

"God, *please* do something," he'd respond. "You're driving me crazy."

By then, Carolyn had lost the fragile nerve that had driven her so relentlessly during her adolescent years. Helmut's reaction made her feel abandoned, as if he didn't *want* to take care of her; as if all he wanted from her was to be left in peace. Carolyn wanted the *option* to go out and do something, but she certainly didn't want to feel that she *had* to. She should have some choice about how she lived her own life.

But Carolyn's concern with choice was superficial and false. She would far rather live *without* choice—as she had been doing since the day she married—than risk experiencing her own individuation. So she kowtowed. She took it as a command when Helmut began grumbling about the bills at the same time that he insisted she start to entertain on a different level. He was becoming *known* in the academic world. "No more of this postgraduate cheese-and-crackers stuff," he bellowed. "And no more jug wine. These people are used to estate bottled."

At this point, what Helmut really wanted was a second income in the family, something that would help spruce up their lives a little. He was *beyond* the style in which they lived. He was publishing regularly now; he was being *spoken* of in his field. Instead of boosting him, he complained to several of his most intimate colleagues at Yale, his wife and family were holding him back.

A Wifely "Flight from Self"

Carolyn's phobic avoidance of life became increasingly apparent as she did nothing to develop a new course of action for herself. Responding not to any inner dictate to grow and develop, but merely *reacting* to pressure from Helmut to create a stage that he might illuminate with his brilliance, she tried desperately to become cleverer with the family budget. She took a free university extension course in wine selection. She extended her culinary repertoire, becoming skilled at producing exotic meals that required little meat. Instead of cheese and crackers, when company came, there were her own *caponata*, fresh-baked herb bread, and the darkest of Bordeaux, which she had learned to ferret out of the most god-awful neighborhood liquor store for under four dollars a bottle. To upgrade the appearance of their apartment she haunted thrift shops, looking for small hooked rugs, brass lamps, quadruple-plated silver serving bowls—things that would help create an ambiance of comfort and success. Carolyn had never read *The Second Sex*. If she had, she would have found riveting Simone de Beauvoir's remarks on the dangers, for women, of excessive involvement in the home. "In this insanity . . . the woman is so busy she forgets her own existence," De Beauvoir expounded. "A *household, in fact, with its meticulous and limitless tasks, permits to woman a sado-masochistic flight from herself . . .*"

If Carolyn was too busy to sense the implications of all her busyness, not so Helmut, who was beginning to feel that his wife was a failure. His colleagues' wives *did* things, even if it was only to go back to graduate school. "God, Carolyn, *caponata* again?" he would say, five minutes before the guests arrived. "I think *maybe* the Aronsons have had that stuff the last three times they've been here."

I would need a year, Carolyn told herself. I would need a manager, a booking agent, an accompanist. I would have to travel at least four months out of that year, sometimes for weeks at a time, and *then*, at the end of it, maybe it'll turn out I don't have what it takes to do opera anymore.

She thought about medical school, but it was too outrageous an idea to contemplate for very long. It would take two years just to get ready, then four years of med school, then internship, and residency . . . With horror Carolyn grasped that she would be over forty and just starting, and that life between then and now would be difficult— awfully, impossibly difficult. Helmut would simply never accommodate himself to the havoc her going back to school would create.

Always, at this point in the fantasy, Carolyn's eyes would fill with tears. "Probably I couldn't even get *into* med school."

It was easier for Carolyn to think of herself as "not bright enough" than it was to face the degree to which she depended on Helmut for everything. As a result of her dependency, Helmut got away with murder. A petty tyrant whose every wish was acceded to, he wasn't even faithful to her anymore.

Only in the wee hours of those nights when Helmut stayed over in New Haven would Carolyn allow herself to think about how *often* he stayed over in New Haven. How easily the routine had been established. Once or twice a week he'd call with an excuse—the weather was bad and he was going to stay at a friend's house; or he'd be using the library late and no sense in trying to take the milk train home.

The sham of it! And for how *long* it had been going on this way! Except for his academic brilliance, which seemed to shine ever brighter with each passing year, Helmut had disappointed Carolyn in virtually everything she had ever hoped for from him. He was father to the children only in that he provided for their physical needs. Though he was home more than most men, he hardly ever saw his children, except for the ritualized excursions they made on Saturday afternoons.

As for his relationship with *her*—well, Helmut hardly made a fit companion, since he rarely talked to Carolyn anymore except to remind her to take care of things he needed: to get his shirts from the Chinese laundry; and couldn't she get him out of having to go to those awful parents' meetings at Timothy's new school? and would she see to it that her mother didn't come to visit until after New Year's? Her mother *certainly* wouldn't fit in with the department people they were entertaining on New Year's Eve.

At the age of thirty-two, eleven years after she'd gotten married, Carolyn began having sudden and prolonged weeping spells. Even *thinking* about a change—a job, a little vacation by herself, just the tiniest way out of the nightmare her life had become—made her feel unbearably tired and listless. She felt herself to be going through her days on a conveyor belt, making the same dismal rounds: the school, the butcher's, the children's floor of the library, the liquor store. She lost weight but hardly mourned the loss of her looks, for her body had become all but useless to her. She began lying awake nights, plagued by the memory of strange dreams, images fraught with violence and death. Helmut was putting pressure on her to get out of the house and get a job. He wasn't satisfied with her anymore. It made her angry, yet she didn't dare face him with her anger. *Who did he think he was, demanding of her that she change after all she had given up for him. She had given up her life! He? He had given up nothing.* Like a nasty mother bird, he was trying to nudge her out of the nest before she was ready. No, she was *not* ready. Someone had clipped her wings. Someone had neglected to teach her how to fly.

When, finally, Helmut decided to leave Carolyn, she was forty and still had not learned. The divorce almost ruined her. It took her a long, long time to put the pieces of her life back together. It took a long time to discover that she, not he, had been the instrument of her martyrdom. It took a long time to teach herself what no one can hope to escape in this life: responsibility. All the rushing about and errands and preoccupation with things of the family had made her *feel* responsible, but that was spurious. From the day Carolyn Burckhardt had met Helmut Anderson she had not made one independent decision concerning her own life. She had become a helpmate—a grown-up in name only. By the time she was several years into the marriage, her phobic avoidance of life had increased to the point where she had given up *all* authority and handed it over to Helmut, who she hoped would save her.

Women over thirty in particular are caught in the middle. We've been groomed and educated for dependency—for motherhood, for wifedom; for what is really, when we sit down and analyze it, an infinitely extended childhood. When marriages break up, women are often profoundly shocked to find themselves in charge of their own lives for the first time. Deep down they had always believed that to be supported and taken care of by someone else was their God-given right.

The question that must be asked now is: How did women get this way?

CHAPTER **IV**

Becoming Helpless

I had been the indulged and protected first child for longer than most. My parents sent me across the railroad tracks and into the little village school when I was five. I started young partly because I knew how to read and Holy Name of Mary School could be persuaded to accept me early, partly because my only sibling—a brother —had just been born.

Feeling confused and not a little rejected, I went off to be taught by black-garbed nuns in a peculiar institution where I would never once be comfortable, from first grade through twelfth. Learning came easily, and I was often bored. Other children struggled, going over the same things with sister again and again. Sometimes my quickness made me smug, but mostly it made me feel peculiar.

I skipped half the second grade and half the fifth, which put me into sixth grade in St. Thomas Aquinas, a chaotic school in a little mill town in Baltimore, when I was nine years old. It was the nearest parochial school to where we lived. The kids there were poor, hostile, and if smart, didn't like showing it. I spent most of my time trying to avoid getting beaten up after school. When IQ's were tested at the end of eighth grade, the principal, in typically unenlightened fashion, announced the scores to the class. My score was highest, and from that moment on the kids looked at me as if I were the enemy

—odder, even, than they had previously imagined. "She thinks she's so smart," the girls would hiss at one another behind my back as I passed them on my way to do equations on the blackboard.

Thankfully, I was sent to a private high school in the country, although it turned out that the girls there were almost as uninterested in learning as the kids in the mill town. Though I had grown sassy and rebellious as a consequence of never fitting in, I was also deemed a "leader." I was elected class president, yearbook editor, and head of the Field Day marching routines. This newfound power I took home with me, using it to do battle with my father, who had suddenly taken an interest in my intellectual development. I was always trying to show him that I was smart, that I knew things, that I was beginning to think. He was always trying to show me how much better off I'd be if I'd simply recognize how little I knew about *anything* and accept his tutelage. Science was his field—science and math. I got less and less adept at math as my high school years progressed. By the time I reached college, my "science anxiety" was such that I almost failed freshman chemistry.

For many years I thought that my problems had to do with my father. Not until I was in my thirties did I begin to suspect that feelings about my mother were part of the inner conflict that had begun developing in me when I was very young. My mother was an even-tempered person, not given to screaming or fits of temper, always there, always waiting when my brother and I came home from school. She took me to dance lessons when I was very small, and later—until I was well into my teens—insisted that I practice the piano every day. She would sit by me and count, as regular and predictable as a metronome. Equally predictable was the afternoon nap she took, the small retreat from the reality of her daily life. She was given to illnesses of a chronic variety: headaches, bursitis, fatigue.

On the surface, there didn't seem to be anything so unusual about her life: she was the typical housewife/mother of her time. And yet . . . that peculiar elusiveness, and the little illnesses, so many of which, I think now (and so does she), were related to unexpressed anger. She avoided confrontation with my father and appeared to us children to be thoroughly intimidated by him. When she did speak out on some issue, the strain it caused her was palpable. She feared him.

In comparison with my mother, my father loomed large and vivid in my life—forceful Father with the big voice, big gestures, rude and sometimes embarrassing ways. He was didactic, authoritarian, and no one who knew him could easily dismiss him. Dislike, yes; there were certainly those who could summon forth that sentiment. But no one could pretend he wasn't there. He forced himself upon the consciousness of those with whom he came into contact; his personality impinged. You thought that he was lavishing attention upon you, but often the conversations seemed to spring more from some hidden need of his own.

I loved him. I adored the sureness he exuded, the idealism, the high, edgy energy. His laboratory in the engineering building at Johns Hopkins University was cool and impressive with its big, cold pieces of equipment. He was The Professor. My mother would refer to him, when speaking with others, as "Dr. Hoppmann." She referred to herself as Mrs. Hoppmann. "Mrs. Hoppmann speaking," she would say, when answering the phone, as if to take refuge of some sort in the formality of the phrase, and in the use of my father's name. We were, in fact, a rather formal family.

In his work—which was his life—my father dealt with chalk, numbers, and steel. In his laboratory were machines. On his desk was a massive paperweight someone in the Metallurgy Department had given him, a hunk of smoothly ground steel with a cold, precisely cut cross at the top. I liked to heft the weight of it in my hand. I also wondered why anyone would ever admire it, as it was neither beautiful nor inspiring.

In the face of my father's demanding personality, my mother seemed to have difficulty holding her own. She was quiet and dutiful, a woman who'd grown up as the fourteenth of sixteen children in a Nebraska farm family. Somewhere along in her sixties, she started—quietly, determinedly—to live her own life, almost in spite of my father. My mother grew tougher and more interesting with age, but when I was growing up she was not tough at all; she was submissive. This same submissiveness was something I saw in virtually every woman I met, growing up—a need to defer to the man who was "taking care of" her, the man on whom she depended for everything.

By the time I entered high school I was bringing my ideas home from school—not to Mother, but to Father. There, at the dinner table, he would dissect them with passionate disdain. Then he would

move on, digress, go off on a trip of his own that had little to do
with me, but always infusing the conversation with great energy. His
energy became my energy, or so I thought.

My father considered it his God-given duty to point me in the direction of truth—specifically, to correct the mistaken attitudes
inflicted upon me by the "third-rate intellects" who were my
teachers. His own role as teacher was more fascinating to him by far,
I think now, than my fledgling development as a learner. At the age
of twelve or thirteen I began to pursue what was to become a life-
long ambition: to get my father to shut up. It was a peculiar, mutual
dependence that we had: I wanted *his* attention; he wanted *mine*.
He believed that if I would only sit still and listen, he could hand
me the world, whole and flawless, like a peeled pear on a silver plate.
I didn't want to sit still, and I didn't want the peeled pear. I wanted
to find life on my own, in my own way, to stumble upon it like a
surprise in a field—the ruddy if misshapen apple that falls from an
unpruned tree.

When I would complain to my father about his methods of argument and his apparent need to be right above all else, he would
laugh at me and say that I misperceived him. This taloned thrust-
and-parry, he explained, was how one "sharpened" one's mind. The
fact that he involved me in it, he said, only showed his basic respect
for my ability to "take it."

The messages I began receiving from my father, beginning at the
age of twelve or so, confused me. I believed my father was training
me for combat in the tough, abrasive world of grown-ups and ideas.
(Didn't he tell me that was what he was doing?) Yet he seemed to
be interested quite personally in the win-or-lose. Even then, there
was a level on which I knew that combat had little to do with com-
prehension.

In my twenties, when I began to write, it did not occur to me that
I was entering a field as far from my father's as possible. I started out
writing what I thought of as "little things," short, personal mood
pieces, subjective stuff—nothing very adventuresome, I thought. Certainly nothing that demanded Real Thinking. I did not believe myself capable of that. Real Thinking was for men. Real Thinking was
for professors, fathers, priests.

Aside from some strenuous tilting with a few of my college
teachers, I had little experience in learning to develop a rational posi-

tion on anything. Even in college I was more a jouster than an independent thinker. The kind of mental and emotional development that comes in isolation, when one is up against oneself alone, was something I was too frightened to engage in for almost twenty years. I would try to gain clarity by differentiating myself from some strong and forceful Other—anyone, male or female, on whom I could project that internalized image of my father. The "clarity," needless to say, would be short-lived. I would pull from the Other like a rubber band, glimpse my differentiated self for a brief moment, then snap back again when the tension of separateness became too great to endure.

Intimations of Helplessness

Psychologists have known for some time that women's affiliative needs are stronger than men's, but only recently have studies of female children begun to zero in on the reason: because of a profound, deep-seated doubt in their own competence, which begins in early childhood, *girls become convinced that they must have protection if they are going to survive.* This belief is bred into women by misguided social expectations, and by the fears of parents. As we shall see, a monumental ignorance shapes the way parents think about, feel toward, and relate to their daughters. In terms of their ability to grow into independent human beings, girl children are hampered by their parents' protective attitudes as surely as if their feet had been bound.

Girls are trained very differently than boys. The training leads to their becoming adults who stay stuck in jobs beneath their capabilities.

It leads them to feel intimidated by the men they marry, and to defer to them in the hope of being protected.

It even leads—as we shall see—to the crippling of women's intellectual abilities.

Long praised by teachers for being diligent and dutiful in school, we who rely on dutifulness to get us by in the professional world soon find ourselves being treated as if we were not quite grown up. Virtuous, perhaps. *Nice*, perhaps (as in "Isn't Mary nice to take care of all those back orders for us?"). But childlike. Not to be taken seriously. And, like the good slaves on the old plantations, easily exploitable.

Since time immemorial, men have pointed out that on the grand scale of things, women haven't really accomplished very much. Where, you will hear, are the women plasma physicists? How come there are no female Bartoks? (The questions are usually raised in an effort to squelch any suggestion that women are as intelligent as men.) New studies make it increasingly clear that *women prevent themselves from advancing.* We sabotage our own originality. We downshift—avoiding the heady speed that's possible in the upper gears—as if we had been programmed to do so.

And indeed we have.

Psychologists have begun to take a close look at how women conduct and feel about themselves in relation to how they were taught to behave and encouraged to feel as children. Shockingly, the picture has changed very little in the past twenty years or so. The way girls are socialized continues to predetermine an agonizing conflict over the psychological independence that's necessary if women are ever to spring free and take their place in the sun.

Learning to Lean

We like to think that as parents we're doing it all differently—that *our* girls will not suffer the effects of the discriminatory and overprotected upbringings to which we were subject. But research shows that most of today's children are being locked into the same kinds of artificial role differentiation that you and I were taught.

Male dominance—and female collusion with it—can be observed firsthand in nursery-school children.

"You stay here with the mommies and babies. I'm going fishing," says little Gerald to little Judy as he trots off.

"I want to go too," calls Judy, running after him.

Gerald turns and repeats, "No, you stay with the mommies and babies!"

"But I want to go fishing!" Judy cries.

"No," insists Gerald. "But when I come back I'll take you to a Chinese restaurant."

While supervising a playroom in the nursery school where she works, Laura Carper observed this scene between two four-year-olds, and reported it recently in *Harper's*.[1]

"Another scene I observe now and then goes like this," she wrote. "Three or four little boys seat themselves around the play table in the play kitchen. The boys start issuing orders such as 'I'd like a cup of coffee!' or 'Bacon and eggs!' or 'Some more toast!' and the girl runs back and forth between stove and table, cooking and serving. In one such scene the boys got completely out of hand, demanding cups of coffee one after another while the girl was racing around in a frenzy. She finally gained control of the situation by announcing that there was no more coffee. Apparently it never occurred to her to sit down at the table herself and demand coffee from one of the boys."

The girls in this nursery school are acting out an ancient trade-off —waiting on the master in exchange for being protected. Caseworkers, counselors, and other professionals who work with or study young women have come to deplore the continuing existence of The Cinderella Complex—girls' belief that there will always be someone to take care of them. *"With all the intense focus on women's roles, there has been practically no change in the preparation of young girls for adulthood,"* said Edith Phelps, executive director of Girls Clubs of America, at a recent conference. "Their preparation remains destructive at worst—full of conflict at best."[2]

Studying adolescents at the University of Michigan, psychologist Elizabeth Douvan found that up until the age of eighteen (and sometimes past that) girls show virtually no thrust toward independence, aren't interested in confronting authority with rebellion, and don't insist "on their rights to form and hold independent beliefs and controls."[3] In all of these respects, they differ from boys.

The data show that dependency in women increases as they grow older.

They also show—strikingly—that girls, from the time they are quite young, are trained *into* dependency, while boys are trained *out* of it.

How Does It All Get Started?

Girls begin the game of life a step ahead of boys. Verbally, perceptually, and cognitively, infant girls are more skilled. At birth they're developmentally ahead of the game by four to six weeks. By the time they enter first grade, girls have a full year's edge.[4]

Why, then, are they already waiting tables and serving up the easy-overs at the age of three or four?

Eleanor Maccoby, a Stanford psychologist specializing in psychological sex differences, thinks "the key to the matter is whether or how soon a girl is encouraged to assume initiative, to take responsibility for herself and solve problems by herself rather than relying on others."[5]

Psychologists say that the die of independence is cast before a child reaches the age of six. Some now believe girls are prevented from taking a certain crucial turn in their emotional development precisely *because* the way is made too easy for them—because they are *over*protected, *over*helped, and taught that all they have to do to keep the help coming is be "good."

What's encouraged in the goose, however, is not encouraged in the gander. Much of what is considered "good" in little girls is considered downright repulsive in little boys. Physical timidity or hypercautiousness, being quietly "well behaved," and depending on others for help and support are thought to be natural—if not outright charming—in girls. Boys, however, are actively discouraged from the dependent forms of relating, which are considered "sissyish" in male children. Gradually, says Judith Bardwick, "the son will be pushed towards and rewarded for independent behavior . . ."

Why little boys and *not* little girls grow up learning to be independent, why they're not afraid to strike out on their own (or, more accurately, why they do it *in spite of being afraid*), and why they begin developing personal standards for self-esteem virtually before they're out of diapers—these are questions that researchers like Bardwick and Douvan are examining anew.[6] They have developed a theory having to do with the constructive effects of stress. In their view, the small boy has no choice but to deal with the stress of being restricted from his "core instinctual behavior" (which includes such no-nos as biting, hitting, and masturbating in public), and also of being "masculinized" out of his dependent behavior. This stress, they believe, is ultimately beneficial: the experience of having to deal with restrictions, and with the occasional loss of adult approval, helps set the young boy on the right road—the road to finding, and living by, his own lights.

This process of switching over to an independent mode begins, in boys, at the age of two. During the next three years they gradually wean themselves from their need for outside approval and begin developing independent criteria for feeling good about themselves. Most boys have accomplished this vital step in the maturation process *before they turn six.*

With girls it's a far longer row to hoe. In important, frequently cited developmental studies, Jerome Kagan and H. A. Moss found that both *passivity* and a *dependent orientation toward adults* appeared consistently in girls all the way into adulthood. Indeed, it was found that these two personality factors were the most stable and predictable of all female character traits. The girl who is passive in the first three years of life can be counted upon to remain passive in early adolescence; by the same token, the girl who is passive in adolescence can be expected to be excessively dependent on her parents when she reaches adulthood.[7]

As they grow older, girls tend to *increase* their reliance on others. In a kind of Catch-22 of gender development, female children use their advanced perceptual and cognitive abilities *not* to advance the process of separation from Mother, *not* to become involved in the satisfaction of mastery for its own sake (they are much more likely to achieve mastery for the sake of approval), *not* to pursue increasing independence, but to apprehend and anticipate adult demands—and conform to them.

Bardwick and Douvan think that in part girls' troubles stem from insufficient stress when they're young. Because girls' behavior is generally pleasing to adults from the start (ordinarily, they do not bite, draw blood, or masturbate publicly), daughters need do nothing more developmentally challenging than continue being the way they are—verbally and perceptually skilled, nonaggressive, and extremely clever at second-guessing what's wanted of them by those on whom they depend.

Adults, for their part, do not interfere with or thwart the instinctual behavior of girls—*except for their gropings toward independence.* These they systematically stymie—as if their girl children, by reaching out and taking chances, were courting death itself.

Overhelp and the Crippling of Girls

Dependency training begins very early in the life of the girl. Female babies are handled less frequently and less vigorously than boys.[8] In spite of their greater sturdiness and developmental maturity, girls are *thought* to be more fragile. Receiving less physical stimulation, they may not get the same kind of encouragement boys receive for their early exploratory ventures. Apprehensiveness about the girl's safety is exhibited by her parents before she's even out of the crib.

A 1976 study showed that parents make a sex distinction when they interpret the meaning of babies' cries. The same infant's crying was perceived by parents as *fear* if the child was thought to be a girl, and *anger* if the child was thought to be a boy. Moreover, Mother *responds* differently to the crying. When her baby girl cries, she's more likely to drop what she's doing and run to comfort her. (Apparently, parents are more comfortable ignoring squawks from baby boys.)

Another notable difference is that the mother will *increase* her contact with a baby girl who's irritable, but *decrease* it with a son—even when the son is *more* irritable.

Such early conditioning, says University of Michigan psychologist Lois Hoffman, could well signify "the beginning of a pattern of interaction . . . in which the daughters quickly learn that the mother is a source of comfort and the mother's behavior is reinforced by the cessation of the crying."

In other words, girl babies learn that help comes quickly if you cry for it, and *mothers* of baby girls learn that the crying will stop if you run to help them. Precisely the opposite lesson is reinforced when the interaction is taking place between mothers and sons. Because male infants are thought to be tougher, Mom doesn't trip over the vacuum cleaner running to comfort her baby boy. As a consequence, he is not so systematically reinforced in the idea "Help will come speeding my way if I cry for it." There are times when he has to solace himself. Occasionally, he discovers, this *works* for him. He is able to comfort himself. Bit by bit he learns to do this on a more regular basis. *Bit by bit he learns to become his own emotional caretaker*.

As any infant turns toddler—crawls, stands in the crib for the first

time, finally takes its first steps—parental anxiety begins to mar parental joy. There is glory in the child's achievement combined with a
new ambivalence because Baby will now begin incurring risks: fool-
ing with electrical outlets; examining the contents of jars on low
shelves; walking too fast and taking spills. Like fortune-tellers gazing
into the same globe, Mama and Papa are able to envision these catastrophes the moment the baby begins to crawl.

The potential catastrophes don't loom quite so vividly in parents'
minds if the baby is a boy. Ambivalence about a child's first moves
toward independence is greater, research shows, when the child is female. Billy, that tough little fella, will make it. Deborah needs a lot
of watching over, a lot of help. When Billy takes his first steps,
Mommy and Daddy are alight with happiness. When Debbie takes
her first steps, the happiness is tinged with the beginnings of
worry. Baby Deborah, unfortunately, looks up and sees anxiety in
Mommy's eyes.

This early indication of anxiety on the part of Mother—what some
researchers call "apprehensive oversolicitude"—leads the child to
doubt her own competence. "If Mommy's afraid I can't make it, she
must know something I don't know," thinks little Debbie.

Coming out of their greater fear for their girl children is the parents' tendency (one might more accurately say *compulsion*) to protect—to jump up and catch the baby before she stumbles; to be
sure the little thing doesn't hurt herself. If Baby Boy hurts himself,
it's considered part of the maturing process. "There, there, Billy,"
Mother coos. "You'll learn." If Debbie bumps her head it's time for
panic—and guilt. Mommy should have been watching more carefully. Mommy should have made *sure* that nothing happened to little Debbie. After all, little Debbie is "just a little girl."

*This is the point at which parents begin inculcating their small
daughters with the idea that so far as risk-taking and the evaluation
of their own safety are concerned, they should not trust themselves.*

And self-trust, as we know, is crucial in the development of independence.

Often, fear begins in little girls because of attitudes held by their
mothers. Anxious mothers instruct their children to avoid behavior
that might make *them*—the mothers—anxious. Teaching her little

daughter to avoid risk, the anxious mother inadvertently prevents the child from learning how to deal with fear.

The only method both humans and animals have for learning to master fear in new situations is to approach and withdraw from the frightening situation repeatedly. "The repeated arousal of the fear response in small, controlled doses leads eventually to extinction of the fear response," explains Barclay Martin in *Anxiety and Neurotic Disorders*.

Mother doesn't want Debbie to even encounter the fear-inducing situation, so the child gets no experience in learning to control her response to it. Children who have no experience in dealing with the fear response are likely to become adults whose lives are ruled by fear. In essence, little Debbie will remain fear-prone through elementary school, high school, college, and on out into the terrifying cold world of adults. There, she will cope by trying to "manage" her fear, to "stay on top of it," to keep it at bay. Fear—the quelling of it, or, preferably, the utter avoidance of it—will end up becoming a chief motivator (or *de*-motivator) in Debbie's life. As a result, of course, she will have great difficulty developing self-confidence.

Studies show that girls—especially smarter ones—have severe problems in the area of self-confidence.[9] They consistently underestimate their own ability. When asked how they think they'll do on different tasks—whether the tasks are untried or ones they've encountered before—they give lower estimates than boys do, and in general underestimate their actual performance as well. One study even showed that *the brighter the girl, the less expectation she has of being successful at intellectual tasks.* Duller girls have higher expectations for themselves than bright girls do.[10]

Low self-confidence is the plague of many girls, and it leads to a host of related problems. Girls are highly suggestible and tend to change their minds about perceptual judgments if someone disagrees with them. They set lower standards for themselves. While boys are challenged by difficult tasks, girls try to avoid them. Even at preschool age, little boys demonstrate *more* task involvement, *more* confidence, and are *more* likely to show incremental increases in IQ.

By the age of six, the cards are in on *probable* intellectual development, just as they are in on *probable* independence development. By this age a predictive picture will have emerged. The six-year-old whose IQ is going to increase in the following years is the child who is already competitive, self-assertive, independent, and dominating with other children, according to Eleanor Maccoby. A six-year-old whose IQ will *decline* in the following years is passive, shy, and dependent. "On this evidence," says Maccoby, pointedly, "the characteristics of those whose IQ's will rise do not seem very feminine."

All of this relates, in girls, to the development of excessive "affiliative needs," by which is meant the need to experience *relationship* above all else. Given her *felt* incompetence, it's not surprising that the little girl would hotfoot it to the nearest Other and cling for dear life.

Lois Hoffman describes, below, the developmental sequence that leads girls to become adults who need excessive support from others.

> Since the little girl has a) less encouragement for independence, b) more parental protectiveness, c) less cognitive and social pressure for establishing an identity separate from Mother, and d) less mother-child conflict, which highlights this separation, she engages in less independent exploration of her environment. *As a result, she does not develop skills in coping with her environment nor confidence in her ability to do so. She continues to be dependent upon adults for solving her problems, and because of this she needs her affective ties with adults.*[11]

As we can see, the problems of excessive dependence follow female children right into adulthood. Yet a restricted and overprotected childhood is generally something of which women are not aware. They do not think of themselves as having been hobbled in their efforts to become independent as children—and so when dependency problems crop up to plague them in adult life, they are dumbfounded. Those who end up going into therapy will begin to recall the strange, fear-enhancing proscriptions of their parents: the warnings, the curfews, the entreaties not to "tire" themselves—frail butterflies whose wings might cease to support them at any moment.

Ruth Moulton says the major psychological problems of many of her women patients stem from "the early inhibition of all assertion and sometimes of all physical activity, which was considered either dangerous or 'unladylike.'" Two of Dr. Moulton's patients had literally been tied into their beds at night as girls. She says the childhood histories of her women patients reveal many such examples of "excessive restriction and overprotection." All lead to the fact that as girls, these women were made to feel weak—unable to use their bodies, unable to defend themselves physically and verbally. What Moulton calls a "good girl syndrome" develops. Grown, these women want to play it very, very safe. They keep *themselves* restricted.[12]

The final behavioral clincher in the training of little girls is *overhelp*—parents' tendency to jump in and help their daughters when they don't really need it, or when they should be learning to falter and self-correct (a process utterly fundamental to the development of confidence and self-esteem). Little girls don't get the *chance* to self-correct. They are picked up, dusted off, and set to spinning again, like those little gyroscopic ballerina dolls that dance or decline according to the whim of the owner.

Why is "overhelp" so destructive? "Mastery requires the ability to tolerate frustration," explains Lois Hoffman. "If the parent responds too quickly with help, the child will not develop such tolerance."

"Independence results from learning that one can accommmplish by oneself, can rely upon one's own abilities, can trust one's own judgment," says Judith Bardwick in her book *The Psychology of Women*. Girls are consistently reinforced in the notion that they can achieve only with the help of others. Eventually they internalize the idea that they can't succeed in meeting life's challenges on their own.

There are certain "dependency diseases" which afflict only women. One of these is anorexia nervosa, the bizarre starvation syndrome in which adolescent girls diet themselves right out of existence in a sadly paradoxical attempt to get some control over their lives. Each year one out of every hundred teen-age girls plunges into one of these emaciating anorexic regimens. Some 10 percent of those who do so end up starving themselves to death.

"Girls with conforming personalities feel obliged to do something that demands a great degree of independence in order to be respected and recognized. When they get stuck, the only independence they feel they have is to control their bodies," said Dr. Hilde Bruch, an authority on the the disease.

Anorexia affects mostly twelve- to twenty-one-year-old women—

rarely men—who are well educated, highly motivated, and come from financially comfortable backgrounds. Treating them, says Dr. Bruch, can be a long, painstaking affair. "The conviction of being inadequate and unworthy is so deep-seated and of such long standing that [such a girl] withdraws behind the mask of superiority whenever she experiences the slightest self-doubt or encounters disagreement. She must be assured she is a worthy, adequate individual before she can be cured."[13]

Other victims of neurotic dependency are battered wives. The fact that they are so often financially dependent upon the men who beat them makes for a vicious kind of entrapment. It's *emotional* dependency, though, that puts a double lock on the trap. "There's a kind of panic that many women have about being able to make it in any way other than being dependent on their husbands," said Kenneth Mac-Farlane of the former Department of Health, Education and Welfare. "They've been taught their whole lives that they can't. It's a conditioning process."

In situations in which they have no effect on their environments, animals begin to give up. New studies show that the same thing happens to humans. Stay long enough in a situation in which you feel you have no control, and you will simply stop responding. It's called *learned helplessness*. The phenomenon was named by Martin Seligman. Diane Follingstad of the University of South Carolina began to use some of Seligman's ideas about learned helplessness in a treatment program she devised for battered wives. Follingstad teaches these women to *un*learn, in a relatively short period of time, what it has taken their parents and society years to inculcate. "With human females there's the feeling of being out of control, that things in their lives are caused by chance, luck, fate. It's not 'If I do X, I'll get Y,'" says Dr. Follingstad. Having been "shaped" to believe there is nothing she can do about the situation, the battered wife goes on being battered. Only after she begins to disengage from her belief in her own helplessness can she break out of the vicious cycle of dependency and its brutal effect on her life.[14]

The concept of learned helplessness has caught the imagination of many psychologists, who've begun to look for signs of it along the developmental path. Carol Jacklin of Stanford's Psychology Department told me that there are new studies indicating that helplessness is being taught to our own daughters by their grammar-school teachers. "Teachers say nice things about boys concerning their academic work and bad things about their behavior—throwing chalk and making noise. Girls tend to have more compliments given them about their nonacademic work—how neat and clean they are, how pretty they look today, that sort of thing."

This kind of reinforcement pattern, says Jacklin, means girls can actually have the *experience* of failure in academic work even if they're doing well. And girls are notoriously ill-equipped for dealing with a situation in which they think they've failed, or might fail. "All of us have been in situations which at least *seem* like failures. The question is, Do you persevere, do you try harder, or do you give up? The conclusion—and I think it's sad," says Jacklin—"is that girls give up."

Once established, the young girl's dependency is systematically supported as she proceeds through childhood. For being "nice"— nonchallenging, nonconfronting, noncomplaining—she's rewarded with good grades, the approval of her parents and teachers, and the affection of her peers. What reason is there for her to turn deviant or nonconformist? The going is good, so she conforms. Increasingly, she patterns herself after what's expected of her. Rewarded for little more than good behavior and competent memorizing skills, the girl succeeds. Life is good—and basically easy.

Until puberty. That, for the American girl child, is where things begin going askew.

Adolescence: The First Crisis in Femininity

A "crisis," in the language of developmental psychologists, is a period of stress and disruption, an unsettled time during which anxiety about one's abilities or identity increases. In the process of resolving our developmental crises, we grow in maturity and psychological health.

For girls, adolescence brings with it a unique developmental stage —what Bardwick and Douvan refer to as "the first crisis in femininity." Before they turn twelve or thirteen, girls are more or less free to behave as they like. With puberty, however, the trap door begins to swing shut. New and quite specific behavior is now expected of the young girl. Subtly (and often not so subtly) she will be rewarded for her "success" with boys. Regardless of how much her daughter may be accomplishing in other areas of life, the mother of a fifteen-year-old girl who isn't dating starts to get worried. Gently but firmly, she pushes her daughter to become a heterosexual partner. The message the girl gets—inevitably—comes in loud and clear: it's not good to be too competitive with men. What *is* good is to please the boys, to "get along."[15]

It is at this point that girls are faced with what certainly has become *the central problem of femininity in our culture: the conflict between dependence and independence.* What is the proper balance between the two? What is "right"? What is "appropriate"? An overly dependent girl, one with no opinions and no "personality," is thought mousy and unappealing, but an overly *in*dependent girl is no prize either. Boys might pal around with her, but romantically they don't find her very compelling.

No girl growing up in our society needs to be told any of this: she *knows* it. And so she begins to shift her priorities. In adolescence her chief developmental task becomes one of achieving "successful" relationships with others. As she learned to do in childhood, she continues to depend on feedback from others as her main source of self-esteem. Toward the end of high school or college, many young women will suddenly flip-flop their values, rejecting achievement in favor of an all-out pursuit of social acceptance.[16] When this happens, the task of developing achievement skills and independence is brought to an alarming halt. *Because of the way society sets them up, women never again experience the need to develop independence—until some crisis in later life explodes their complacency, showing them how sadly helpless and undeveloped they've allowed themselves to be.*

Handicapping the Adolescent Daughter

Not least among the shaping factors in the life of the young girl is the particular family in which she grows up. Here, within the confines of Mommy and Daddy's living room, she will be encouraged to break away and become her own person, or she will learn to play it safe.

Examining the childhood histories of female patients who became accomplished professional women, Ruth Moulton uncovered certain fascinating trends in the way they grew up. Often the father intrudes, blocking the girl's burgeoning independence, and the mother stands by and lets him. Out of the crucible of her parents' conflicting claims upon her emerges the bright, eager, and usually underachieving woman.

First, let's take a look at the elusive mother. In terms of her own development, she has taken a back seat to her husband, copping out on her own life long ago. Her posture of submission imbues her with what one daughter describes as a "wispy, evanescent quality." A surprising number of women I interviewed concluded, almost apologetically, "I can't tell you much about my mother. There's a vagueness there, something I can't quite get hold of."

One woman who's been doing graduate work in psychology and happens to have made considerable progress in moving out from her own dependency is still struck by how lacking in substance her mother seems to be. "It's strange, considering she's alive and I see her fairly often. I just don't have a very clear sense of who my mother is—or of what our relationship is all about. I think I never have."

Another woman described the "empty spot" she experienced growing up, a gap in her relationship to her femininity. "My father was the one who ran my life. Now that I have children of my own, I often think back and wonder, 'Where was my mother, back then? Why did she just let my father take over? Didn't she *care*, or was she just weak?'"

"My father came first," says a Missouri painter who consistently faces a work slump whenever she commits herself to submitting paintings for a show. "My mother was defined by him. If she behaved well he would love her, buy her presents, and take care of her —she was a queen. He *did* take care of her. She behaved; she ran the house. He bought her presents all the time."

"Was she smart?" I asked.

"I don't know," the woman replied. "I think she may have been, once. She stopped thinking."

One reason Mother remains shadowy is that she was intimidated by the forceful, vivid personality of her husband. The peacemaker, a kind of half-person who chooses to tag along safely behind her husband, Mother is protected from the more abrasive aspects of life in the world. Huge fights, open power struggles—these were not characteristic of the girl's relationship with her elusive mother. There may even have been a kind of eventless calm, an aura of peace deceptive in that it disguised the paralyzing paradox that lay at the core of everything: *Mother was there (ah, how endlessly, endlessly there). But she was also not there.*[17] Unwittingly, the girl in such a family grows up with an increasing sense of disengagement from what psychologists would call her "feminine core."

"I felt guilty all the time," an account executive at a New York ad agency told me. "I *lived* with guilt because I never felt feminine. My father encouraged me to stand straight, wear high heels, and look 'the lady,' but I didn't want to act 'the lady.' It had something to do with the fact that my mother was a 'lady' and she was a placator. Mom doesn't make waves; she doesn't ask questions; she doesn't want to know."

The split, then, takes place in relation to a central distinction the girl makes: Father is active; Mother is passive. Father is able to rely on himself; Mother is helpless and dependent.[18]

A special bonding will sometimes occur between the girl child and her father. They are like pals. He will tell her how she reminds him of himself. She will feel flattered and encouraged, imagining herself to be quite special. Pamela Daniels, a Wellesley social scientist, recalls "the small, momentous rhetorical ritual my father and I often performed in company. 'When your Daddy tells you to do something, what do you do?' he would ask, and my response was 'Do it!' No father was more proud, no daughter more obedient."[19]

How shocking, then, is the abrupt withdrawal of Father's involvement when later his pride-and-joy tries to strike out on her own.

The Betrayal of the Father

"Frequently the father will encourage his daughter until the point where he becomes afraid of her knowing more than he does," Ruth Moulton observes. "Or else he's afraid that he'll become sexually attracted to her. Often a father who turns on his daughter in adolescence will be the same father who gave her all kinds of intellectual encouragement when she was younger."[20]

"I was groomed to be a concert pianist from the time I was five years old," a young mother from Washington, D.C., told me. "Then suddenly, when I was ready for college, my father asked what I was planning to major in. 'Music, of course,' I told him. No, he said; music was too hard a field to make a living in. 'Major in early-childhood education. That way you can always be a teacher.'"

The woman did as Daddy told her and proceeded to major in early-childhood education. After college she taught for a few years, then married and had children. Once voted New York State's "most likely to succeed" high school student, she has long since given up her musical ambition.

Sadly, she told me, "I haven't played in twelve years." In fact she doesn't even own a piano.

Many young women who begin to succeed intellectually or creatively find themselves in the position—suddenly and without warning —of having all support from Father withdrawn.[21] It is a shock—and it is experienced, on a profound level, as betrayal.

"I was obeying his wishes to the letter," Simone de Beauvoir wrote of her adolescent relationship with her father, "and that seemed to anger him. He had destined me to a life of study, and yet I was being reproached with having my nose in a book all the time. To judge by his surly temper, you would think that I had gone against his wishes in embarking on a course that he had actually chosen for me."[22]

The girl has little insight with which to objectify what is happening with her father. "I kept wondering what I had done wrong," De Beauvoir recalls. "I felt unhappy and ill at ease, and nursed resentment in my heart."[23]

The resentment, certainly, is there, but the young daughter is perplexed by it, believing in Father as she does, believing in *his* description of the situation—which is that he is worried about her. Or he wants to train her. Or he thinks she's better off marrying and "indulging" in her talents on the side, since she won't be able to support herself anyway.

Sometimes it turns out that the father is competing with his daughter just as strenuously as he might compete with a son. So long as he's ahead in the race, fine; he feels comfortable and the camaraderie remains a pleasant one. But when the girl shows signs of pulling out in front, the trouble begins. Father may become outwardly hostile, criticizing her "for her own good," or (more insidious) he may turn dour and self-pitying. We've heard a lot about the guilt-pushing mother, but virtually nothing about the father who does the same. Yet in the particular family constellation we're describing here, it may well be the father who attempts to curtail his daughter's efforts by making her feel guilty.

The year she graduated from high school, Hortense Calisher confided in her father her wish to be a writer—specifically (then) a poet. What was his response? He brought out a notebook of his own poems, she tells us, "never before mentioned, flicked now under my eyes only tangentially, and at his death lost, saying, 'Looky here. I wanted to. But you can't make a living off poetry, m'dear.'"

How *dare* she attempt to succeed where he himself had failed? was the unspoken implication. Taking the separate stance that's required of those who must actively pull themselves up and out of the hand-icapped-daughter syndrome, young Hortense snorted, "I don't *want* to make a *living* out of it!" And then she proceeded to *do* it.[24]

Strange things can happen when fathers feel that their daughters are slipping out from under their control. In her several decades of practicing psychiatry, Ruth Moulton has seen a striking incidence of fathers who lash out vindictively the moment their daughters try to pull away. One man she knows tried to insist that his daughter get married as soon as she finished college. "The girl didn't *want* to get married then; she wanted to go to law school," Dr. Moulton told me. "In spite of the fact that she *knew* what she wanted, it was virtually impossible for her, at first, to pursue it."

What Daddy thought of her was too important to this woman. Risking his rejection was too potentially devastating. "She had to go through a lot of depression and a lot of therapy," said Dr. Moulton, "before she was finally able to stand up to her father and go her own way." Still, Daddy kept popping up at all the crucial moments in her life. Just when she thought she'd emotionally "dealt" with him, something would happen to remind her of how pernicious her need for his approval was.

"Eventually the woman was offered a fellowship to study in Europe. Again, her father was infuriated," Dr. Moulton recounts. "He wanted her to stay home and study at the state university; she wanted to go to Europe and finally did, despite him."

After that, their relationship was never the same. "Ten years later, when her father died, the woman realized she'd really lost him at the point when she'd first begun to disobey him."

For some women the point of departure or separation from Daddy and what Daddy wants doesn't occur until they're much older. Meredith, a woman who'd toughed it out in New York for eighteen years, recently had to face up to the infantile relationship she had with her father when she lost a job she'd held for some years with a big publishing company.

She had lost the job for reasons having to do with office politics. A "good worker," Meredith had never contemplated leaving "Big Daddy" (as she now describes the paternal corporate structure), but when Big Daddy left *her*, she envisioned several alternatives, any one of which could lead to personal growth. She could establish herself as a free-lance editor; or she could go after a job with another publisher; or she could go back to school and train for something entirely new.

"I felt the time was right to at least consider a new profession," said Meredith. She was thirty-nine. She thought she could make use of what had happened to her, turning it from something negative into a springboard for change. But her father—who'd been telling her what to do since the first date she had to turn down at age fourteen because the boy wasn't "right" for her—had other ideas. "Dad was horrified that his daughter had been fired and wanted to 'do something about this right now.' He knew someone who knew someone who knew the publisher—that sort of thing."

Having become aware of her father's long history of intrusiveness in her life, Meredith resisted his attempts to take over and bail her out. "Who knows?" she told him. "Maybe I'll go back to school and become a psychotherapist."

All right, if a new profession was what his daughter wanted, he could go along, but *psychotherapy*? Law was the profession for any girl of his.

"If you go to law school I'll pay for it," he told her.

If, on the other hand, she insisted on training to become a therapist, he would *not* pay for it. Psychotherapy wasn't "right for her."

"Once again," Meredith told me, "it was, 'If you do things *my* way, I'll take care of you.' Really that sums up my relationship with my father over all these years. When I think about it, I could cry."

Though thinking about it *always* had the effect of making her feel helpless and a little weepy, Meredith has finally arrived at a new insight: either she would be Daddy's Little Girl for the rest of her life, or else she could begin taking the steps, however anxiety-provoking they might be, toward managing life on her own.

"I'm finally admitting after all these years that I'm a princess," she says. "My parents told me what to think, what to do, what to wear. In our family you never did anything *separate* from, or *different* from. You did everything together. You went shopping together. They were picking out my clothes until I left home when I was twenty-one. To this day my driver's license is still at my father's address, in Rhode Island. Whenever it needs to be renewed I have to go home to do it."

Drawing the connection between her dependency on her parents and how devastated she felt upon losing her job, Meredith says, "I was afraid I couldn't *exist* without the corporation. I didn't have any money saved. I didn't have any insurance, because the company had always provided the "fringe benefits"—just like Daddy. Suddenly the effect that my father had had on my life became painfully clear. I saw that if I wanted things to change I was going to have to forget about what *he* wanted and go ahead and do what *I* wanted."

For the first time in her life Meredith has become realistic and forceful in her own right. She decided things were financially too unstable for her to change careers at that point, so she set herself up in a free-lance editing business. She rented a small office in a first-rate location in Manhattan, hired a small but competent staff, and went after—and got—top clients. Today, two years later, she's doing fine, both professionally and financially. "Now," she says, "I have the money and the confidence to change fields if I want to. For the first time in my life I *know* what I'm capable of doing on my own because I've actually gone out and done it."

The Betrayal of the Mother

Daughters often experience the problems in their lives as stemming from their intense, overbearing fathers, but in fact both parents contribute to women's difficulty in growing up and getting free. The Elusive Mother tends to be almost as dependent upon her daughter as she is on her husband. She sins by omission, by *not* supporting her daughter's efforts to move out on her own.

Dr. Moulton tells of a bright professional woman who'd gone through conflict for years because of the demands of her dependent mother. Finally she got herself through school and completed a Ph.D. She married, had children, and continued working part time. Though she'd worked long and hard to free herself from the clutches of a dependent mother, now that she was comfortably settled in a dual-career life she found it very hurtful when her mother sought revenge. The woman swooped down on her daughter with all-out disapproval: she shouldn't be working; terrible things would happen to the children; her place was in the home; and so on and so on. The *coup de grâce*, in this story, was that Mama made such a ruckus the woman's father offered to *pay* her if only she would stay home with her children "and rest." That way, the woman told Dr. Moulton, "Mother wouldn't worry about it and upset *him*."

"Even as a kid I was always vaguely worried about my mother," another Daddy's Girl told me. "It always seemed she wasn't getting as much recognition from my father as I was. When the paper arrived at the breakfast table, it was usually *me* he discussed the editorials with. My mother was always clearing the dishes or getting the biscuits out of the oven."

In such triangles mothers will sometimes vie openly for their husbands' attention. Usually, though, it's a slowly deteriorating hope for their own future, tinged with envy, that they communicate. They feel anxious and don't know why. They are disgruntled by their daughters' turning toward a larger world; inwardly, they experience their daughters' outward reach as rejection.

It isn't just Mother's passivity that hurts her daughter. Often there's a great fluster of concern for the girl's "welfare" that neatly undercuts her strivings toward independence. Mother tries to restrict Daughter's activities so that she doesn't "overdo"; she asks Dad to tighten up the girl's curfews. She pushes for the "right" boyfriend (the guy next door), the "right" college. In sum, as Ruth Moulton puts it, the mother "is often clearly jealous of the girl's drive for freedom and individuation, fears being shown up as inadequate and bypassed by her daughter, and needs to vindicate her own limited way of life even though it may not have been happy or satisfying."[25]

The Proof of the Pudding

Once we've had all this training in dependency, how do adult women actually fare? Not very well, as you might expect.

In the last decade psychiatrists, psychoanalysts, and social scientists have brought tremendous scholarly energy to the subject of woman—her infancy and childhood, her adolescence, her early adulthood and mid-life transition. What is emerging is a whole new psychosocial picture of womanhood. Studies have shown, for example, that women are unwilling to recognize other women as leaders. In one study, University of Delaware researchers presented to a mixed group of subjects a slide showing men and women sitting at a conference table with a man seated at the head, then a slide showing a woman seated at the head. *Both* male and female subjects tended, in the second slide, to perceive a man as the leader of the group. (Only when she was sitting in an all-female group did a woman end up as leader.)[26]

Competition tends to be more difficult for women than for men. Put us in a competitive situation and our confidence drops. Positive feedback will raise women's confidence, but take away the verbal support and it's back to square one.[27] Even in helping or nurturing situations, women—it turns out—feel inadequate unless they know exactly what to do. Because of a fear of behaving incorrectly, they're too rigid to feel comfortable swinging with it and improvising a solution.

One study set out to discover how men and women respond in an emergency situation in which they think someone has suffered a seizure. The women reported feeling far more uncertainty about what to do. They were preoccupied with the issue of whether or not they were doing "the right thing." Even while they were in the *middle* of the situation these women were obsessed with thoughts about being unable to cope.[28]

A friend of mine illustrated this same phenomenon with a vivid anecdote concerning her husband's death. "From the moment he died until his memorial service was over," she told me, "all I thought about was whether I was doing the right thing—notifying the 'right' people, choosing the 'right' psalms. I was utterly, morbidly preoccupied with whether or not people would *like* the service—as if one could be right or wrong in the matter of deciding how one would like to memorialize a man one has loved and lived with for twenty-five years."

Even actual success, in the case of women, does not always breed further success. Studies show that we tend not to reap the psychological benefits of our accomplishments because a peculiar, internal disruption prevents us from *assimilating* success. When a woman solves a difficult math problem, for example, she has the option of attributing her success to her ability, or to luck, or to the fact that she "tried hard," or to the problem's being "easy." According to "attribution theory," which analyzes the effects on people's lives of what they see as the causes of things, women are likely to attribute success to external sources that have nothing to do with *them*. "Luck" is a favorite.

While we avoid taking credit for success, women leap at the opportunity to take responsibility for failure. Men tend to externalize the reasons for their failure, putting it off on something or someone else. Not so women, who absorb blame as if they were born to be society's doormats. (Some women like to speak of their willingness to take blame as if it were a form of altruism. It isn't. Women take the blame because they find it scary to confront those who are actually culpable of wrongdoing.)

Given our socialization into dependency, women are also poor risk takers. We resent being in the position where risk is even a possibility. We hate tests precisely *because* they're risky. We avoid new situations, job changes, moves to different parts of the country. Women are afraid that if they should make a mistake, or do "the wrong thing," they'll be punished.[29]

Women are less confident than men in their ability to make judgments, and in relationships will often hand over the decision-making duties to their mates, a situation which only ensures that they will become *less* confident in their powers of judgment as times goes by.

Most shockingly of all, women are less likely than men to fulfill their intellectual potential. In a major study of sex differences in intellectual functioning, Dr. Eleanor Maccoby of Stanford concluded: "In adulthood . . . men achieve substantially more than women in almost any aspect of intellectual activity where achievements can be compared—books and articles written, artistic productivity and scientific achievements." In fact, as women proceed into adulthood, they get lower and lower scores on "total intelligence," owing to the fact that they tend to *use* their intelligence less and less the longer they're away from school.

Other studies show that *the intellect's ability to function may actually be impaired by dependent personality traits.* The dependent or conforming type of personality relies heavily on "outside cues"—or cues from others—and this can hamper the internal process of sequential analysis.[30]

Envy and Competitiveness: The Vicious Cycle

A study conducted several years ago uncovered something very interesting about what happens to women when they work in collaboration with others. The amount of self-confidence women have is in inverse proportion to the performance level of their partners. Remarkably, *the higher the partner's performance, the less likely the woman is to attribute competence to herself.*[31]

Confidence and self-esteem are primary issues in women's difficulties with achievement. Lack of confidence leads us into the dark waters of envy. We see men as functioning without hang-ups—and like girls who envy the unfettered freedom of older brothers, we find it easier to focus on how "lucky" the men are and how "unlucky" we are. Sequestered in an unfair situation, we don't have to *do* anything about achieving the competence and self-esteem we so admire in others.

At the same time, we feel competitive. Thirty years ago, the psychiatrist Clara Thompson pointed out that women are indeed disadvantaged by living in a competitive culture whose atmosphere is likely to make us feel less valued. In such a situation, competitive attitudes toward men are inevitable. Yet, as Dr. Thompson warned, envy must be recognized, *seen*, and fully comprehended; it can too easily be used as a cover-up for something that is far more crucial to women's independence—our own inner feelings of incompetence. These must be dealt with—directly—if we are ever to achieve confidence and strength.[32]

When I met her, Vivian Knowlton, a young lawyer, was caught up in a vicious cycle of envy which kept her oblivious to the inner problems holding her back.

"I'm baffled about what's happening in my life right now," Vivian told me. (As with other women in this book, I've changed the name as well as certain identifying details.) We were sitting in the living room of her pretty, brown-shingled house in Berkeley, California. "I make a good salary and I like legal work. The thing is, I don't *feel* good. I go off to work every day with this kind of a cloud of anxiety hanging over me.

"Three years ago, when I first started working," she recalls, "I was turned on every morning. I'd whip out the door, swinging my briefcase, and practically run to the bus stop.

"Things began going stale after about a year. I thought I was doing pretty well on the job, but in retrospect it was mostly because I was so good at taking on assignments and doing what I was told. I got to be a kind of glorified gofer. Whenever someone wanted some garbage work done, it always ended up being given to me."

Vivian rarely asserted herself with the senior partners in her law firm, telling herself she was just starting out and that this was a learning experience. (Who was *she* to challenge people who'd been practicing law for twenty years or more?) During her second year, she began to admit that she wasn't working up to her capabilities. "I clammed up at meetings, feeling very timid about expressing my ideas. If someone *else* needed support, though, I could be thrillingly articulate."

Things plodded along for another three years. Vivian was never actually called on the carpet, but neither was she praised. "I'd become a C person and I was used to being an A. It made me sad. Where was the bright, together woman who'd ranked so high in her class at law school?"

There was one other woman in Vivian's office, a senior partner. "Natalie was incredibly self-assured. It was tempting to try patterning myself after her. I even caught myself imitating her hoarse whiskey voice. It was crazy. I felt as if I'd lost all sense of who I was and was clinging to the little quirks and mannerisms of someone else just to get by."

"Why Is It So Much Easier for Men?"

Vivian was ambivalent about the two young men who'd been hired at about the same time she had. "Paul and Hurf began carving niches for themselves right from the start. Paul dug into tax havens, something our firm had never been involved in before. That didn't stop Paul. He went out and learned about it, and then convinced old Hodgkins and Pearl it was the thing to do."

Paul's willingness to take the initiative was enraging to Vivian. "He seems to view the office as a base of operations for his personal flings in the business world," she said, bitterly. "You get the feeling he doesn't give a damn about the firm, or even about *law*, for that matter."

For Vivian, Hodgkins and Pearl has become the equivalent of the Adult. She feels rebellious toward her employer and at the same time envies Paul, who doesn't *have* to rebel, who's sufficiently independent to be able to take his own stand vis-à-vis "the office." Unintimidated by "the boss," Paul is far more innovative and self-directed than Vivian, and thus more valuable to the firm.

Hurf is not so brashly aggressive as Paul, but he too takes the kind of personal risks that would make the panic rise in Vivian's throat.

"Hurf's thing is courtroom law," she says. "Usually they don't let someone so inexperienced go out and represent the firm in court, but Hurf pushed. He kept asking and asking. After a while I felt embarrassed for him."

It's not unusual for women to feel that the men they work with are "insensitive" and "pushy." Yet everyone else, Vivian noticed, seemed to take the men's aggressiveness in stride. "Every time Hurf approached the senior partners, he had a better and better reason for being given what he wanted. Finally, he laid it all out at a meeting."

Hurf did what so many women, once they enter the professions, find a frightening prospect. At the risk of being disagreed with, or, God forbid, turned down, Hurf stood up in front of everyone at the biweekly staff meeting of Hodgkins and Pearl and *sold* himself. "I have a unique background for handling the Wilkinson case," he announced. He proceeded to tell how his brother-in-law was a manic-depressive and that he himself was familiar with the biochemical aspects of the disease, as well as with the civil-rights precedents in cases involving psychotic episodes. After revealing his personal expertise, he expressed the belief that Hodgkins and Pearl would save money if it let him represent Wilkinson in court.

"I can't take anything away from Hurf," Vivian told me. "He got himself the job, and he got himself into the courtroom. He was perfectly straightforward about what he was doing. Still, when stuff like that happens, I wonder why I'm not going anywhere. I keep getting the feeling that, somehow, I'm being overlooked."

"It Isn't Fair!"

Because justice—or rather, injustice—has been so central a problem for women, the issue of "what's fair" can easily be used as a mechanism to defend—and hide—feelings of inadequacy. Like the youngest child obsessing on the negative treatment received from the family, women use the unfairness with which they've historically been treated to wall themselves off from further negative treatment. Isolated by their feelings of victimization, they remain trapped. As with battered wives, a system of negative reinforcement is in effect. It's a painful cycle. In an objective, clinical sense, women *are* less confident than men. We were reared in such a way as to prevent us from accomplishing the psychological separation that leads to self-confidence. Culturally, this may be a reality, but it's self-defeating for women to stop here. And yet this is precisely the point at which many women give up.

"It isn't *fair* that I ranked in the top fifth on the law boards and now I'm sitting around sifting through the dust of *their* reports, and doing research on *their* cases," says Vivian Knowlton. "It isn't fair that I lived virtually without a social life the three years I went to law school, holing up to get those A's, and *now* I'm spending hours under a fluorescent light looking up old codes from morning to night."

Things weren't running according to any of the rules that had governed Vivian's life until then. Professional life was demanding a degree of independence she had never needed in order to get her A's in college. In a very real way, the rules had changed. "It makes me feel cheated, as if I'd been built up for something big and exciting—the whole world of law was put out there for me to devour—and now there's this awful let-down."

Vivian actually believes that everything her male colleagues do is somehow "effortless." She feels competitive and envious toward the men, but she also feels that way toward Natalie, the senior woman. It seems as if "they" have something she doesn't have, something they use to gain success. *This is the most insidious catch in contemporary feminine psychology.* Vivian *uses* her sense of cultural disadvantage to disguise from herself many of her most painful emotions —feelings that are preventing her from achieving the true confidence and self-esteem without which she hasn't a chance of getting free.

Women retain their dependency needs long past the developmental point at which those needs are normal and healthy. Unbeknownst to others—and worse, unbeknownst to ourselves—we carry dependency within us like some autoimmune disease. We carry it with us from kindergarten through college and graduate school, into our careers, and into the convenient "arrangement" of our marriages. Like the sliver of glass in the ice maiden's heart, dependency lodges deep in the center of our relationships with our husbands, our friends, and even our children. Much of the time—for many of us, *all* of the time—our unwillingness to stand on our own two feet goes unnoticed because it's *expected*. Women are relational creatures. They nurture and need. This, we have been told for many, many years, is *nature*.

And although it cripples us, we have let it go unquestioned.

CHAPTER V

Blind Devotion

Five years into the marriage. From the beginning, my goal had been to get my husband to perform at a level that would make me feel safe in the world. His competence was my competence; his failures, however, were his own. It was a neat, if inequitable, arrangement. I never questioned this attitude—never, in fact, identified it.

In the summer of 1967, my ambition for my husband's success soared when he received his first, long-coveted magazine assignment. *The Atlantic Monthly* was interested in having him trace the connection between rising food costs and the amount of money spent for advertising national brands, the bill for which was unwittingly paid by the consumer. *The Atlantic*'s approval of the project gave Ed the impetus to pursue it, even though there was no guarantee the resultant article would ever be published.

That summer, he spent his after-office hours researching and writing the piece. I was thrilled by this turn of events (I must have foreseen some grand and glorious future arising from it) and found myself energized by my new role as amanuensis and editor. It was hot as hell in New York that summer, but the sweat that poured in our cramped little apartment was like a healthful purge. Gone now were the toxins of failure and frustration. As soon as Ed got home from the office I'd serve supper. Then I'd wheel the babies out into the playground and stay until it grew dark. At eight thirty or nine, after bathing them and putting them to bed, I'd go into the dining room to edit what Ed had written in the intervening hours. It was something I had learned at *Mademoiselle*—how to look at other people's sentences and paragraphs for structure and clarity. I had begun writing my own little pieces about mothering and housekeeping, but was quite in awe of these larger ideas Ed was trying to untangle—ideas having to do with government and industry and the burgeoning consumer movement. When Ed's ideas were murky I could recognize and point out the need for clarification, but I knew little about the subject matter and believed one needed something extra—a graduate education? bigger brains? to have been born a man?—in order to deal with such complex stuff.

Part of my problem, of course, was the fact that I was twenty-nine years old and had not yet developed the habit of reading the newspaper. Any Queens construction worker watching the news over his five-o'clock beer knew more about economics and politics than I did. Somehow, these things didn't seem relevant to my personal life. Who ran the country, and how, and why; what money was and how it functioned—these things were of no visceral concern to a woman with three small children who was relying, for her welfare and theirs, on the efforts of another. The women's movement was just getting started back then, but it didn't emphasize the idea that women needed to assume greater responsibility for themselves. Rather, it seemed to suggest that they needed to be *given* certain things—things which, traditionally, had been withheld: professions, equal pay, a say in their present lives and in their future dreams. The irony is that while we began wishing for more, we continued relying on others (men, primarily) to supply it. Women, it seemed, had entered adolescence: we wanted freedom, but we didn't yet want its responsibility. We didn't want out all the way.

Of course, we thought that we did. The fact that Ed and I never had enough money was a problem I believed I was doing something about. What was I doing? Helping him. Making the way clear and buttressing his self-image so that *he* could do better. A possible new career of free-lance article writing seemed a way out of the futureless job of writing for a trade magazine and earning a meager $7,500 a year. Clearly this was too little money for a family of five living in

Manhattan; but there seemed no way out—unless, of course, Ed provided it.

It's true that society had locked women up with the full responsibility for child rearing. We were imprisoned in our homes—tethered to the awesome knowledge that no one but us would take care of the babies. There were no day-care centers when I first began waging my campaign to get Ed to function on a higher, more remunerative level. It would doubtless have been difficult to arrange babysitting and have so much as a nickel left over after paying for it. But looking back, I know now that I could have done *something*. I could have laid out a plan, begun at the bottom, and worked up (as eventually I had to do anyway). The cause of my inertia was not lack of day care. I didn't really want to assume responsibility for myself, so I did nothing to begin the process. I had run from independence at the age of twenty-four, and I had no reason to want to embrace it now. Inwardly I still yearned to be taken care of, and I was willing to work very, very hard and put up with an awful lot in exchange for it. I was willing, in fact, to be a slave.

We didn't like to think of it that way, of course; he didn't, I didn't. We preferred to imagine ourselves as contemporary and enlightened. I was no wimpish woman, throwing up during pregnancies and fainting when something frightened me. My phobic symptoms had vanished. Marriage had made me powerful and strong. I had energy enough to take care of three children under the age of four, the house, the food, the laundry, *and* phone the senators' offices and make appointments for Ed. I had energy enough to become a kind of alter ego for him, supporting him with my feigned strength.

The fiction was that Ed needed my help that summer because he could work only in the evenings on the *Atlantic Monthly* project. The truth was that he was afraid—afraid to get started (he might fail), afraid to ask senators and congressmen to give him interviews (they might say no), afraid to begin working on a new and more challenging level, one that would test his abilities and could end up dashing forever his most grandiose fantasies. I didn't know this then, having never faced my own demons. I thought Ed's fears "unrealistic." At the same time, I liked to think that I *believed* in Ed, that I knew he "could do it." With great panache I lined up a full schedule of Washington appointments in one afternoon of phone calling.

"My husband is doing a piece for *The Atlantic Monthly* on food prices," I would tell the aides and secretaries. I felt efficient and calm. I was not unnerved by associating with the power of the press (the senators' doors swung open immediately), because in fact it was not *my* power-by-association, but my husband's. I felt strong and effective precisely because I was acting on behalf of my husband, my own image protected, my personal talents untried. I would have made a top-notch executive secretary, cutting through swathes of red tape, making plans, arranging details, and seeing to it that the other guy—my boss, my protector—always got what he wanted.

Giving your life over to the master can end up being enormously frustrating. As a scheme for avoiding the anxiety that goes with autonomy, it doesn't always work. There were times—many times—when Ed would give vent to his own frustrations by going on a drinking binge. Such episodes would plunge me into despair, for they would bring with them a recognition of my own helplessness—how vulnerable I was, how lacking in the ability to *do* anything, how utterly, futilely dependent.

In the bleak morning after, I would feel, mixed in with the misery, an obscure sense of relief. Some bottom line would have been reached, and with it a recognition of the lie being lived and the energy being wasted in the living of it. The rumpled bathrobe, the day-old beard, the foul odor of alcohol offered a nasty glimpse of the truth: the marriage wasn't working. Its safety and protection were falsehoods. Each of us was using the arrangement to avoid the central issues in our separate lives.

This glimpse, of course, I would dash from in panic, as if fleeing rocks in a slide. I wanted the sure footing of the familiar, and by late afternoon of the day following the binge we would both sink into it: the guilt, the apologies, the avowals to change, and, ultimately, forgiveness.

For nine years I lived the life of a married child playing at being adult. I had my children christened and inoculated. I paid the bills and begged at the bank for loans when things were rough. I cleaned and diapered and tried to make it work, against odds that some goddess in the heavens would have laughed at had she looked down upon us. For that goddess would have seen that all my efforts were regressive. They were devoted solely to keeping the walls of my prison intact.

The Escape Hatch of Marriage

The view women hold of marriage doesn't really seem to have changed much over the years. In a study that led to their recent book *Husbands and Wives,* Dr. Anthony Pietropinto and Jacqueline Simanuer found that many women still view marriage as a fortress. In choosing husbands they are looking for the prince, someone who will rescue them from responsibility. Good sex, stimulating companionship—these are secondary. Give them a pedestal high above the dangers of authentic living and they'll be happy just sitting there.

The educational backgrounds of the women in the study had remarkably little to do with their attitudes toward love and marriage. One woman, a homemaker who had a postgraduate degree, told the authors she'd picked her man because "I was the center of his life. He went out of his way to make me happy. I felt he could be a good provider and give me financial security." (Financial security was high on the list of what many of the women in this survey wanted from a husband.)

Said another college-educated woman of the man she succeeded in snaring, "He is really my best friend and always has been and always will be. I chased him till he fell in love with me and wanted to marry me."[1]

A Southern woman told me that when she married she wanted "this intense, romantic, sexy, exciting, loving relationship." In hindsight, though, she saw the romantic fallacy of her expectations. "I wanted to be able to stay home safely with the children and have *him* bring excitement, love, and adventure to the doorstep."

What's striking in these women's responses is the amount of sheer self-involvement they express. The wives seem obsessed with getting proof of how much they are loved. Most importantly, they perceive themselves as having a *claim* on male-provided security.

Typical of those who make such claims is the woman who sets her cap for a doctor. More than any other single factor, doctors' wives say they want "security" from marriage. But in the end, the conflict and hostility they exhibit toward the men who provide them with all this security is stunning to behold. A survey of the real-life experiences of women who'd chosen to marry doctors (the results of which were published in a magazine called *Medical/Mrs.*) got down to bedrock. Was being a doctor's wife all it had been cracked up to be? the magazine asked its hundred thousand subscribers. "Is it actually what you expected and what society promised?"

Not on your life, to hear the women who've gotten stuck in this miserable existence tell it. "A doctor's wife has much more expected of her than other wives and not much emotional support or positive feedback," one woman complained. "We can't rely on our husbands for anything, not even to pound a nail in the wall."

The frustration experienced by a Maryland doctor's wife was plain to see, especially in her use of italics. "*Cannot* make him realize that extra hours put in do not increase his salary or status but subtract from family—has prevented me from having time for a life of my own because *I do everything to run our house and keep three children in peace!*"

"The sad part is," wrote another woman, a twenty-nine-year veteran of marriage to an M.D., "I have been forced to create a life of my own, separate and apart from him." (Many older women, and not a few younger ones, believe that being "forced" to have a separate life is actually a sign of pathology in a relationship. The woman whose husband does not take up the slack in her life, providing her with both a reason to be and an escape from her own developmental problems, has gotten a bum deal.)

Doctors' wives discover, to their apparently universal dismay, an inverse ratio between the amount of financial security they get from their husbands and what they crave even more: *emotional* security. "Feedback," "support," "friends and family life"—all of these are areas in which the physician-provider doesn't give as good as he gets, the poll revealed. In fact, many a Medical/Mrs. thinks her husband is a dull and limited fellow. Unlike her, he has no "outside interests" to enliven his existence. He doesn't really *do* anything. (Having no separate existence of her own, the wife finds it difficult if not impossible to grasp that her husband *enjoys* that part of his life which is separate from her.) To add insult to outrage, the doctor husband behaves like a petty demagogue around the house.

"Do you suffer due to the 'God' status your husband enjoys?" the magazine survey asked, impetuously, and 48 percent of its readers shouted, "Yes!" One wife, obviously at her wit's end, remarked,

"The biggest problem is my husband's failure to realize that while he may be God at the hospital and his word is law, different expectations are encompassed in a healthy family relationship. He tends to give orders to me and our children; we all resent this. . . . He is a neurosurgeon and I do understand the pressure he faces in the operating room, but I'm 36 years old now, my children 11 and 12, and I'm getting tired of the whole routine. Until I can find a better way out, I intend to ignore him a lot."

How aggrieved these women sound! They want security—yes—but security to them means more by far than just someone to pay the bills. It means nightly cuddling. Someone to sit next to them during Junior's Little League games and Alice's piano recitals. Someone to help put in the vegetable garden and join in a game of golf once in a while. Instead, what they have ended up with is ego with a capital E. Three-piece suits from J. Press and a big gas guzzler for him; a Subaru—and Hubby's rules and regulations coming down from on high—for her.

"He is a very controlling person—of the food that is to be served, the house, the money, of course, and my time," complained the neurosurgeon's beloved.[2] The doctor no doubt feels justified in his domination of the domestic scene because, deep down, he feels that he's paying for his wife's security with his *life*. The more she complains about his absence, the more time he spends "at the hospital," avoiding her. He feels righteous about the way he lives, even smug. He tends to isolate himself from his more threatening feelings, such as the anger he has toward the demanding, childlike woman with whom he lives. He prefers to act out his anger, willfully frustrating her efforts to tame and domesticate him. He has great leverage, after all, for his wife can do nothing, go nowhere without him. All he has to do to circumscribe her activities is cancel her credit cards. Just the threat of economic disenfranchisement is enough to keep most non-working wives in place. And so, feeling it's more than anyone should really have to put up with, the doctor's wife, with a great sigh of sadness and depression (for doesn't she, after all, deserve better than this?) breaks down, finally, and attempts to make "a life of her own."

"Togetherness" was the Fifties term for describing an ideal marriage—a cozy, intimate relationship in which wives and husbands shared everything: ideas, opinions, dreams, epiphanies. In the Sixties, togetherness was supposed to have been blasted out of existence, exposed as an unhealthy interdependency, one that allowed neither man nor woman to grow, change, or develop. (Women's magazines in particular came in for a beating for having historically taken the position that women should want, need, and promote this stifling "togetherness.")

Whether a backlash has occurred in the intervening years or whether, in their innermost selves, women never *wanted* to break out of the togetherness cocoon, it seems that marriage still offers, for many women, an escape hatch—a retreat from autonomy that's stamped with society's approval. The outward style may be more liberated, but the inner fear women experience pushes them toward a merged, symbiotic existence that's fundamentally no different from the Fifties picture of the devoted couple going hand in hand toward the rosy horizon of their future.

The issue we're addressing here is what psychologists call "separation-individuation," and it has to do with whether *any*one—man or woman—can withstand the experience of being primarily and fundamentally alone: one who stands on one's own two feet, develops one's own ideas, and has a unique and personal way of looking at life. It is *lack* of separation-individuation that wrecks a lot of marriages.[3]

There's Safety in Fusion

"Fusion" is the word used in the literature of marital psychology to describe a relationship in which one mate, or both, afraid of being separate or alone, give up individual identity in favor of an attempted "merged identity." Statements like "I can read his mind," "We think alike on everything," and "We can actually *feel* each other's feelings" do not reflect intimacy; they reflect fear—the fear of growing up and standing alone.

The desire to merge, symbiotically, with another has its origins in childhood, and the deep desire for "reengulfment" with the mother.[4] Psychologically, the first phase of separation is a precarious time in the development of the young child, who, still uncertain of his or her identity and anxious about separation, is tempted to regress to a time

in early infancy when he or she was not aware of any separate existence at all, but was fused with the all-encompassing, all-protective
mother. Joan Wexler and John Steidl, who teach psychiatric social
work at Yale, believe that adults who try to fuse with their mates are
acting out of a regressive impulse similar to a toddler's. "Ambivalent
about autonomy, frightened by their separateness and feeling needy
and alone," say Wexler and Steidl, such people "yearn for and try to
recapture with their mates the primitive, continual empathetic exchange of a young pre-verbal infant with its mother. This attempt at
fusion . . . is an attempt to remain merged, to never be alone, and to
deny separateness or differentness."[5]

In marriages that stay fused year after year, both husband and wife
are firmly planted at a psychologically infantile level of development.
Wexler and Steidl describe the phenomenon chillingly, as "two gray
figures locked in a repetitious, deathly dance."

How do couples go on this way?

With great calculation. They have ways of protecting themselves,
taking "measured strides and scrupulous care" to avoid having to see
the disturbing reality: that things have changed radically, and the
marriage has become bitterly disappointing.

Men, of course, are partly responsible for maintaining this bind,
but women feel themselves in greater jeopardy and can be positively
brilliant at keeping the balance struck. The more dependent they
are, the more vigorous their efforts to (for example) structure a
"proper" family life—sit-down meals, schedules for rising and retiring; in general a rather humorless insistence on the family's doing
"what's right," which tends to translate into "Do it my way." Hubby
is expected to be dependable and predictable. When he goes out of
town on business he plugs into the family structure with nightly
check-in calls. In varying degrees of extremeness, dependent wives try
to construct of "family life" an elaborate social network, a web of
children and relatives and carefully selected friends in which the husband is ensnared, a stiff and shiny-winged fly.

Some women control through a critical insistence on keeping all
family members on their toes. Others do it through blind devotion.
The blindly devoted make themselves indispensable to husbands
who, they genuinely believe, couldn't make it without them. There
are many ways to keep the seesaw of a fused marriage balanced. So-

licitousness and excessive concern for the welfare of the partner is one of them.

Blind Devotion

The most poignant story I have ever heard on the subject of blind devotion belongs to a woman I'll call Madeleine Boroff. Because of the nature of the story I have had to change a great number of details so as to protect the privacy of those involved. But what you will read here is true in its most important aspects—the dreams, the illusions, the self-deception.

Madeleine is a woman whose particular kind of attractiveness has a lot to do with her apparent competence, her ability to remain calm in the face of crisis. It is a quality she was fortunate to possess, given the turn her life had taken, almost from the day she married. Bright and energetic, Madeleine had left off being a girl to marry and become a woman when she was eighteen. A year and a half later she gave birth to her first child, and the whole scenario of her adult life —an almost picaresque struggle with adversity—was under way.

"That whole welfare mess that Manny and I were involved in a few years back has suddenly come to life again," she told a friend on the phone one rainy winter morning. It was only a few months after her fortieth birthday. "Would you believe I've been summoned to court? My lawyer says I could actually end up going to jail."

To everyone who knew her, the idea of Madeleine Boroff's going to jail seemed preposterous. With four children and a husband who was far from stable, she had been the family's emotional mainstay. During years of tumult, she had been the Competent One, a nonimpulsive woman who had been responsible for keeping the family afloat. Word had gotten around that the Boroffs were living on welfare (Manny had lost his job again), and months later it began to seem as if they were staying on welfare a lot longer than their intelligence and education would seem to warrant. Still, jail! Jail was an institution for those whose intent was criminal, not for struggling, emotionally overwhelmed members of the upwardly striving middle class. And not for *mothers*.

Among the women who knew her, the immediate reaction was anger. Madeleine had worked hard to keep things functioning and to keep the children on an even keel. Now, after twenty-two years, she was on her own, trying to piece together a life by working as a receptionist and going to school nights to finish up a degree she'd put off years ago, when fleeing to Rome with Manny had seemed a thrilling course.

The details of what happened during the period when the Boroffs were living on welfare had never been entirely clear, but one thing was obvious: if *anyone* was to be sent to jail, it should not be Madeleine. Madeleine Boroff was a good woman. Living through hardships that would have devastated most wives, she had gotten four children from infancy into adolescence more or less unscathed. At forty she was still attractive, still slender, still hopeful. She had given a tremendous amount to others. Shouldn't she now have the chance to live for herself?

Several weeks after the initial alarm, Madeleine could anticipate the clang of the slamming door. "You're not going to believe this," she told her friend, "but I've been sentenced. Twenty-one days in the Hartford Penitentiary. Manny has already served. He only got two weeks." She gave a dry laugh. "I guess the judge thought I had more time to spare."

It would turn out, of course, that the judge had not really been concerned with who had more time to spare. The judge had been concerned with the idea of fraud, and he'd decided that Madeleine was guilty of it; guiltier even than her husband. She had been the one, after all, to sign up for welfare in Massachusetts when they were already on the rolls in Connecticut.

Initially, it had not been easy to fathom. The idea of a woman you know being ordered to leave her children and go to jail was so appalling it distracted from any underlying principle of justice. The old sanctification of motherhood had once again clouded the issues and implied a double standard of ethics. In their annoyance over Madeleine's having to "put up with" yet another indignity, her women friends overlooked completely the relevant questions. *What, in fact, had Madeleine's life to date been all about? During those many years, had she really been true blue—to her children, her husband, herself? Or had she been desperate rather than devoted, a woman blinded by insecurity?*[6]

Scenes from a Marriage

Several years before being fired from his most recent job, Manny Boroff had moved his family out of their apartment in Springfield, Massachusetts, to a big old house in Thompsonville, a little town on the Connecticut River. For a year Manny had been the agency account executive for a major Massachusetts bank, and the salary he commanded was such that he decided to get his family out of Springfield and into a terrific house, one that was a bit dilapidated but loaded with charm.

True to the pattern of his life so far, it was not long after the move that Manny found himself out of a job again. Employers were initially impressed with Manny's cleverness and good looks, but soon disappointed by his inability to follow through on responsibilities. He was the sort of guy who'd begin a job by sending the sales figures skyrocketing. Then, once his mark had been made, down the hill he'd go, like a skier out of control, arrogantly missing appointments, arriving late to work, and finally, when caught, lying to cover his tracks. It was always getting caught in a lie—or series of lies—that did him in. But in telling his story to Madeleine he would put the onus on "them," finding increasingly subtle ways of getting her to side with him against his insensitive and moronic employers.

This time, though, things felt different to Madeleine. As the months passed in the house in Thompsonville, a safe-feeling routine established itself. Manny would hunker in his third-floor study, working, he said, on a novel. Madeleine felt hopeful. She baby-sat and sold bread to supplement the unemployment payments. It was a new and, in some ways, invigorating life. With Manny home, it was fun plotting and scheming and planting the herb garden together. Each morning Manny would be up early, whistling, repairing things around the house. Afternoons he stayed upstairs, working on the novel.

For a year the whole thing had a peculiarly idyllic appearance. Who wouldn't like a life of gardening and writing in the lush Connecticut River valley? But after fifty-six weeks the unemployment insurance ran out, and the Boroff budget suddenly sagged under the strain. Forthwith and efficiently, Manny applied for Connecticut welfare. He did *not* go out and look for a job. He wrote (or at least tried to), and Madeleine encouraged him. Working in advertising had always frustrated Manny and made him drink too much. All his life he'd wanted to be a writer, wanted it desperately. Madeleine found hope in the change her husband was apparently trying to make, a change she hoped would lead to a more stable existence for all of them. She cajoled, she analyzed, she "supported" her husband —in the interest of her own security at least as much as in his.

As the months passed, it grew harder and harder to make ends meet on the meager, though constant, welfare payments. The Boroffs' mortgage payments were $350 a month, and everyone had to be fed. In addition, there were the four or five gallons of wine they somehow managed to consume each week (though Madeleine had to admit it was mostly Manny doing the consuming). So one day, a couple of weeks before the bank's foreclosure date and with no other means of income in sight, Madeleine, not knowing what else to do and believing it would be only another month or so until Manny got his outline and sample chapter submitted to his agent, took the bus into Springfield and applied for Massachusetts welfare. As proof of address she used the lease on the old Springfield apartment, which they'd been smart enough to hang onto and sublet.

It had been surprisingly easy. Well, if not precisely easy, not as hard as one might imagine, either. The checks would be sent to their Springfield address. To expedite the process, she told the welfare worker her husband had run out on her. The system beams most fairly on abandoned women with children. Besides, Manny had convinced her that *he* had already had enough hassle, what with having to show up at those Connecticut welfare hearings to defend his case every few months. It would be hell if he had to do the same thing in Springfield. So Madeleine had agreed that it was *her* turn to deal with "the welfare hassle."

It was a scary step for her to take—but not, apparently, as scary as facing the inner fears and low self-esteem that had been pulling her just a little bit lower every year. Blindly devoted to Manny, Madeleine was also blind to her own stifling dependency—her need to stay merged with her husband, as closely attached as a barnacle to a ship. It made no difference that the ship itself was rudderless. More than anything Madeleine was terrified of ending up alone. To avoid that she would do virtually anything—steal from the government, if need be (though neither of them quite thought of it as "stealing" at the time). There was an ironic, entrepreneurial efficiency with which Madeleine managed the double-welfare scheme. She arranged that their subtenants would mail the Massachusetts payments to their Connecticut address. Then they would simply cash them somewhere —anywhere other than at their local bank in Thompsonville, which had been cashing the Connecticut welfare checks for over a year.

Coming up against reality has a strange, how-could-this-be-happening-to-me? quality for those who, in their innermost souls, don't really feel themselves to be adults. For Madeleine, being found out was doubly ironic. By the time the two welfare departments caught up with the Boroffs, Madeleine had finally summoned the courage to break free. In *spite* of the kids. In spite of her fear that Manny would go down the drain without her. She wished to make some move for herself even if it *did* mean abandoning him.

That last is a trick of the dependent personality—believing that you're responsible for "taking care of" the other one. Madeleine had always felt more responsible for Manny's survival than for her own. As long as she was concentrating on Manny—*his* passivity, *his* indecisiveness, *his* problems with alcohol—she focused all her energy on devising solutions for him, or for "them," and never had to look inside herself. It was why it had taken twenty-two years for Madeleine to catch on to the fact that if things continued as they had always been, she would end up shortchanged. She would end up *never having lived a life.*

She did recognize this, finally, and made the wrenching move to break away—not only from Manny, but from her whole dependent life-style. She put the drafty old house she loved so much on the market, settled her debts (the judge, by the way, had let her do her "term" on weekends), and moved with her children to Seattle. There she lined up a job with an insurance company, planned to go to school nights, and hoped fervently that she would be able to make for herself a new life. From the time she was eighteen until she was forty—years when people are supposed to reap, and grow, and experience the world—Madeleine Boroff had been hanging on, pretending to herself that life was not what it was, that her husband would get his bearings before long, and that she would one day spring free to live her own inner life—peacefully, creatively.

For twenty-two years she had not been able to cope with what it would mean to face down the lie, and so, without intending any harm, but too frightened to live authentically, she turned her back on truth.

It may seem dramatic in its surface details, but in its fundamental dynamic Madeleine's story is not so unusual. The go-along quality she exhibited, the seeming inability to extricate herself, or even *think* of extricating herself, from an utterly draining relationship—these signs of helplessness are characteristic of women who are psychologically dependent. For them, marriage functions as a reinforcing agent. Instead of strengthening a woman's character, it deteriorates it. Instead of building self-confidence, it leads to self-doubt. Instead of providing an experience in which women can grow and develop individual resources, marriage all too often ends up having quite the opposite effect: it reinforces their dependencies and takes away from their autonomy, leaving them with only a vestige of the resilience and strength they at least appeared to have before they took "the plunge."

Jessie Bernard, a sociologist at Pennsylvania State University, notes in her book *The Future of Marriage* that "Women who are quite able to take care of themselves before marriage become helpless after 15 or 20 years." She tells the story of a woman who'd managed a travel agency before she married but who, by the time she was widowed at fifty-five, had been so buffered against life's realities she no longer knew how to get a passport and had to ask friends how to go about it.

"Girls are reared to accept themselves as naturally dependent, entitled to lean on the greater strength of men, and they enter marriage fully confident that these expectations will be fulfilled," observes Dr. Bernard.

The counterpart of this fantasy, of course, is that men will be parentlike: strong, unwavering, willing and able to protect and give succor. The myth is that women are the nurturing ones in a marriage, but that myth does not take into account the other side of the picture: that women look to men for the same kind of protection, support, and encouragement that children expect from their parents. After they marry, women are brought up short; their husbands, they

discover, are far from the supermen they had imagined during court-
ship. Men are as easily hurt as anyone, and in trying to achieve personal fulfillment they have their own insecurities to struggle with.
Upon making this discovery, says Bernard, some women act like children "who come to realize that their parents are not really omnis-
cient." They are disappointed and angry.

After she was married for a while, Madeleine Boroff discovered
that her charming young husband was not at all what she had imagined him to be. No tower of strength, he leaned heavily on her—and
on the entire family. They were the armature he hoped would
bolster his collapsing confidence. That bold, opinionated way he had
of talking, and his flamboyant dismissal of convention, were nothing
but fearful attempts to gain esteem in the face of his repeated failures. Anyone else looking at Manny Boroff could see these things,
but Madeleine would not. She conspired with her husband in his
fantasy that he was in charge of things: the king pin.

"Some people control by being dependent," says therapist Marcia
Perlstein, "by keeping the man feeling as though he's the boss." This
is often true in relationships in which the man has self-esteem problems. "The way he feels big in the world is by being big *to* somebody," Perlstein goes on. "By staying just the right amount of small,
and by controlling that balance very carefully, the woman can keep
them both symbiotically merged and 'happy.'"

Madeleine was so enmeshed with her husband, she couldn't
see—was afraid to see—how overwhelmed he was by the demands of
adult life, and by the emotional chaos created by his own inner
conflicts. When Manny had delusions of beatnikism and insisted
they go off and live in Rome before their first child was born, Madeleine too became entranced with visions of the Via Veneto, and followed him like a loving puppy. She wasn't sure about how or on
what they would live; but then, that wasn't *her* problem anyway.
Years later, when Manny felt the time had come to get out of "the
slums of Springfield" and buy a house in the country, Madeleine also
wanted to buy a house in the country, though she would never have
come up with the suggestion on her own and had no idea how they'd
manage the mortgage payments. When Manny felt he had to have
his chance at Being a Writer No Matter What, Madeleine organized
the entire family toward helping him fulfill his dream.

Until, one day, the equation didn't work anymore. She saw,

finally, that the children were getting older and would soon be lumbering out of her life, at which point she would be left to live out her last days with the Great American Outline Writer and his jug of junk wine. As it has been for so many other women, the departure of the children was like a slap in the face, awakening her—so rudely—to the dumb servitude of her existence. *What would she do now? Who would she be? For she saw that she wasn't anyone separate and identifiable at all; she was only a part of "them."*

The "Good Woman" Syndrome

The woman who devotes her entire life to keeping her husband straight and her children "protected" is not a saint, she's a clinger. Rather than experience the terrors of being cut loose, of having to find and secure her own moorings, she will hang on in the face of unbelievable adversity. If she's really good at it, she doesn't even appear to suffer much. This is the woman who "looks on the bright side." Who appears tough and sinewy in situations where most would be reduced to mush. Who is, at all costs, "terrific with the children."

The Good Woman does her damnedest to please others. In terms of her own developmental tasks, however, she's gotten about as far as high school. She "uses marriage in the service of regression," as the psychologists put it, meaning that she unconsciously hopes to return, through her relationship with her husband, to an earlier, safer time. For the Good Woman, according to ego psychologists Rubin and Gertrude Blanck, marriage becomes "a way of being taken care of and supported . . . a way of *acquiring* a home instead of making one . . . an opportunity to relieve conflict instead of mastering it."[7]

A cover-up that's used to mask inner neurotic drives, such a relationship must be continuously and delicately manipulated. "Some women who come into treatment with me have a very finely tuned sense of what's going to work in their marriages," says Marcia Perlstein.[8] "Of course the arrangement doesn't *really* work or they wouldn't be starting therapy in the first place. Outwardly the mechanism may seem to be functioning, but inwardly these women aren't happy. They feel an acute lack of meaning in their lives. Their only sense of competence is tied up with being able to control—to get what they want through dependency."

In a dependent relationship there are different ways of maintaining the desired balance. Sometimes the wife pretends that her husband is superior. Bringing this off can require major contortion acts. Some women *do* so little—*limit* their lives so severely—that they actually *make* themselves less competent. Comfortable only when they feel smaller than their husbands, they placate, appease, and effectively turn their backs on themselves—their own needs and talents and interests.

(Leon Salzman, a psychiatrist, says this is similar to the denial used "by the prisoner, slave, or member of a minority group who comes to accept the derogatory view of his own status *in order to achieve maximum security and advantage*."[9] In other words, there are *advantages* to remaining in a state of thralldom—advantages so great that many women prefer to remain slaves rather than forfeit the security slavery provides.)

Another trick is to do quite the opposite—to diminish men by noting how like children they are. "Men are all alike," you will hear in the playgrounds, and kitchens, and living rooms of America. "I was at a dinner party where all the women were housewives and all their husbands were hotshot astrophysicists at Cal Tech," said Barrie Thorne, a sociologist. "All the hotshot husbands sat on one side of the room talking about black holes and all their wives sat on the other side of the room talking about what babies their husbands are."[10]

When women do this it's a sure sign they're suffering. By sharing with one another the comforting "all-men-are-babies" cliché, they can vent some of the pain of their girlish disillusionment without risking change. They never have to *do* anything about their lives. They simply, comfortingly, complain. (Or if they are Good Women, they *don't* complain.)

The dependent wife often veers back and forth between building her husband up and tearing him down. Madeleine Boroff, for example, would magnify Manny's writing talent because it provided her with a rationalization for putting up with his destructiveness—remaining a slave to it. "My-husband-the-genius" is a seductive game. It allows us to continue leaning on these "geniuses" even when they're patently dull-witted.

Madeleine also diminished Manny, choosing to think of him as fragile and in need of her protection. Acting the protector helped her to salvage a little self-esteem. As Big Nurse, a woman whose self-confidence is a slender reed can gain an illusory potency. "See how well I cope?" her every act demands. "*Trust* me. *Rely* on me." (And inwardly, "*Never let me go.*")

Under the guise of helping their husbands, many women have an emotional investment in keeping their husbands weak. Weak, men will always need their wives. Weak, they will never leave. (This, actually, is a paradigm of the alcoholic's wife: outwardly competent and well organized—but inwardly afraid that if left alone she would dissolve in a pool of butter.)

The Good Woman, of course, has the same character structure as the Good Girl, who learned passivity at Mother's knee. The disadvantages of growing up obedient, docile, and nice are beginning to be seen in all areas of a woman's life. One of the newest studies finds a correlation between the "good girl syndrome" and difficulties in achieving orgasm.[11] Dagmar O'Connor, a New York psychologist who has treated more than six hundred women patients in a sex-therapy program at Roosevelt Hospital, compared nonorgasmic patients with women who were orgasmic. In the nonorgasmic group, 88 percent described themselves as having been "good girls" as children and teen-agers. They were obedient, did well in school, never had conflicts with their parents. Interestingly, only 30 percent of the orgasmic women fell into that category. The study indicates at least a tentative correlation between psychological independence and the ability to experience orgasm. Women who are psychologically dependent can find terrifying that moment of merger with the other, when the boundaries of personality and identity dissipate. Unsure of their identities to begin with, dependent, vulnerable, and helpless, they find the moment of passionate abandonment unbearable, and refuse to give themselves up to it.

The Second Time Around: Pursuing the Myth of Safety

Much as they are willing to give up for it, women often discover that marriage brings them no real safety. "It's like that song, 'You Can't Even Run Your Own Life, I'll Be Damned if You'll Run Mine,'" a woman I'll call Jessica told me. "It's not long before you find yourself wondering, 'How can this person who's loaded with faults be in charge of me?' "

Before her recent remarriage, Jessica had lived alone with her children for five years, during which time she'd gone back to school to become a dental assistant. Soon after starting her first job, in the little apple-growing community in Massachusetts where she lives, Jessica abandoned her barely gained independence for a handsome new husband. Ben, it soon turned out, wanted a baby. Jessica already had three children from her earlier marriage, but at thirty-four she thought she was old enough that she'd better comply now if she was going to comply at all. Ben had never had a child. How could she deprive him of a baby if a baby was what he wanted?

But a baby was not all Jessica would give Ben. She liquidated $13,000—savings from the sale of her previous home—to offset some debts belonging to her new husband. Now, with the baby a year and a half old and another on the way, she's not so happy she was so "giving." "I wanted to wipe the slate clean of Ben's debts so he and I could have a fresh start. But now when I think that I no longer have the house I owned, and I no longer have the thirteen thousand dollars in the bank, and I no longer have a profession, I feel stuck. I think to myself, 'If anything goes wrong, if for some reason I should want to get *out* of this relationship, it would really be hard.' "

Jessica's attitude is a clear illustration of the new feminine conflict. Emotionally she wants the luxury of being taken care of, but she's smart enough to know she's paying a high price for what Jessie Bernard calls "the pitfalls of too much security." Jessica discusses her "situation" with a kind of passivity, as if she has had no say in her decisions. "Suddenly I'm no longer financially independent; I'm no longer professionally independent. My resentment of the situation will occur, and I'll blow up. The reason is because I'm not in control of my life anymore. I lost it."

Sociologists have found that women make far greater personal adjustments than men do in an attempt to keep their marriages on an even keel. When they marry, most men have no intention of changing the routines of their lives. They figure that basically they'll do the same things, *think* the same things—in general, be the same person—only now they'll be married instead of single.[12]

Women don't look at it this way. We *become* wives in the same way that we *become* mothers. We expect to change, to soften and blur whatever line exists between "me" and "him." In essence, we expect to merge. And while it may not be something we give conscious assent to, if the shape resulting from the merger is more informed by *his* ideas and attitudes than by our own, we hardly question the arrangement. "Dwindling into a wife," says Jessie Bernard, "involves a re-definition of the self—an active re-shaping of the personality to conform to the wishes or needs or demands of husbands."[13]

"Dwindling into a wife" also involves relinquishing skills. The bottom line for many married women today is that they would have no way of supporting themselves, because any skills they may have developed before they married have long since atrophied. As women who've been through it will tell you, there's a pathetic fallacy involved in believing you can "drop out" for six or seven years while the children are young and then pop back into careers again as if nothing had happened. You may need new training, a period of reevaluation. You are not the same person you were when you married. "It's such a subtle thing that happens," said the woman who gave up her career *and* her $13,000 nest egg. "When I was living alone, divorced and single, I felt as if I were able to do just about anything. I had *responsibilities*. As soon as I get into marriage again I begin to look to the other person to do all kinds of things for me. If he doesn't do them, I feel, 'It isn't fair!' "

Dependency, by its very nature, creates self-doubt, and self-doubt can lead all too quickly to self-hatred. Comparative sex studies show that wives perceive themselves in a far more negative light than husbands perceive *them*selves. Wives worry obsessively about things like how they look, how "attractive" they are. If they have trouble adjusting to some aspect of the marriage, wives are quick to blame themselves, tending to attribute the problem to their own shortcomings. Even when it's the husband who is creating difficulty in the relationship, women feel as if the fault were theirs.

Of all the women I talked with while researching this book, those in their thirties who had divorced and remarried but *who had not gained self-sufficiency between Husband No. 1 and Husband No. 2* were the most poignantly resigned of all. "When we got our divorce, I felt I was in limbo until the next husband came along," said a woman from Little Rock. "I was just waiting for the next husband."

"I'm not *trained*," said a woman with a master's degree who so far has never earned a salary. "I've never had to think in terms of supporting myself and my family, and it's really hard to begin thinking in those terms."

"The day comes," said another, "when you say to yourself, 'Hey, there's really something about this person that I don't like, something I wasn't aware of before I committed myself, something that, as I've grown and changed, I can't quite accept.' Then it's 'Okay, what am I going to do with it?' You contemplate divorce, you contemplate separation, but it's not so easy the second time around."

The woman who gave up her nest egg says, "You come to a point where you realize there are certain things you might like to change but probably aren't going to—you can't change 'the nature of the beast.' I get depressed about it sometimes, and then I think, 'Well, there's got to be some *angle*.' First I kept thinking I'd like to change things, but now I think acceptance is really where it's at."

Women who don't complain, women who are stoic and "strong" in the face of marriages that don't nurture them are usually women with an unhealthy degree of dependency. As wives they are incapable of confronting their husbands because to do so effectively they'd have to experience their own angry or hostile feelings, and that would be far too dangerous. These are the women who love not out of a choice bred from inner strength—a tenderness and generosity they can afford because they feel whole and estimable within themselves. These are the women who "love" because they are afraid to stand alone.

Out from Under

Dependency feeds on itself. Ultimately the dependent woman will find herself in a position of real enslavement. Humiliated, she will look to her "oppressor," the man on whom she depends. At this point she finds it difficult, if not impossible, to look within. "*He's* the reason I have no life," she will tell herself.

Marcia Goldstein, a psychotherapist in Berkeley, California, specializes in helping couples work through their fused, symbiotic relationships. Sometimes her clients end up staying together, able to enjoy more satisfying lives as individuals as well as able to be more

loving and less angry toward each other. Sometimes they end by
splitting up. But as the following "history" points out, the departure
from a relationship that has little going for it other than a fused dependency for both partners doesn't have to be devastating to either.
It can truly be an escape into freedom.

The man in this story (we'll call him Al) had a history of getting
into relationships before he was really ready. "A passive-aggressive
type, he would appear to go along with things and then later resent
it," the therapist told me.

The woman, whom we'll call Lyn, was an active, outgoing person,
a teacher and a school administrator. Over the almost four years she
was involved with Al her effectiveness and her self-confidence
drained away, so that she seemed a different person than she had
been "before Al," as her friends noted. The more she went out to Al,
it seemed, the more he withdrew. He would complain that she was
intruding in his life; she would back off again, her self-esteem
dashed.

A frustrated artist, Al wanted a chance to find out if he could really make a career for himself in commercial art. Lyn would encourage him to go into his studio at night and work, and then she would
hang around waiting for him, "in case he wanted a late supper or
something." Al, *feeling* her presence waiting for him, felt smothered
by it.

Al and Lyn had truly become "two gray figures locked in a repetitious, deathly dance." The emotional stress involved in trying to con-
tain their anger and resentment sapped both partners. Al was always
frantically clawing for some "space" for himself, the kind of solitude
that would allow him to work in a free, spontaneous way. The truth
was, though, that he was inwardly afraid to free himself, because he
didn't want to experience his aloneness; so he externalized, blaming
his problem on Lyn.

Lyn, for her part, was frightened by Al's moves away from her. His
being separate—an individual in his own right—she felt as the anni-
hilation of their togetherness. "In fused adult couples," Wexler and
Steidl observe, "the mate is seen as the whole world, as entirely responsible for one's well-being or misery. If the partners happen to be
in tune with each other's needs the world goes well. If one mate,
however, doesn't respond as expected, the relationship goes
badly. . . ."

Keeping a fused relationship in a state of balance requires that both partners stay precisely as they are. There is no room for growth or change in such a rigid transaction. Eventually, one partner or the other is likely to blow it by wanting more, by expressing disappointment, or by feeling threatened. That's what was happening with Lyn and Al, according to their therapist. Though consciously Lyn felt she was being reasonable and mature, in fact she was terribly disturbed by Al's evenings alone in the studio. "When the other person isn't present," explain Wexler and Steidl, "the relationship is felt as lost and this is experienced as the loss of one's self. Utter dependency is interpreted as togetherness."

How do people get out of such a lock-up?

"Lyn and Al tried a three-month separation," Marcia Goldstein told me. "It's something I'd done with other couples—an experiment to break the clinch, to give them a breathing space, and possibly some new perspective on themselves. The first month they live separately but monogamously, concentrating on developing their individual lives. The second month they can be nonmonogamous; if they wish, they can use this time to experiment with the possibility of another kind of relationship. The third month, monogamy again—a time to reevaluate and determine what they have in their relationship and what they don't have."

When the three months were up, both Lyn and Al were asked to decide, independently, what they wanted to do—whether they wanted to split up or stay together.

In Lyn's first session after the trial separation she delivered what her therapist describes as "the classic dependent response." "She began by saying how she knows it's going to take time, but she really loves Al and she knows he really loves her, and even though he's been remote from her, if he's willing to give it a try, then she's willing to give it a try—blah, blah, blah. It all sounds very reasonable and balanced, but it masks her belief that she can't possibly cope without Al." In fact Lyn had made no decision at all at that point; she was desperately clinging to "the relationship."

In the meantime, the therapist had already seen Al and knew that he had decided to break up with Lyn. How would Lyn, with all her dependency on her lover, take it?

"Actually, beneath her surface preoccupation with Al, a lot had been going on in Lyn's life," Marcia Goldstein told me. "She'd gotten a better job. Also—and this was very important—she'd been in much better contact with friends during her separation from Al—women friends, even some of her old boyfriends. They'd taken walks and gone on picnics and had some good conversations. Like so many dependent women, Lyn had previously just locked herself up with her one-and-only. She'd gotten to the point where she couldn't even *relate* to other people anymore."

Lyn still thought she was deeply dependent on Al, but it was a conviction based on old ideas about herself rather than on the reality of her new life. "Knowing that Lyn had begun to develop a solid support system for herself, I asked her if she was willing to take the relationship with Al at all costs. She thought for a while and said, 'No. If he'd continue resenting me, and continue blaming me as the sole reason for his not doing his art work, if he were to feel that he was doing me a favor by staying with me, then no, at this point I *wouldn't* take it.'"

When Lyn came to the following session, with Al, she was in an emotional state which Marcia Goldstein describes as "courageously vulnerable." She told Al, in essence, "I'm not going to lie to you; we've been through too much together for me to pretend." She told him, "This relationship means a lot to me, partly through history, partly through habit, but mainly because I genuinely care for you. And if I could have you *wanting* to be in it, if I could really have you, have all of you, and with the commitment that we'd still each try to live our own lives—if you were willing to do all that, then I'd want the relationship. But if you have even the slightest hesitation, and don't want to, even though it would be painful, I'm really ready to split up."

Said Marcia, "Al told Lyn he couldn't do it, he couldn't give her what she wanted; and the two of them split up right there in my office. I found it incredibly beautiful. It was Lyn's graduation out of dependency."

Since the separation, Lyn is "more tender, more vulnerable, and more loving with her friends," says her therapist. And she's getting ready to go off on a trip to Europe. "That's something important; when people really get out of dependency, they get out in a positive way. They experience the *freedom* side of independence rather than the isolation side. If they're still *feeling* dependent, regardless of what they may be doing, then they experience the isolation side, the self-pity: 'I'm all alone in the world and destined never to be intimate again, never to be happy.' Lyn's saying to herself, 'I don't have to worry whether he loves me or not. I can go to Europe for three months; then I can come back, settle down, build on my job.' That's the true barometer of whether or not you're really springing out of dependency: if you haven't that kind of energy, that kind of *confidence*, then you haven't yet sprung free."

CHAPTER VI

Gender Panic

How, when you have dared nothing in life, do you begin to dare? What gives you the little push, the impetus to move out to the edge of what's familiar and step off?

For many women it is a feeling of despair.

When I began, finally, to write, it was not at school, not at *Mademoiselle*, but in a little five-room railroad flat just north of Greenwich Village, when my second baby was a month old. I remember the night so clearly, for in no way had I anticipated what was to happen. The rush had come from nowhere (or so it seemed on hindsight)—a sudden, compelling urge to write, to put down words on paper. Those words were a beginning, for they came directly from my head to the paper, with no Others to intervene. It was glorious and focused, the first utterly independent experience I'd had since marrying. The apartment was quiet, nondemanding. My husband was asleep on the living-room couch. My son was having his midnight feeding. I remember cradling him to my breast with my left hand and beginning to scribble down words with my right. As the baby sucked, my mind filled impetuously with the shape of something I wanted to communicate to others. I wrote nonstop, as if fevered, barely pausing to put the baby down. I sat alone, aware only of the smokestacks on neighboring rooftops as the morning light began to rise.

What impelled me to begin writing was that I didn't want to be alone anymore. It was an old aloneness, one that long preceded the aloneness I'd felt in my marriage. It went back to the little parochial school in Valley Stream, Long Island, the strange, disaffected nuns, my own frail body; the spaces between my teeth; the perception of myself as always too young, too thin, never in tune with the world around me: my parents, my schoolmates, my friends. For years I had been both maverick and leader, both insider and outsider. I had existed, always, slightly to the right of my own image of myself, and it was a lonely, self-alienated way to live. So the motivation, when I finally began to break out, was to say: "Look at me. I have something in common with you. I have these feelings that surely you must recognize." I think that then, as now, I was writing specifically to create a sense of communion with other women.

In the beginning, the feelings I wrote about were safe enough—the frustrations involved in being a young wife and mother trying to make a go of things in a big, noisy, dirty city. In my loneliness, I imagined that the women who read my articles would actually be able to *see* me making the dress from the Vogue pattern in a living room with a fire escape outside the window, and broken toys all over the floor. I imagined that they would *know* that all I sometimes wanted was to be able to get the eyeliner to go on smooth and wrinkleless, and go out and forget I was not yet thirty and feeling used up, a girl who had somehow turned old and tired without ever having had the chance to bloom.

As time passed the frustrations grew deeper, and the risks involved in writing about them became greater. Seven years after my first article was published, I was ready to begin talking. Not coincidentally, I was also ready to leave my marriage. The two things, it seemed, coincided—the need to throw off the false security of my relationship with my husband and the need to use my writing as an act of self-definition. I had begun thinking for myself. My husband's opinions, which in the beginning I'd clung to out of a kind of childlike fascination and later because I'd become completely alienated from my own mind, had become ordinary to me. I recognized that I saw most things differently than he did, that there was much he considered important that didn't compel me in the least.

To be truthful, I saw also that this man could not protect me in the world. I had come to a point where it seemed less dangerous to live alone than to continue in a marriage that submerged us both in deception. Strangely, this realization came at the end of a year in which Ed had had nothing to drink. We were ordinary, workaday people with no claim to specialness. Without crisis, our life together began to feel spiritually and emotionally arid.

Through writing, *with* the writing, I had begun to come into my own. To write demands the solitary use of one's mind and emotions. There is no one to cheer you on as you lay down paragraph after paragraph, no one to say, "Good girl, you're on the right track." You alone decide, and the decisions are endless. There are many ways in which one can come to know—and accept—oneself. There are many ways to begin to engage straightforwardly with life. Writing happened to be the way that process began for me.

Why is it that we have chosen to remain merged, undifferentiated creatures who still avoid the process of self-definition? How *many* of us belong to that hidden statistic—that enormous reservoir of untapped talent buried beneath the surface of middle-class womanhood?

"People kept telling me I was creative," a woman wrote to me from the well-to-do suburb of Bedford Village, in New York's Westchester County. "Some of my friends, with incredible patience, are still confident that I will burst upon the professional artistic scene like a welcome comet. While *they* are, and have been, typing EKG reports from 9 to 5 every day. And while I have been sitting in a stupor trying to decide what to *do* when I grow up. Help me. I'm about to sit down at the piano again, or go out into the garden and pick cabbage worms." (The writer of this letter is thirty-seven.)

A suggestion of an answer as to why women are so inhibited about exercising their talent came from Ann Arbor, Michigan, in the late Sixties. Struck by the peculiar panic she herself had experienced during her long haul to a doctorate in psychology, Matina Horner began to suspect that success—the *idea* of success—meant something quite different for women than it did for men. Women don't seem to go *after* success the way men do. They hedge their bets. They feel just as anxious when things go well as they do when rejection or failure seems imminent. Doing well—getting really good at something, *suc-*

ceeding—seems to scare the hell out of an awful lot of women who have what it takes to produce something substantial during the course of their lives.

Horner decided this was a phenomenon worth investigating. Undertaking studies that would eventually catapult her into the forefront of a new field—female psychology—she began by testing 90 women and 88 men at the University of Michigan. In the end she identified something that no one until then had even conceptualized —women's tendency to become so clutched about even the possibility of succeeding that it shuts down the very *will* to succeed. She called this phenomenon *Fear of Success.*[1]

Immediately apparent, as the data rolled in, was the high percentage of women afflicted by this fear—so many more women than men, as it turned out, the problem could be considered in some ways unique to the female psyche. It was not simply a question of being insecure about whether they had what it takes. *The more they had to offer, the more anxious they were.* "The very women who most want to achieve and who are most capable of achieving," says Dr. Horner, "are those who suffer the most from Fear of Success."[2]

It may have caused controversy in academia, but the rest of us— reading about Fear of Success in the media—felt an instant rush of recognition. Could it be that women actually *make* themselves unsuccessful? Could it be that concern about men and love and emotional security, all wrapped up in that heavily freighted term, "femininity," was a significant if not the major factor in what was holding us back?

The Crisis over Success

The technique Dr. Horner used to uncover this strange, previously unidentified fear is called "projective story completion." With it, she was able to dig into students' unconscious attitudes to find out what they felt, rather than what they thought they felt, or would have liked to feel. The men and women students were asked to write imaginative stories based on a "clue," a lead sentence designed to get test respondents thinking and feeling along certain lines. This was the clue for the women students: "At the end of first term finals Anne finds herself at the top of her medical school class." (For the male students the clue was the same, with "John" at the top of the class instead of Anne.)

The students' stories were then analyzed by the research team. The idea in "story projection tests" is that the respondents' real attitudes and expectations are buried in the plot of the story.

Dr. Horner considered it a sign that Fear of Success was operating if students made statements indicating they expected *negative consequences* to follow on the heels of any outstanding academic success. Negative consequences included the fear of being socially rejected, or losing one's eligibility as a date or marriage partner, and fear of becoming isolated, lonely, or unhappy as a result of succeeding.

Word of what Horner was working on jumped from university to university the way lightning jumps to the rod. There were tremendous differences, she found, between how men and women respond to the prospect of success. The male students were eager about the possibility of developing brilliant careers; such a prospect sent the women into tailspins of anxiety. Ninety percent of Horner's men not only thought success in the work world was something they'd be quite comfortable with, they also thought it would help them gain points with women. Sixty-five percent of the women Horner tested found the idea of success anywhere from disturbing to out-and-out terrifying. The main reason, according to Dr. Horner, was this: *The women thought doing well professionally would jeopardize their relations with men.* It was as simple as that. Women with boyfriends thought they'd lose them. Women without boyfriends thought they'd never get them.

Rather than risk a life without love, women apparently will give up a great deal—drop out, turn their backs on their ambitions, flee anxiously into the anonymity of The Eighty Percent. Not for them the fate of moldering lonely and unloved on the cold throne of professional excellence. *More than anything, women want to experience themselves in relationship to another.* This is primary; it takes precedence over everything.

Disasters Befalling "Anne"

Let us see how the women at the University of Michigan actually handled the disturbing situation in which Anne found herself in medical school.

A large majority of women wrote stories expressing the idea that Anne might as well have been a leper for all the isolation she could expect as a result of her anomalous brilliance in med school. This brilliance was going to get Anne into so much trouble it wasn't worth exhibiting. One woman suggested that Anne immediately bring herself down from her Number One position in the class. By slacking off on her own studies and helping out her friend Carl, Anne could soon marry, drop out of med school, and "concentrate on raising [Carl's] children."

Consistently, the theme in the women's stories was that Anne could hardly expect to have the affection of a lover if she persisted in excelling so ostentatiously. The women expressed a kind of anxious annoyance with Anne. She was not "happy," they said. Or they found her unattractively aggressive. This "Anne," they suggested, had no qualms about trampling over others—family, husband, friends—in her obnoxious pursuit of her own ambitions.

Mostly the women seemed concerned about being socially rejected. "Anne is an acne-faced bookworm," one wrote. "She runs to the bulletin board and finds she's at the top. 'As usual,' she smarts off. A chorus of groans is the rest of the class's reply."

Another, questioning whether a woman of such brilliance and ambition wasn't a little abnormal, decided Anne should beat a fast retreat. "Unfortunately Anne no longer feels so certain that she really wants to be a doctor," this student wrote. "She is worried about herself and wonders if perhaps she isn't normal. . . . Anne decides not to continue her medical work but to take courses that have a deeper personal meaning for her."

Some of the students' stories were bizarre in themselves. One woman found the idea of Anne's enjoying her success so revolting she punished her with startling brutality. "Anne starts proclaiming her surprise and joy," wrote the student, only to have her classmates become so "disgusted" with her behavior that "they jump on her in a body and beat her. She is maimed for life."

However extreme, these women's fears that success will crimp their social lives are not entirely without foundation. Traditional ideas of what's desirable in women continue to be surprisingly prevalent among the cream of the bachelor crop, today's snappy young Ivy League men. A recent study of six coed Northeastern colleges and universities uncovered a startling fact: *the vast majority of male stu-*

dents expect to marry women who'll stay home and not work. They see themselves as breadwinners, while their wives stay home with the kids.[3] "Maybe after the kids go to school," they say. *Maybe.*

In her book *The Future of Marriage,* Jessie Bernard says aggressiveness, drive, and will to succeed—the qualities required for getting high-paying jobs in our society—"are precisely those *not wanted* by most men in wives." Today's up-and-coming professional men—those in the Ivy League schools, at least—are still looking for mothers for their progeny. They are *not* looking for professional women who can function in the world with as much sophistication—and independence—as they.

It's beginning to be apparent that this conflict over working is strongly related to class. In Matina Horner's studies the women who were the most disturbed about the possibility of future success tended to come from middle- and upper-middle-class homes with successful fathers—fathers not unlike the current Ivy League men, who want nonachieving women for wives. In these homes the mothers either didn't work at all or worked in less than a fully committed, professional way.

The women who weren't so hung up on success came from lower-class homes with mothers who were often better educated than their husbands, and who usually worked throughout their lives. The daughters of these women didn't experience a conflict between achievement and femininity because they had grown up seeing the two happily integrated in their mothers.

The relation between class distinction and women's conflict became even more obvious when, in later studies, Horner turned up a fascinating parallel between white women and black men.[4] Both, it turns out, are notably more anxious about succeeding than are white men and black women. Only 10 percent of the white men had problems with Fear of Success, and only 29 percent of the black women.

The results of Matina Horner's Fear of Success studies were so provocative, she wanted to go a step further and see how the attitudes women expressed in their story-completion tests jibed with the way they actually performed in real life. Does Fear of Success lessen the likelihood of actually succeeding? *Were women who were anxious about success in fact less likely to succeed?*

The same college students used in the earlier study were given tests involving both competitive and noncompetitive tasks. The results, says Horner, "made quite clear" that when women expect the worst from success, they go out of their way to avoid it.

The *process* constitutes a kind of self-fulfilling prophecy.

Expectancy of nega-   arousal of
tive consequences ⟶ leads to ⟶ Fear of Success.

Fear of Success ⟶ leads to ⟶ less success.

Once Fear of Success is aroused in women, their levels of aspiration plummet like mercury after a cold front hits. It's not that women court failure; they avoid success. For example, even though their grade-point averages were in the top percentiles, the high-FOS women were opting for the less challenging, so-called "feminine" occupations—housewife, mother, nurse, teacher. It was as if, by avoiding the tougher careers, they could prove to themselves that they were still okay as women. For the individual woman, avoiding success may not be as blatantly self-destructive as seeking failure, but the effect of this phenomenon on women in general can't be underestimated. *This tendency we have to scale ourselves down, to step back from our natural abilities rather than risk the loss of love, is a consequence of what I have referred to earlier as Gender Panic—the new confusion about our feminine identity. Rather than experience the anxiety of doing (and possibly feeling unfeminine as a result), we don't do.*

Women are playing a sad game of self-denial. College women high in FOS lower their aspirations progressively as they move from freshman through junior years, Dr. Horner discovered. If Julia enters college with her hopes set on becoming a doctor, she's likely to have decided, by the time she's a senior, that nothing would please her more than being a paramedic. The sophomore history major with eyes for law school ends up thinking, along about the fall of her senior year, that teaching second grade would be a terrific thing to do, and maybe she'll just pick up a few education credits so she can get her teaching certificate. Mom says the decision she's making is sensible; so does Dad.

And so does boyfriend Jim. "Teaching is something you can always go back to later," he assures her, "once the kids are grown."

What about the women who scored *low* on Fear of Success? Their futures looked rosier by far. Surprisingly, though they had *less natural talent* than the high-FOS women, they were aiming for graduate work and careers in rigorous scientific disciplines—math, physics, and chemistry. In this respect, low-FOS women are like men. It's often the case that men have aspirations that exceed their actual ability. This only gets them farther along in life than they might have gotten otherwise. *Men are stretchers. They may generate their own brand of anxiety by skating out on the thin ice beyond their God-given capabilities, but at least they get to the middle of the pond. Women are shrinkers. They pull back from their possibilities, aiming well below their natural level of accomplishment.*

As a result, many never get to leave the edge of the pond.

By the time Matina Horner published her initial results, in 1968, many thought that surely women must have outgrown such pathetic fears—if, indeed, they ever had them to begin with. What, after all, had been the point of the women's movement if not to broaden and de-rigidify the cultural boundaries of femininity? Horner's original studies had been conducted back in the dark ages of 1964. College women these days were hell-bent for busting out and making it . . . *weren't they?*

Horner continued her studies, only now she used as her subjects the "liberated" young women of the late Sixties and early Seventies. What she found contradicted all of our media-formed impressions of the New Woman: to wit, an even *higher* proportion of women were showing Fear of Success.

And collapsing in competitive situations.

And lowering their career aspirations to an interest in jobs that were less challenging, more "feminine."

In 1970, Horner reported, "*The negative attitudes expressed by white female subjects have increased from the 65% found in the 1964 study to a current high of 88.2%.*"[5]

The High Price of Squelching Ambition

Remember how much encouragement young girls are given for *avoiding* anything that makes them anxious and you'll begin to understand how these ambitious, academically gifted women can be so willing to give up on themselves. They want to escape Gender Panic.

The potential loss of their feminine value should they do what they're capable of doing makes them so apprehensive they begin looking around for options that are less threatening. They try to make themselves Women, with a capital W. And the effort backfires. Success-anxious women may succeed in keeping themselves more or less *ordinary*, more or less in line with the acceptable image of the Girl Next Door, but they'll soon find themselves prey to a host of other problems. "Aggression, bitterness, and confusion," says Horner, are the lot of women who squelch their potential.

A young Washington woman who'd quit her job as congressional aide soon after she married began feeling bored and dissatisfied. But instead of identifying—and dealing with—the problem as her own, she found it easier to be angry at her husband. "I felt a kind of gnawing frustration whenever my husband went on a business trip," she said. "Why was *he* getting to take off for parts and people unknown and not me? He'd come back from these trips all high and excited, and I'd force myself to seem interested, but inside I was furious and resentful."

"I always envied the lives of my friends who didn't have kids," said another, an actress who had felt almost from the minute she married that something had been taken away from her—though in fact it was she who had given something up. "I missed the life of the theater and felt that fate had gotten me tied down too soon." (Not recognizing that it is they themselves who are running from the very thing they want so badly, women often have the experience of being acted upon—the victim. *How could this be happening to me?*)

For some years, until she finally got sufficiently fed up to do something about her life, this actress found herself envying friends she thought had more freedom than she. "Once I tried collaborating on a theater piece with a single friend, but the woman had so much more leeway in her life for doing research and bopping around town, I felt tense and stupid by comparison."

The comparison leaked over into other areas of the friendship. "I envied her thinness and the kind of clothes she could afford because she earned a salary while I always had to wait until there was enough money in the household kitty to buy a new pair of shoes for myself. The relationship got worse and worse. Next to this woman I felt bovine and clumsy, dragged down by mothering and constantly having to tend to these runny-nosed kids who were always hanging around whenever we wanted to work on our play. Finally, I started avoiding my friend altogether. She'd burst into my toy-and-diaper-strewn apartment all fresh and enthusiastic, her mind going clickety-click and talking a mile a minute, and all I could think of was how soon I had to start the children's lunch. It makes me sad now to think of it, but I finally backed off the project. It got so I couldn't stand the sight of this free young thing."

Women pay a high price for their anxiety about succeeding. Matina Horner and her co-researchers concluded that able young women often inhibit themselves from even *seeking* success. In mixed-sex competitive situations they will do more poorly than they could, and many who end up succeeding in spite of themselves try to downgrade their performance afterward. These women are not comfortably experiencing their own power and excellence. Confused and anxious, they will lower their career aspirations rather than feel that discomfort.

Some, withdrawing from anything that smacks of competition, sabotage their entire futures. The worst part is that they have no idea that their lives are being ruled by Gender Panic.

The "Good Life" of the Working Wife

Consider, for example, the story of a woman I'll call Adrian Holzer. A bright, high-energy sort who had almost always had a job, Adrian had long ago forgotten her adolescent ambitions, having relegated them to the junk heap of childish dreams. Now, for some reason, those dreams were back, pricking at her conscience like letters left unanswered. It was an uncomfortable sensation, one that made her feel unsettled in her life, as if, somewhere, she had taken a wrong path. Just when she'd begun to think things were on such a smooth and pleasant track, something unexpected rose up from within to change her inner life.

One winter afternoon as we talked together over a bottle of wine, Adrian poured out her old dreams—and began to find she had some new fears.

"It wasn't so long after having the kids—only three or four years—before I was back at work again, but life felt different than it had when I was single. I no longer had any sense of 'future,' of a future for myself. Living day to day is something mothers do, you know. I took that day-to-day mentality back to work with me. Two years had drifted by before I even thought of saying, 'Hey, what about a promotion?' Then I was mad because I had to ask."

At thirty-four, Adrian had gone back to work doing corporate public relations at the Ford Foundation, "a prestige job with a prestige image," as she put it. "I was getting a decent enough salary, considering I didn't have to support myself with it. But I've been getting this feeling that I'm cut off somehow. The truth is, I don't really give a good goddamn about the concerns of the Foundation. I've always been content to be a working wife with a 'good' job and a good pair of leather boots. If I could go out to lunch with my girlfriends, have a little 'mad money' of my own . . . well, that was freedom enough for me.

"Four years went by!" she exclaimed suddenly, refilling her glass. "Four of those years you don't even *notice* but which turn you thirty-eight anyway."

Adrian's mid-life epiphany was typical of the woman who lowers her sights at twenty and doesn't figure out what's going on until she's almost forty. Now the lunches were boring; the job was boring. "It's weird, when I think about it. Everyone in college always assumed I'd go to graduate school. I had really good grades. There was a time when I wanted to go into the Foreign Service."

What did she do instead? Like so many women, she made a crucial trade-off. "I became a wife. Then I became a wife who happens to work. If Gerry were to die tomorrow I don't know what I'd do, really. When I think about that—what it would be like, now, if I were alone—it's frightening. Widowed and still doing PR for a big, bland nonprofit Daddy?" She looks up, startled. "I don't think I could even *afford* this job if I weren't married."

The thought caught her up short. What kind of situation had she gotten herself into if she wouldn't be able to live on her salary as a single woman? The picture began to get clearer. "My husband supports me and my kids wave good-bye every morning so I can go off and write press releases in my Diane von Furstenberg dress," she said.

Self-recognition was beginning to hit Adrian Holzer, bringing with

it a question she has spent the better part of two decades avoiding:
"*Why am I doing what I'm doing?*"

Following right on its heels was an even more disturbing thought:
"*If not this, then what?*"

These had never seemed questions she had to ask herself. Women
are, they don't do. When they choose to work, it's still something
that comes second to being a wife and mother. That, at least, is how
Adrian and her friends had always experienced it.

But the imminence of a fortieth birthday was changing things for
Adrian Holzer. There was a sense of something overlooked, something passed up. Walking into her mind late at night (indeed, in all
the odd moments) was the girl-woman of twenty, that enthusiastic,
hopeful creature. Slender, with lank blond hair and vivid ideals, the
girl she once was had been lost to Adrian for years. Now she was suddenly here, blooming like some forgotten flower. With her appearance, all the little lunches, the dinner parties, the shopping for the
kids' clothes at Saks had turned into empty rituals. A friend's husband, only forty-three, had had a *heart* attack, for God's sake. Life
was no longer timeless and free.

Things had changed at home too, with the children getting older
and Gerry spending so much time in Washington. People didn't
seem to need her as much. She felt herself to be more separate, more
alone. And so the new questions came piling in—"*What will I be
doing five years from now? Ten?*"

Ten! Ten seemed impossible. Forty-nine years old and still having
the gang over to smoke dope and watch *Saturday Night Live* on the
big Advent screen? Forty-nine and still going to the spa religiously,
three times a week, to grind away the cellulite on the Nautilus ma-
chine and hope to hell she wouldn't have to go four times a week
next year? She was tired of spending Christmas week in Bermuda,
tired of visiting her folks on the Vineyard for two weeks every August, tired of the utter predictability of it all. But most of all she was
tired of the spongy, two-dimensional stuff that went on in the empty
spaces of her own brain. Obsessional thoughts. Low, disgruntled
complaints. Adrian did not *like* dissatisfied women, she told herself.

Now, suddenly, she was one of them.

There was, of course, a background leading to all this. Had Adrian
gone to the University of Michigan instead of Smith, she might well

have been one of Matina Horner's early subjects. Her aspirations had
been cut back many years before. At the turning point though, in
1964, about six months before she graduated, she was quite unconscious of what was going on.

Adrian had told her boyfriend at the time that she was planning
to go to the Georgetown University School of Foreign Service. "Foreign Service!" he'd shrieked. "That'll take forever!" Threatened, he
had tried to make a joke, "Stick with me, kid, and you'll never need
to be a spy."

What Adrian had heard was "I can't wait around for all this
graduate-school stuff." Finally, she didn't persist. The fact was, she
hadn't felt *sure* enough of herself to persist. She and her boyfriend
never really talked about it after that. He went off to film school in a
blaze of glory, and she traipsed along to New York after him. About
a year into her "career" as a time buyer for J. Walter Thompson, she
stopped seeing him. By then, Gerry had wandered into her life.
Sweet Gerry, who'd said, "You can do anything you want to do. I
make enough money for both of us." So Adrian had stopped worrying about what she should *do* with her life. Marriage, the kids, Gerry
—gradually all that took precedence over developmental issues. She
was not a growing, learning, changing human being; she was—quite
properly—a wife.

It's remarkable how easy it is for women to give up stimulus and
challenge. After a while we don't even feel the loss. We choose comfort and security over stimulation and the anxiety it often engenders.
Part of Adrian's problem is that her life has been too easy—easy
enough to buffer her against the existential terror that belongs to us
all. Even now her anxiety remains in the realm of vague apprehension. She has not yet received that terrifying dictate from the
inner self which says, "*Watch it, or you'll soon be missing in action.*" The way Adrian experiences things still depends upon some
action taken or not taken by Gerry. If he should die (or if, God forbid, if he should start spending even *more* time in Washington),
then a full-fledged crisis would be upon her. Short of such a crisis,
Adrian will probably continue on, never sensing just how insecure
she really feels, until some other external event forces that knowledge on her.

It's too bad that women on the brink of self-knowledge so often
seem to require something catastrophic to jar them into facing the

truth about themselves. After that afternoon in which Adrian revealed so much to herself—but not quite enough—I couldn't help thinking that she might have done well, at this point in her life, to encounter someone like Sulka Bliss.

The Withdrawn Mommy

I met Sulka (whose name is also fictionalized) at the Center for Displaced Homemakers in Oakland, California. This place has about it the look—and sound—of serious disenfranchisement, like a labor camp. *Center for Displaced Homemakers.* It could be the headquarters of some small, struggling political party that is never going to make it. Immersion heaters and instant coffee are what you notice; Styrofoam cups and green metal waste-paper baskets. The women who work here are volunteers, displaced homemakers themselves who are hoping "The Party" will pull them together again. They are not deadbeats, these women. Many, when married, lived comfortable—too comfortable—lives. When their marriages fell apart, so did the world around them. Here, at least, there is order—a desk to sit behind, a phone, voices to fill in the empty spaces. Here there is work to do for others who are less fortunate even than they: women who've just gotten the boot and who don't know what's happened to them. Women with puffy, tear-swimming eyes and bitten fingernails. Women who wake up on coffee and go to sleep on Valium doused with vodka.

Sulka Bliss had not yet gone the pills-and-booze route, but when I met her she was certainly depressed. "I don't know how to do anything anymore except take care of the kids," she told me. "I doubt if I could even type thirty words a minute."

Without skills (and clearly without self-esteem), Sulka had one thing going in her favor that most employers would never hear about, if only because few of them ever show an interest in *potential:* in high school Sulka Bliss had tested out with an IQ of 135.

"When we got those scores back in ninth or tenth grade, I remember being surprised," she told me. " 'Maybe I'll be a scientist,' I said to myself. I had always been a whiz at math, but girls never grew up to be scientists in those days, and my brother teased me about it. Even my mother thought I was showing off when I said I would like to become a chemist."

After high school, Sulka ended up going to a junior college for two years and then getting married.

Time had swaddled Sulka's ambitions. So long ago she could hardly remember it, she had been a thin, high-strung, and energetic young woman. When the babies came along, she got fat. She enfolds herself now in comforting folds of cotton, hand-batiked with Crayolas and Rit dye. Embarrassed by her size, Sulka takes special pains with her personal appearance but has given up on almost everything else. The geraniums on her patio have gone to hell. The *patio* has gone to hell. The mortar between the bricks needs pointing. The paint under the eaves has begun to flake and peel. *Amazing, thinks Sulka, how a house can begin to fall apart in less than a year.*

It had been a year almost to the day since Dick had left. He had not left because she'd gotten fat (as she liked to think sometimes). No, this man had had one foot out the door ever since he'd gotten his doctorate in molecular biology—the degree Sulka had *given* him, in a way, by working to support him as he swung triumphantly through graduate school. In addition to working full time as a secretary she had typed on the side, weekends, and had held off having kids so Dick could get himself established. "You can quit now," he'd told her, when the degree had come through in the same month as the job offer from California Institute of Technology. Soon Dick was ensconced in an office at CIT: tall windows, old oak desk, blackboard, students, and a laboratory supported by government grants.

Sulka had quit with a vast, contented sigh of relief. Now she would pot her begonias. Now, no doubt, she would become implanted with child.

Sulka dusted and polished and sang for a year, took to making her own breads, and in the spring of 1965, gave birth to their first child, a daughter. She and Elsie lived together in the sunny California house, so close they could almost have been one. Things were happening in Dick's life, but then, his entire existence had begun to have a remote feel to it, just as *her* life was becoming increasingly remote from him. They entertained several times a year, they went out to departmental parties from time to time, but these things did not interest Sulka much. Home was where her heart was, the nest.

She had more children, gaining weight with each pregnancy that she could never seem to throw off afterward. By 1970 she was very round and jolly, with three jolly little kids who seemed to attach themselves to her like those stuffed cotton piglets attached to the big mama pig with metal grip fasteners. It was okay with Sulka. She made her own clothes (nothing in the stores fitted her anymore) and combed and braided her long, glossy hair. Whenever you saw her—at the supermarket, the library, the movies in the evening—her kids were with her. Dick, usually, wasn't. Sulka never looked as if she minded. Scientists are preoccupied and obsessive. Dick was no different from any other. She had what she wanted. Dick didn't bother her.

Then, in the early Seventies, things came together in Dick's life with sudden intensity. He and his research group were involved in some big technological breakthrough, and they often stayed over in the laboratory at night, sleeping for a few hours before getting up and going back to work. When Sulka saw him, which was only occasionally, his face glowed and his eyes clouded over, as if to veil out the world lest it interfere with his thought processes. Sulka sometimes imagined the inner workings of his brain to be like one of those Rube Goldberg machines—detailed, complicated, and, ultimately, ludicrous. Dick was a doer. He did and he did—but where, Sulka sometimes wondered, did all his activity get him?

Where it got him (quite suddenly, it later seemed to her) was into a new, mysterious business, one that all kinds of huge corporations were pouring money into, something called recombinant DNA—genetic engineering. "It will be the savior of the energy crisis," Dick had announced one night, a bit high on wine, his eyes all aglow. "In fact, it will be the savior of the whole future!"

Sulka remembered that word "savior" because it had seemed, in the foreshortening of retrospect, that he had left the very morning after he made that statement. Did Dick somehow identify with his work to the extent that he had begun thinking of *himself* as the savior?

As women who are about to be left by their husbands so often do, Sulka began, frantically, to analyze Dick, to pick apart his motivations and see him in a cool, "objective" light. She was going through a process of trying to gain control. It was, of course, too late for anything. The emotional disaffection—indifference, really—had begun long ago. Dick was soon gone, off to conquer new worlds: new job, new money, and, inevitably, new woman.

"Just think," Sulka said, weeping, that first time she'd pulled herself together and gone to the Center—not liking the label "displaced homemaker," but feeling pretty much at the end of her rope and in need of help from *someone.* "No sooner does he become successful than he leaves me with three kids to take care of and barely enough money to make the mortgage payments."[6]

It was not until she'd gotten some psychological counseling that Sulka could begin to stop viewing her life as utterly determined by her husband and see, instead, how big a role she herself had played in what had happened in her life. Slowly it came to her that she'd given up on herself years ago, even before she left high school. She'd had plenty of support for doing it, of course, from her parents and friends—even from the school guidance counselor, who'd pointed her with her 135 IQ toward a "career" in clerical work. *Nevertheless, Sulka had gone along with the whole program.* She had acceded. There were reasons why she felt so weak, useless, and untried; now she was beginning to see that at least *some* of those reasons had to do with her!

Marrying and putting a husband through graduate school had been a safe and ego-enhancing course for Sulka to take at twenty-one. "Isn't she wonderful!" everyone had said then, as she brought home the weekly paycheck. "He's so lucky to have her." Indeed the challenge of supporting *two* of them had been stimulating to her even if the work *was* dull. But what Sulka didn't recognize was that *the challenge was superficial.* She wasn't really up against anything in terms of developing her own potential. And always, while she trundled off to work every day, was the underlying knowledge: "This will soon be over."

And it soon *was* over. With the loss of the job and the return to the nest, all traces of Sulka's independence had died. The challenge that stimulates growth was gone; accordingly, she stopped growing. Now, ten years later, she was paying the price in lost self-esteem and, worse somehow, in lost courage. Sulka would be able to get back her old typing skills a lot sooner than she'd be able to develop real confidence and strength.[7]

If Sulka Bliss had known Adrian Holzer, sitting pretty and still protected on the other side of the country, she might well have looked up from her own misery long enough to tell her, "Go all the way with your life; don't wait a minute longer. Taking the path of least resistance isn't really safe at all. It only *feels* that way!"

Caught Between Two Worlds

Intense and unresolved ambivalence about roles and success has been correlated with serious psychosomatic symptoms in women. It used to be that bored housewives, those left behind to wipe down the refrigerator shelves and gather dust balls day after day, made up the largest proportion of women alcoholics. Now the disease has swung over into the ranks of the "doers," the active ones, the ones who are saying good-bye to Johnny and rushing out their front doors each morning to catch the 8:05 into the city. "Married women who work have significantly higher rates of both heavy and problem drinking than either single working women or housewives," says Paula Johnson of the University of California at Los Angeles. The fact that married men who work are not afflicted with a similarly high proportion of drinking problems raises, she says, "the distinct possibility that this type of non-traditional role for women leads to an increased rate of alcoholism."

It's not, I think, the *role*—the combining of work and marriage—that's driving women to drink so much as the disturbance they feel about *choosing* the role. The distinction is an important one. *To choose means to act freely and with full cognizance, recognizing that there'll be consequences, and committing oneself to accept the consequences, whatever they may be.* This isn't easy for anyone, but it's especially hard for women, who aren't accustomed to doing things that leave them open to risk and anxiety.

Not knowing what the upshot of their new choices will be, women are afraid. We do not move forward wholeheartedly but hold back, hedging our bets, trying to achieve in a competitive world without giving up our old-fashioned, "feminine" ways—our perfumes and powders, if you will. We "let" the man open the car door or light our cigarette, saying to ourselves, "What harm can it do?" It's not the act itself that's harmful but the feeling in us that it engenders—the feeling of "How nice it is to be taken care of by a man."

In little ways, women show that they want to remain pampered and waited upon—by men, especially. They say it makes them feel delicate and womanly. They like those little gestures of protectiveness. Inwardly they recite the *Cosmopolitan* credo: I can be sexy and successful at the same time.

But they fool themselves. Wanting to be protected and wanting, at the same time, to be independent is like trying to drive a car with the brakes on. To get things done, one has to be aggressive when the occasion calls for it. One has to be able to stand up for one's beliefs, to argue for them if need be.

One also has to be able to withstand friction. Women are all too likely to avoid making statements that could conceivably be interpreted as hostile. *That* behavior, they feel, might leave them standing alone. Fearing isolation, women do not cultivate in themselves the techniques and talents needed for professional advancement. As Lois Hoffman of the University of Michigan has observed, *"Driving a point home, winning an argument, beating others in competition, and attending to the task at hand without being sidetracked by concern with rapport are all hurdles women have difficulty jumping, no matter how innately intelligent they may be."*[8]

Women are in effect pushing themselves forward and holding themselves back at the same time. Our inability to maintain a positive, well-rounded image of ourselves as *feminine workers* thwarts our fondest aspirations. In fact, our entire relation to work is *reactive*. Women work when men "allow" them to work (which means, of course, when men need them to work). Because of the current state of the economy, men need us to work now, so the working wife is suddenly sanctioned. Women feel that the new freedom to work— *and* be wives—comes not from within themselves, but from without. They have been given permission. "My husband is happy we can still go out to dinner once a week, due to *my* salary," complained a high school teacher, sensing the self-interest in her husband's attitude, "but before we were hit by this monstrous inflation he used to drop these little remarks about the messiness of the house and how my working affected our kids. No doubt his attitude will switch back again once the economy stabilizes."

No doubt. The attitude of the entire country "switched back again" after World War II, when women, no longer needed for running the factories, were told to get back to their hearths. And we did.

And, apparently, we have learned nothing from the experience.

Women are reactors. Ours is not a stand-up, self-generating position. We still make our primary decisions according to what "he" wants, what "he" will allow. Because, deep down, we still see "him" as The Protector.[9]

It's illuminating to watch what happens to a woman when her marriage breaks up. Suddenly she begins to flourish. "Aha!" she thinks. "So *this* is what it's like to be a grown-up." Now that she's been forced into a position of financial responsibility, now that it's *she* who must meet the mortgage payments and buy the children's shoes, ambivalence vanishes. What a relief not to have to struggle with the inner issue of Gender Panic anymore, not to have to worry about whether what one is doing is "right," or to fear that others might possibly view one as tough, invulnerable—*unfeminine*.[10] Her salary goes up; assignments proliferate. There's a new and healthy connection between work and money, a professionalism that's now *allowed*. The woman appears to be on her way!

But isn't she still reacting? Isn't she simply following another dictum—one that's as old as the animal kingdom itself? She has become the mother tiger taking care of her young, and who could possibly fault her for that?

Watch the same woman remarry or begin living with a new man, and you'll see the moving picture begin to run backward—*fast*. Now the woman is "home again." A feeling of safe berth sets in.

So, uncannily, does an attitude of deference.

"I began doing little catering things," said a woman who, at thirty-three, was two years into her second marriage. "Whenever I went into the kitchen for coffee, I'd bring *him* a cup too. When I first caught on to the fact that I was waiting on him, I thought, 'Well, it's nice, I love him, what could be wrong?' 'Like a sandwich, sweetie? A beer?' Soon, of course, it had frozen into a one-way street, with me doing all the fetching and him sitting there doing nothing. And I *knew*, having been through it all before, that these things are significant. They're not 'nothing.' They mean a *contract* is operating: *'You take care of me in the world, and I'll take care of you at home.'* Suddenly *he's* going for it, and *you're* going for it, and before you know it you're right back where you started."

A woman who'd been alone for several years after her marriage ended found her attitudes toward her new lover beginning to change almost as soon as she began sharing a living space with him. "My work started becoming just a little *less* important, his just a little more. It wasn't six months after we'd started living together that I was thinking of *his* future as *our* future. *My* future had somehow dropped out of the picture."

Living in two apartments they had been two people with two different careers, and neither career was more important than the other. "Living together in one apartment I felt myself becoming a wife again." Merged. Undifferentiated. One half of a whole, and not the more exciting half at that.

Just as it happened back in school, the priorities switch and we hardly even see what's happening. Partnering takes precedence over independence. We begin sharing everything—our projects, our ideas, our innermost insecurities—so that we don't have to be so alone with it all. It's so easy, suddenly, to begin going to *him* to get backup and validation for virtually everything we do and think. As a young patient of Dr. Moulton's put it, boldly, "I need a man to lend importance to what I sense is important."

Once a man is on hand, a woman tends to stop believing in her own beliefs. After a while she only "senses" them, at best. Slowly she begins to abdicate, turning her back on her own authenticity. A peculiar thing is working itself out—the old primal replay. Unwittingly, she is restructuring things to look—and feel—the way they did between Mom and Dad, with Dad the chief focus of family life and Mom the happy adjunct. "I married a man as unlike my father as I was unlike my mother," Celia Gilbert, a writer living in Cambridge, recalls in amazement, "and yet, insofar as I could bring it about, our marriage was made to resemble that of my parents."

Why does this happen? We *say* we hate all that. We say we don't want to live with a man the way our mothers lived with our fathers— docile, compliant, never having what it truly takes to be in a position of independence: ample money of one's own. But it is a superficial declaration. Emotionally, if not intellectually, the decision to live *contra* mother (which so often is the way we experience it) is terrifying. Mother may not have had it so good, but at least we know *how* she had it.

The young girl gets her definition of femininity from observing the women around her. Forever after, she "knows" what it is she's supposed to do. Should she choose to go against this, according to psy-

chiatrist Robert Seidenberg, she will be making a decision so fundamentally disturbing that it constitutes a *moral crisis* for her. "The
little girl who sees her own mother and aunts and grandmothers
invested completely in household matters and disdainful of women
who are active in the world," Dr. Seidenberg writes, may actually end
up feeling that any other roles for women are "unnatural and
immoral."[11]

What will happen to the woman who deviates from the model
supplied by her own mother? Inside, the woman feels like a child expecting that something bad will happen if she takes that step toward
independence—separating from her mother and going her own way.
Also, she wonders, where will she find gratification in life if she
rejects the path taken by her mother? *The woman without an adequate role model is in a deep psychological quandary. She doesn't
want to be "like her mother." Neither does she want to be "like her
father." Whom, then, will she be "like"?* That confusion of gender
identity is the essence of Gender Panic.

The Frantic Wife/Mother/Worker

Backing off from ambition—like the women in the Horner studies
—is one "solution" to the problem of Gender Panic. Another is trying to hang on to the old domestic role at the same time we pursue
our new, demanding careers. The negative effects of this "multi-role
solution"—the fatigue, the anxiety, the resentment over having to do
too much—are widely discussed among women today. Books and
magazine articles have begun to appear on the subject. But no one is
talking about the *cause*. Why is it women are driving themselves
frantic with overwork? It has to do with our unconscious conflict,
which remains hidden.

> "Work has become a place you go to that takes the entire day
> and which you have to leave each evening so you can go home
> to Job No. 2—chef, maid, housekeeper, and nanny."

> "I am so tired all the time that more and more often I wish I
> were only working a few hours a week, although it would cer-

tainly be nice to earn the same amount I now make in a forty-hour week."

"If I could only have an hour in the middle of the day to just sit in my home entirely alone with no demands from my child, my husband, my dog or cat, my employer—just time to sit all alone . . ."

These women were responding to a survey conducted by the National Commission on Working Women.[12] In it, what is often referred to as women's "double burden" of wage earning and homemaking emerged as a major complaint.

Sheer exhaustion is a prevalent symptom among women these days. Natalie Gittelson said the words "I'm so tired" ran like an unbroken thread throughout thousands of letters women sent to *McCall's* in response to a recent survey. "Of course many working women prize their paychecks," Gittelson writes, "and many more report that their husbands prize them even more than they do. But there is enormous fatigue expressed before the sometimes all-but-inhuman demands of the double life—home and job—that so many working women must live."[13]

Once eager to spring out of the house and into the world, women are beginning to cry "Uncle!" *The problem is that they have sprung out into the world, but they have not really left the house.*

"My energies are so divided," one of the working wives wrote to *McCall's.* "I work all day and come home to a dirty house, dirty laundry, and a dinner that needs to be cooked. On weekends my time is usually spent catching up on housework. Dull!"

"Sex is a big problem for us," said another, about herself and her husband. "I spend ten hours a day on my job and four working hours at home at night. I'm always tired."

A third wife wrote, "I'm *convenient* for him. I supply a much-needed second income, take care of his children, home, and am an attractive piece of property. But I feel so pressured from the bills, from having to work. I wanted to at first, but now I feel as if I'm missing out with the children."

In the late Fifties and early Sixties Russian women were rumored to be workhorses. For all their vaunted equality, their lives, we suspected, were dreary beyond belief. The Russian wife's idea of bliss was to work all day as a street cleaner and come home at night and cook and clean. I remember American women laughing about this. Back then we were still more anti-Russian than pro-woman, and we had the feeling that Russian women were being taken for a ride and didn't know it.

Now, twenty years later, here we are doing precisely the same thing. American women are the new workhorses—overextended, fatigued, and emotionally undernourished. Most jobholding married women in America put in 80 to 100 work hours a week, including housework. Husbands no longer earn enough in our inflation-bloated economy to support their families, so they encourage their wives to get out there and bring home the bacon too. Yet for most men, home continues to be a haven where they can rest and be waited on. "Few husbands are willing to assume much of the housework," reports *The Wall Street Journal* flatly in a series of articles on the trials and tribulations of "the new working woman."[14]

In the fall of 1980, three major advertising agencies reported on studies they'd done to see how "the new woman" was affecting "the American husband." Batten, Barten, Durstine and Osborne reported, baldly: "Today's man wants his woman to work at two jobs—one outside the home and one inside the home. . . . The majority [of "today's men"] are not willing to lift the traditional household responsibilities from their wives."

Of the men interviewed by BBDO, more than 75 percent said their wives were responsible for cooking; 78 percent considered bathroom cleaning to be the wife's job. Barbara Michael, a vice president at Doyle Dane Bernbach, concluded in that agency's report: "The major disadvantage that the typical husband perceives in having a working wife is the effect not upon the children but upon himself; a husband has to spend more time on household chores that he doesn't like. And with the exception of lawn and home repairs, he pretty much doesn't like any of them."

On the basis of interviews with 1,000 men, the firm of Cunningham and Walsh concluded: "The working status of women has not had a thunderous impact on their husbands' traditional role at home."[15]

This sort of research may be useful to advertisers, but it certainly doesn't tell women anything they don't already know. I've never met a woman who does an equal share of housework with her husband or her male housemate. *Regardless of whether she works full time or has children, or makes more money than her husband does, when it comes to managing the house and taking care of the children, the woman always does more.* And she complains, continually, I can't "get him" to do this; I can't "get him" to do that.

Why are women so unbelievably ineffectual? Once we start looking into that question we find out that the problem has as much to do with the needs of women as it does with the needs of men.

A national survey conducted just a couple of years ago asked employed women which they found more *personally* satisfying, housework or their work outside the home. "Housework!" was the resounding reply.[16]

"I find it baffling," the senior editor of a large publishing company said, trying to understand the confusing attitudes expressed by his wife. "The other night her mother came to dinner. The three of us worked on cooking the meal together. Afterwards I put on the apron and started washing the dishes, whereupon the two of them chimed out like the Gold Dust Twins, 'No, no, don't do that. *We'll* do the dishes.' 'It's okay,' I said. 'I'll do them.'"

"It's odd," the man continued. "Somehow my wanting to do the dishes when I'd already helped cook the meal was construed by the women as my doing more than my share. It made them very nervous. They didn't *want* me doing more than my share. Yet it didn't seem to occur to them that if they had done the dishes that night it would also have been more than *their* share."

It happens that this man's wife is a successful, highly paid businesswoman. She and her friends spend a lot of time discussing the continuing inequality of women's position in the world. She herself wants a fair shake, both professionally and in her personal life, but apparently, when it gets right down to it, abandoning those old domestic roles is disturbing to her. "It was as if, by doing the dishes, I was taking something away from her," the man reflected. "No, *them*," he corrected, smiling, for he'd remembered what was probably most germane to the whole episode—the fact that his wife's mother was there. (When Mother's on the scene a lot of women find themselves stumbling awkwardly over their newfound freedoms.)

The housekeeping bind has nothing to do with how much money we might earn. "MILLIONAIRE NOVELIST IRONS WHILE THE BIDS ROLL IN" could have been the newspaper headline on September 18, 1979. The writer was Judith Krantz, whose first novel, *Scruples,* had been a runaway best-seller, and whose second novel, *Princess Daisy,* was being auctioned to the paperback houses. What was Judith Krantz doing out in California that day as the bids from New York publishers soared higher and higher?

"My husband and I just got home from Europe yesterday," she told a reporter, "so since seven A.M. this morning I've been doing the ironing."

Ironing! That's what was reported in a front-page "news" story in *The New York Times,* along with the fact that the rights to Krantz's novel ended up selling for $3.2 million—$1 million more than any other novel in the history of publishing. Ms. Krantz had to laugh at herself, of course, saying the ironing was "physical therapy for the waiting."[17]

In the Sixties, the care and maintenance of toilet bowls was an issue for a lot of women. "No matter how much help he gives around the house, there is *one thing he'll never do,*" wives would say of their husbands, solemnly wagging their heads. "It's as if he never even *looks* at the toilet. Toilets are the *woman's* job."

Today the challenge for women is not how to get your husband to do more, but how to earn as much as he does without giving up all the little domestic rituals that convince you you're still "womanly."

"I helped him develop clumsiness in the simplest domestic chores," recalls Cynthia Sears, a Bryn Mawr graduate who eventually separated from her husband and now lives with her two daughters in Los Angeles. Writing of her experiences in a book called *Working It Out,* Cynthia describes a mode of family life familiar to all of us. "When I announced to friends with a certain pride (disguised as exasperation) that he had never changed one diaper, never gotten up with a sick child at night, never given the girls a meal, I didn't see that my 'tolerance' had actually deprived him of a real sense of participation in raising our children. The only thing I could see was the immediate benefit of avoiding any criticism or complaint." When she was thirty-one, says Cynthia, "I went into therapy. By that time I was feeling resentment as a physical sensation—a constriction of the chest and a pounding of the blood."[18]

Besides helping us avoid our anxiety about ambition and achievement, hanging on to the role of Chief Honcho in the Home helps us ignore other issues as well. Sheer, exhaustive busyness can smoke-screen a lot of things.[19] We all know about women—some of us *are* those women—who could afford to hire household help but don't. Why don't we? Precisely because having help would set us dangerously free.

Women are beginning to discover that nothing is more frightening than the escape into freedom. It's a fear made no less threatening by the fact that it tends to detonate like a time bomb the moment basic survival needs have been met and there's no economic need to justify the wife's ambition.

Disguising Conflict with Drudge Work

Talented Evelyn and Richard Melton work at jobs they dislike but which earn them incomes far higher than most of us make. Richard brings home about $70,000 a year as an art director for an ad agency. Evelyn earns close to that modeling. Between them, they have a disposable income of well over $100,000 a year. Through a series of financial errors, however, in which they have acquired more than they can afford to maintain (partly to compensate for the boredom they experience from doing work they've both outgrown), Richard and Evelyn say there's no money left over for hiring household help. Therefore, Evelyn does the housework, and that means—as usual—not just the actual scrubbing of floors and toilets, but all the work having to do with the running of the home and the managing of the children. Three or four times a week she commutes into Manhattan for her modeling work; she also cleans, cooks, shops, and does laundry. She schedules the appointments for everyone in the family and makes sure the appointments are kept. She chauffeurs the kids to their after-school and vacation activities. "It's only for a few more years," she tells herself. Well, five or six years, actually. Her youngest child is in fourth grade. (It's a second marriage for both of them.)

What is Richard doing in the meantime? Well, Richard is extremely busy. Between his weight lifting and his scuba-diving lessons, to say nothing of the evening hours he spends taking photographs and developing prints in his darkroom, there's hardly enough time in the day. It should be said in his favor that Richard is not a dilettante. He is working toward a major life change, planning to switch over, as soon as he thinks he can make it work financially, to what is now a passionate avocation: photography. Richard's conflict about his current situation—working forty hours a week at something he hates when he'd rather be doing something he's discovered he loves —overrides everything. At forty-six, Richard Melton is like a man with death at his heels. To have spent so many years being bored cockeyed working for the agency, only to have found his true love when he was damn near fifty! No way can Richard imagine wasting a second of his precious time doing *housework*. Every spare ounce of energy he has goes into what he calls his "real work"—photography. Between the weight lifting and the concentration he brings to his pictures, his cheeks have hollowed out and his eyes burn with intensity. He's a man harboring a secret within his heart—*the fact that he's been given a second chance*.

Evelyn, married two years to Richard, has turned from an adoring wife into someone who sometimes feels crazy with resentment and anger. Richard leaves everything having to do with the house to her, and she can't seem to get *through* to him. In all these months, the only progress she's made in getting him off his ass around the house is to teach him to make salads. Once in a while he'll break down and tear a few lettuce leaves—mostly when she isn't around to do it for him. For the rest, Richard simply doesn't *see*, doesn't seem perceptually to *take in* that she is constantly doing the housework, the errands, the planning; shlepping to the shopping mall; cleaning and cooking to entertain his friends and family; taking care of his son, when he visits, as well as her own kids.

"You don't have to," Richard will say to her when she complains.

"But *someone* has to," she replies.

He shrugs. *Why* does someone have to? he wonders, in the way that only people who have always had their domestic needs taken care of by someone else can wonder. He decides it's her thing, something she will have to "work out for herself." (Intuitively, he's right about this—she has to take a stand for herself—but he doesn't know how to explain his own feelings of resentment, of being nudged and pushed, so he turns his back on the problem.)

By now the situation has become quite miserable for both of them. Richard is genuinely confused as to why his wife has become so high-strung and volatile. Evelyn thinks it's about as clear as the Jell-O cubes shimmering on her children's dessert plates. There is, however, something she's missing, too. Unconsciously, Evelyn is not *allowing* herself to get through to Richard on the issue of the house. It's strange. She can communicate her likes and dislikes, her fears and resentments on virtually everything else that happens. She's quite good at taking care of herself, really, but she can't seem to acknowledge and break out of her paralyzing entrapment in the *hausfrau* role.

Why?

Because there's something in it for her to stay stuck with the house. Evelyn has no equivalent, in her own life, to Richard's photography—no work she loves, no passionate involvement in anything outside home, Hubby, and *Kinder*. Though she earns almost as much money as her husband, she feels that in terms of his creativity, Richard occupies a separate world, and it makes her feel apart from him and alone. The darkroom, in Evelyn's mind, has become Richard's rendezvous. It's almost a sexual jealousy she feels. When he goes into the darkroom he has turned on his heel and left her, as surely as if he had traveled to the boudoir of another woman.

Jealousy gets the upper hand at times when we're least secure and solid within ourselves. As Evelyn watched her intense and loving husband invest his passion in his art, she started coming to grips with a crisis in her own life—namely, what to *do* with it. Long unchallenged by work that used only the tiniest portion of her talents, she had learned to lose herself in a lot of home-and-children-related activity. There was a time when buzzing around being the Complete Homemaker made her feel *useful* at least. Not anymore, though, which is part of why she's feeling so freaked. Times—and the standards for women—have changed.

Ten years ago Evelyn had what many considered an enviable life, including a glamorous career and financial independence. People marveled over how silkily she combined her work with her domestic life. She excelled in the kitchen. She had filled her home with lovely antiques ferreted out at auctions and yard sales. Each year she gave elaborate birthday parties for her children and large holiday dinners. On Thanksgiving it wasn't unusual to sit down in her home at an extended table covered with white damask and silver—along with twenty-nine other people.

But now it was different. Now the goal seemed to be to work at something *demanding*, something gratifying. Women's whole level of involvement in the world had risen a notch.

And partly in consequence, the old multi-role "solution"—acting the frantic Wife/Mother/Worker—no longer works for Evelyn. Still, she tends to cling to it because she's afraid to commit herself to trying something new. Over the past year she's contemplated everything from taking courses in fiction writing at a nearby college to chucking it all and going to medical school, but when it comes right down to it, Evelyn can't seem to make a move. She's been treading the same path for so long she doesn't have to *think* about things anymore. She's been doing everything one is supposed to do to stay ahead in the modeling business ever since she was eighteen years old and first came to the big city. She was *good*, goddamn it. She knew the ropes! Why should she throw it all over now? Not everyone over thirty is still able to make money at it.

But a small voice within disagrees. She needs a new way. She can't really avoid the conflict anymore. It simmers with painful urgency beneath all the surface feelings—the anger, the resentment, the sense of being injured and abused. Externalizing her inner conflicts, she makes Richard responsible for what she herself doesn't feel able to do. Which is get out of the house. *Do* something. Sell off the country home, hire a housekeeper, or make whatever other changes might be necessary so that she could go back to school, or take up a new profession—something that would open her up and fill her with new energy.

Women continue dominating the homemaker role, whether or not they have an outside career, because they still feel dependent on their husbands and need something—a service—with which to balance out the arrangement.[20] It's the reason women invest more in the whole idea of family than men do—why, regardless of how many hours they may put in at the office, they continue cooking the family meals from scratch, toasting their own granola in the oven, stitching up quilts to match the children's wallpaper.

The safety of marriage—of being loved and needed—can be a mixed blessing for the woman who feels the urge to do something on her own but is afraid. Any negative pressure from "him" can be neatly turned into an external distraction from her own inner fears. Work, especially if it's conceived of as the pursuit of one's own personal development and not just "helping out with the bills," is a way of separating or individuating oneself. Thus it can be experienced as *a going-away from the other*—scary business indeed. Better to hang back in "the marriage." "I really *care* about my family" becomes the rationale for making a major retreat in life.

The exhaustion women are expressing now, in relation to their "double burden," is the result of conflict—the clash between wanting to hang on to the domestic security housebound women have always enjoyed and the desire to be free and self-fulfilling. This unresolved, and thus paralyzing, conflict breeds Gender Panic, keeps women in low-level jobs or work they've outgrown, and keeps them overextended at home.

Most of us have not yet made a true decision about our lives. Trying to maintain a situation in which we give up neither our independence *nor* our dependence drains us of energy. Consciously, we blame men for not changing, but unconsciously we're quite willing to have them stay the way they are.

CHAPTER VII

Springing Free

After my marriage was over and I was living once again on my own, it wasn't long before strange, contradictory signs of disturbance came blistering to the surface. There was tremendous fatigue; I experienced bouts of weeping, times when it was impossible to sleep. Yet these symptoms of depression were offset by puffs of unaccountable joy and energy, elated moments that were manic, almost, in that they seemed to have so little reason for being.

Finest were the moments in which I imagined that one day I would actually be *recognized*. I wasn't sure what this meant, only that it was tantamount to a form of rescue. "They" would find me; "they" would recognize my inner character, my hidden talents, and transport me from that big, empty, lifeless apartment and out onto some thrilling frontier where unknown satisfactions awaited. Sometimes, late at night and slightly drunk, I would dance for myself before a mirror. I would wear only a hat, a soft-brimmed fedora with a long, striking plume. I retain that image, in part because it contrasts so sharply with that other aspect of myself—the backwardly shy schoolgirl, young, inexperienced, insecure. This was the part of me that wanted to stay in the background, content merely to get by. This was the shrinker, happy if the rent got paid and the telephone company could be stalled off another month. What else did I need but a little food, a little warmth?

Toward the end of this period of my life, the vacuum cleaner broke down. It was symptomatic that I made no effort to get it repaired. "A broom is perfectly good," I would tell myself as I swept out my apartment day after day. "Brooms are what women used before there were vacuum cleaners."

How frightened I was then, how narrow and constricted my life. I felt grateful when free theater tickets came my way, or I was assigned to write something about the ballet and could go and stand in the wings of the New York State Theater. There my eyes would widen as I beheld a young dancer pursuing excellence, pushing her body up against the fierce, triumphant music of Stravinsky. Somehow I preferred to think of the dancer as magical. I could not reconcile the glory of her performance with the sweat dripping from her body or the contortions of her face when, during a pause in the dance, her back to the audience, I saw her gasp for air as recklessly and as hideously as some old flatfish cast up on the sand. Grounded, she seemed; vulnerable; exhausted by the effort of having fully extended herself. I did not want to see the connection between the magnificence of her art and the torturously hard work she had to do in order to accomplish it. That glimpse from the theater wings presented me with a truth: a woman panting, out of control, and awful —if briefly—to behold. Her efforts stood in painful contrast to my own dreams of glory—dreams which, unbeknownst to me, had a demanding, even a vindictive edge: I shouldn't have to *work* for recognition. It should come to me as effortlessly as a silken mantle floating down around my shoulders.

Strong crosscurrents were at work here. At the same time that my estimation of myself was painfully low, my fantasies about myself were grandiose. The idea that I should actually have to *exert* myself for my accomplishments was humiliating; it seemed to validate that other, awful opinion of myself: that I was a plodder, not very smart, certainly not original—the mousy stepsister whose only reason for being was to keep the home fires burning. Like Cinderella, I yearned for a fairy godmother, a prince—*anyone* who would present me with a way out.

If all one wants is safety, one is content with a dull and narrow life. I was not content. As I sat on my big, empty bed that miserable winter of '73, with the steam pipes clanking and hot air rising from the radiators to fog the windows, my mind blossomed with images of what it would be like to be strong and clear, unbridled by anxiety. At twenty-seven, stuck in another, smaller apartment with three young children, I used to have fantasies of myself in a miniskirt and boots flying up Fifth Avenue on a bright red Honda. Now I dreamt of other things, of writing strong and free: intense bits of poetry would come to me as I lay wakeful in the middle of the night. I didn't use them, then, for my writing, but they signaled to me the intensity of my inner life. I dreamt, also, of traveling, of coming and going with new friends and lovers, secure in a joyful new connection with myself.

Suddenly, and for the first time, I recognized that I was a person who wanted. *I want, I want, I want,* a voice within me cried, though it still seemed as if I couldn't *get.* It was as if I were living within some tough but translucent membrane. I could see through it, but I couldn't get out of it. The things I had come to recognize I wanted were not material but emotional, not quantifiable but tantalizingly evanescent: the freedom to do and to be, symbolized by yearnings for more light, more air, months at the ocean, a house in the country.

Buried, my conflicting desires to be both free and safe kept me bound. I railed, I danced, I wept. The sands beneath me shifted. This was all to the good. A few more years and friends would be gone; people would say that I had changed. I would have become different—a different person. The anxiety would be gone, but so too would the fine flush that came of dancing dreamily before the mirror. If the split that divided me was to heal, there was much that would have to be given up. No more the comforts of safety; no more the glories one can imagine when one is living solely in one's head.

Working Through the Inner Conflict

Once the inner conflict between dependence and independence has been tracked down, identified, isolated from the tightly woven fabric of one's day-to-day life, can the leap then be taken from the small, stuffy room of fear and out into the open plains of freedom?

Not just like that. A process is required. Therapists call it "working through." You don't have to engage in formal treatment to learn how to work through conflict. You *do* have to be systematic and persistent. A vague, generalized awareness that you're in conflict won't get you very far. Work will. There has to be a conscious, deliberate effort to follow up—and separate—the entangled threads of inner conflict if one wants to get off the motionless seesaw of stasis.

The conflict between wanting to be free and wanting to be enclosed and protected is insidious because it carries with it a hidden gain. Conflict allows us to stay exactly where we are. The condition we admit to wanting—independence—acts as a cover for something we want just as much but can't admit to: dependence—the need for delicious, primal security. With these two opposite wishes driving us, we get to stay in limbo. Limbo has its advantages. It may not be very hot, but neither is it very cold. It isn't exciting, but neither is it quite the same as being dead.

You can't work through dependency if you can't identify it: that much is certain. Identifying the tendency, then, is the first step in getting past it. You have to consciously look for the signs. The time in my life when I spent the wee hours prancing in my plumed hat I was also complaining a lot that the reason I couldn't make money as a writer was that "they"—the editors and publishers—didn't do right by us writers. Allying myself with all the put-upon writers who ever lived, I kept myself the victim. I "refused" to do anything that might compromise my ideals, cursed the system, and conveniently continued to do the same work I had always done, over and over again. The idea that I might be *afraid* to try something new, that maybe I didn't have the nerve to take a chance, to experiment, to get behind something unprecedented—that thought never occurred to me. My problems remained comfortably hidden while I went on complaining.

Work wasn't the only part of my life that was being stunted by conflict. My love life was a shambles, buffeted as I was between my need to be loved and my equally strong wish to reject that need. The apparent narcissism of those late-night encounters with the mirror was in sharp contrast with how I felt when I looked at myself in the harsh light of day. "You're getting old," I would say, scrutinizing my face in the mirror for new signs of decrepitude. "You don't look good anymore." That preoccupation with aging—with anything that made me feel negative about myself—should have been a sign.

I was having, at that time, a limited, unfulfilling relationship with a man who was married. While I danced vaingloriously at night, in daylight I feared I wouldn't be able to "hold" this man whose very remoteness I found fascinating. Not getting the love the other part of me needed, I blamed the man for being shallow, for not having the courage to fling himself into a mad, passionate relationship with me. It was projection, pure and simple, of course. *I* was the one who lacked courage. I went on seeing this man several afternoons a week for an entire year, thereby keeping myself safe—and miserable.

In both work and love, then, I was weighed down by inhibitions of all kinds. I thought that I was experiencing the inevitable fears of a newborn woman emerging from the stagnation of a long, oppressive marriage. It may have been that in part, but it was also much more. The drive to stay down was strong, and it clashed with the equally strong drive to burst out, to excel, to "make a name for myself." The two drives—one expansive and one restrictive—seemed to cancel each other out, leaving me caught in the middle. Fatigue settled down over my life like soot on the neighboring rooftops. I continued working, but it was hard to get anything done. I chastised myself for my slowness. I bit my fingernails.

The Energy Leak

Women who are essentially divided can have whole areas of their personalities eclipsed because they have to use up so much energy in the effort to suppress—or deny—one side or the other of the basic conflict. This is how we try to approximate psychological wholeness. I, for example, was always trying to deny my drive toward dependence—and exhausting myself in the process. As Karen Horney explained it, the part of ourselves we try to suppress is "still sufficiently active to interfere, but cannot be put to constructive use." The process, she said, "constitutes a loss of energy that might otherwise be used for self-assertion, for co-operation or for establishing good human relationships."[1]

This lack of energy is another sign of conflict over hidden dependency. The Energy Leak manifests itself in indecisiveness and inertia.[2] The woman in conflict vacillates endlessly. Should I take this job or that? Should I stay home or go back to school? Should I love him or leave him? The back-and-forth wastes energy like a furnace trying to heat a house when the windows have been left open. The decisions may be trivial or they may be major, but the process is the same: issues get clouded. Procrastination leads to self-chastisement and a kind of aimless, angry frustration.

Such a divided mental state empties us, crippling our effectiveness. It may take hours to write a simple report, for example, or to clean out the linen closet, or plan a menu. For the woman in conflict, even the simplest tasks seem to require an inordinate amount of effort.

Ineffectualness resulting from inner strain usually shows up as well in the way we relate to people. If, for example, a woman wants to assert herself but also wants to comply, she'll end up acting hesitant.

If she needs to ask for something but also feels she should command it, she'll come off quite imperiously.

If she wants sex but has an inner desire to frustrate her partner, she'll have difficulty reaching orgasm. She may blame any or all of her problems on working too hard, not getting enough sleep, "low resistance," or whatever, but her wrought-up state probably has much more to do with the crosscurrents of conflict waging their battle within.

Disentangling

Getting past conflict requires more than doing Band-Aid jobs on all the little cracks and fissures that divide you. It means going after the root causes so that the *need* to be split no longer survives.

How do you do this? By paying scrupulous attention to yourself. By leaving no stone unturned in examining your motives, your attitudes, your ways of thinking about things. When a thread appears— some odd little attitude or bit of behavior you notice that doesn't seem to fit in with the rest of your personality—*follow* it. Don't say, "Oh, that's just a little inconsistency in my character; it's not really me." It *is* really you. And your inconsistencies, if you track them down and study them, will lead you to the mother lode of underlying conflict.

You might notice, for example, that you shuttle between extremes —that you vacillate, say, between being strict with yourself and being self-indulgent. You may recognize that you waver between putting others down and believing, secretly, that they're superior. Or that your need to put *yourself* down interferes with your ability to compete successfully, while at the same time your need to triumph over others makes winning a compelling necessity. Notice especially how you veer between arrogating all rights to yourself and feeling that you haven't a right in the world. (Rather than feel sorry for yourself for the latter, *suspect* yourself for the former. Arrogating all rights to yourself is the same thing as having to have your own way—a dead giveaway of a dependent personality.)

The point to remember is this: personality "quirks" may not be minor aberrations; in fact, they probably reflect major divisions in your personality. Watch them, coolly and objectively, without guiltily berating yourself for being less than perfect, and they will lead to major and previously unrecognized aspects of who you are. By facing —and accepting—these hidden parts of yourself, you will ultimately discover a new, integrated, and forceful self.

For me, strange discrepancies in my attitude toward money ended up revealing major distortions in my relations to others. I will tell you how I followed the dangling threads of my money problem until they led to the giant ball of twine that for years had been winding itself around a central character disturbance: the wish to have someone *else* do the hard stuff; the wish to be saved.

As I described in Chapter I, about five years after my marriage broke up (and a year after I'd begun living with Lowell) I discovered with some chagrin that I didn't want anything to *do* with money. If it came right down to it, I could be perfectly happy living on an allowance. In fact, for almost two years that's exactly how I lived. Lowell paid all the bills; stricken by a pervasive listlessness, I earned virtually nothing. My account at the local bank was almost always empty. (So, increasingly, were the coffers of my self-esteem.)

Here was the predicament: on the one hand, I found it demeaning to have to go to Lowell for money every time I needed to get my shoes repaired; on the other hand (and this was what I had to unravel various long, entangled threads to discover), *I liked the situation more than I didn't like it.*

It took many confrontations before I was willing to hear—and accept—things Lowell was telling me: that I was leaning on him at *his* expense as well as my own; that there were other, more fulfilling things he could be doing with his energies than supporting five people. Finally, I could no longer ignore the justice of this plea.

It was not just pressure from Lowell, however, that was throwing me into conflict. The longer I allowed him to carry the responsibility for my welfare, the worse I felt about myself.

After flailing inwardly and also experiencing huge amounts of anger, I finally pulled myself out of this trough and started doing some productive work. Money began to come in—more of it, in fact, than I'd ever earned before. But the fact that I still yearned to be taken care of showed itself in the way that I handled—or more accurately, *didn't* handle—my new earnings. I had always assumed that if I had enough money I'd be able to avoid the inconvenience of having to manage it. That's a characteristic attitude. *If only I had enough money*, I thought, *I would never have to hold myself accountable!* I would never have to stay on top of things, manage them, be *conscious*, be *aware*; I would never have to recognize how terribly *real* everything is.

My major trick, I discovered, was to avoid keeping a running balance in my checkbook. That way I never knew how much money I had. The longer I neglected to subtract my debits, the fuzzier my whole life-picture became. Not knowing for sure how much money I possessed at any given time, I was able to continue feeling helpless. How could I competently evaluate whether I should spend money on a new pair of boots, or if I could afford to buy life insurance (or if I could afford *not* to buy life insurance)? The mental image I carried was always of the last big deposit I'd made (my deposits as a free-lance were large, if irregular). No matter how many checks I might have written *since* that deposit, I'd still have the original (say) five thousand in mind.

Eventually, some eleventh-hour instinct for survival would prod: "Okay, you'd better tally up." Usually, by the time I'd taken it upon myself to figure out where I stood, whatever money I had remaining was like a sliver of soap in a child's hand. Refusing to take care of my little hoard, refusing to protect it, to put it in a safe place, to take it out only when needed, I'd invariably end up staring at the pitiful remains and wondering, "Where did it all go?"

The refusal to deal with money functioned as both a symbol of my helplessness and the *cause* of it. I never noticed that my assets were diminishing, and so—over and over again—it came as a shock when they ran out. Why this chronic, head-in-the-sand denial? *I didn't want to face the fact that I was going to have to keep replenishing my funds—over and over again—for the rest of my life.*

After many months of pain and confusion, I decided, "Keep your checkbook in order and see what it makes you *feel* like."

What it made me "feel like" was incompetent. The sands were always running out of my hourglass. I was always losing, never gaining. I would never be able to catch up—to create a state of equilibrium between income and outgo.

After a while I began to see that the whole statement-balancing operation was a metaphor. *Not* to keep a running balance is a form of avoidance. I *liked* not knowing where I stood because then I could go on feeling no responsibility whatsoever for the consequences of my behavior. How often my children's dentist bills would get put aside while I shook my head dismally and said, "There just isn't enough money this month!" Yet others I knew who earned less money than I managed to keep up with their bills. Others I knew with less money had medical coverage, and retirement or pension plans—disability insurance—all the dull but realistic provisions the grown-up makes for protecting children and old age. I kept avoiding these realities, believing, somehow, that I was exempt from them; believing that if I just hung on long enough—paid *enough* rent bills, *enough* phone bills, *enough dues*—I would eventually be plucked from the vicissitudes of this nasty, scary, *demanding* life and be saved!

Keeping a running balance is not just good financial policy; it's good emotional policy. It means maintaining a day-to-day, or even moment-to-moment, contact with reality. It means not letting a wellspring of anger develop toward the children, or the man with whom I live. It means not letting things slide, when I'm depressed, but stopping, sitting down, and checking things out: What's going on here? Where are my energies going? Where is my gratification coming from? Does the energy output meet the gratification income, or is there an imbalance? Am I spending more than I'm getting, and if so, how can I get more?

Questions such as these are part of a self-balancing process. I try to take my own counsel. I become responsible for my own happiness or unhappiness rather than shift that responsibility to someone else. Keeping a running balance in my psychic account makes it less likely for me to retain a distorted, unrealistic picture of things. I know what my assets are, but I also know my limitations. Within the framework of these realities I'm able to establish meaningful goals and priorities, to live, realistically, in the present. To keep a running balance means to engage with life's possibilities, to activate one's own change and growth rather than waiting for "something to happen"—to become, in effect, one's own prince.

The Telltale Dream

Sometimes it is only in our dreams that our feelings of helplessness and frustration break through. A youthful, attractive woman of fifty who'd been trying to get up the courage to break out of a miserable eighteen-year marriage described to me the vividness and import of what she called her "fish-tank dream." It preceded by exactly a year the signing of her separation agreement, and it bolted her straight out of bed one night with its energy. She told me:

> I was floating like a dead person inside a huge glass fish tank and trying to talk, but I couldn't make myself understood. Jim [her husband] was standing outside the tank and trying to talk to the "dead" me. The "live" me was standing outside the fish tank, across from him, and shouting, "Don't talk to her! Can't you see that's not the real me? Here! Look at me! *I'm* the real me."

The bitter truth the dream revealed was that her husband never looked her way. Even more important, it revealed that she was actively involved in keeping "the real me" hidden. This was the dream's true pathos, and when she recognized it, sitting up in her bed in the middle of the night, she began to sob. It was not just "him"—the unloving husband—from whom she was hiding. It was anyone with whom she might have had a close and satisfying relationship. As much as she wanted that relationship, as much as she desperately yearned for it, it was lost to her; to let out "the real me" was too scary.

Dr. Alexandra Symonds tells the story of a patient who came into treatment because she'd been feeling depressed. Not long after beginning therapy the woman had a dream. She was hanging outside her apartment building, high above the street, clinging desperately to the windowsill with her fingernails. Inside, her husband walked by. The woman tried to shout for help through the window, but all she could produce was a stifled whisper. Her husband passed on by without hearing her.

The powerful symbolism in dreams like these represents, according to Dr. Symonds, a whole category of women who, though highly accomplished in their professional lives, have inner needs to be taken care of that are deeply frightening to them. A dream is telltale. For some it may provide the first startling clue that something is wrong.

It can also be an indication that old patterns are breaking up and change is occurring. A college professor with a history of finding it difficult to assert herself had a dream that she was a car passenger trying to tell the driver what to do. A few months later, after she'd gained some insight into the fact that she needed to establish more control over her life, she dreamt she was sitting in the passenger seat of a moving car and the driver's seat was horrifyingly empty.

Such a dream may be upsetting, but it may also, as in this case, signify progress. The woman had moved right out there to the frontier recognition that she was alone and unprotected in the world, sitting in the passenger's seat with no driver. (Once *that's* been faced, you may as well decide to sit in the driver's seat.)

A dream can also be a bright harbinger of a new world, one that comes not from fame or fortune, but from having arrived at some inner resolution. After I'd been in analysis for several years I had what I've thought of ever since as my "Harlem dream." In it, Harlem figured as a metaphor for life itself, a strange and motley world teeming with surprise, and gladness, and the potential for danger. Here is how it unfolded:

I am walking up a main street in Harlem, probably Seventh Avenue, with two girlfriends. I have the feeling I haven't been in Harlem for a long time. It's scary, but at the same time I feel it isn't all *that* scary. "I should be able to cope," I tell myself. "There are skills and knowledge for coping in Harlem. Getting along here is not just a matter of fate."

The amount of action and hustle in the streets—crowds of people, noise, moving vehicles—disturbs me. I am worrying about my safety when we stop to look in the window of a *cuchifrito* place, this one specializing in fried fish. My friends go directly into the shop, but I, stunned by the overwhelming variety of things to choose from, stand outside, utterly immobilized. Finally, I walk into the store—push myself to go into the store—hoping that the very act of moving will help me, when I get inside, to choose.

Inside, on the counter, are tantalizing things—broiled scallops for a nickel apiece, huge halves of avocados. Suddenly the thought occurs to me that I might not have enough money. I dig into my pockets and find, with relief, 35 cents. "I'll take two oysters," I tell the tall black man behind the counter. He is dressed in chef's whites; a big *toque blanche* towers on his head. There is a mean, suspecting look in his eye as he pushes the oysters toward me. I fumble awkwardly with my coins, and he shoves my shoulder. "I saw what you were doing!" he shouts. "You were trying to cover the nickel so I would think it was a quarter."

"No, I wasn't," I protest, angry. "I was only confused." I pick up the oysters and walk out of the shop.

Out in the middle of Seventh Avenue some men are playing a street game, snapping a wirelike rope about a foot off the ground. I look at them, decide they aren't out to hurt anyone, and hop over the rope; but I feel angry at my girlfriends for not warning me. "Hey!" I shout. "How come you didn't tell me about this before I stepped off the curb?"

They shrug, and I think, "*Maybe I'm making a lot out of nothing. Maybe crossing a busy street with a lot of hustle and action is just something you go ahead and do.*"

When I get to the other side of the street, my friends are waiting, and the people crowding the sidewalk no longer seem so threatening. It's Saturday afternoon in Harlem. There is sunshine. Leafy trees line the curb. We stop to watch some little girls playing a sidewalk game.

In trying to learn from a dream, I pay attention to what I was feeling and thinking about as it unfolded. This dream began with my feeling anxious and ill at ease in a strange place. Then I had the experience of being presented with a plethora of tantalizing options and finding myself unable to take action on my own behalf. The poignancy of this, as I thought back on the dream, was almost unbearable. *There were good things available to me but I couldn't move in their direction.* Something was keeping me rooted to the sidewalk, frozen.

Then came a crucial moment in the dream. "Move anyway," an inner voice had instigated. "You can't just keep standing there."

In that instant, something in me decided to move.

After entering the store I felt confused and insecure. I had to check and recheck my coins. I fumbled a lot with getting out the proper coins to pay for my food. Finally I had the experience of being hassled unfairly—indeed, quite irrationally—by the man behind the counter. Not only was he wrong, he was *mean* to me— downright, arbitrarily mean.

But so what? This sort of craziness couldn't touch me anymore. Men's meanness, men's arbitrariness was *their* problem. Able now to take care of myself, if someone didn't treat me decently I was free, at last, to walk away. So I did. I told the man he was wrong and walked out of the store.

I got scared in the street—but crossed it anyway.

I got mad at my girlfriends for not protecting me—but saw that I was being silly.

Crossing the street was the thing—to pick up my feet, to watch for cars and trucks, to wind my way through the activity, the action and the hustle—all on my own.

When I got to the other side I felt better, less vulnerable, really quite pleased with the way the afternoon was shaping up. I had crossed the street without getting hurt. I had my oysters (nicely breaded, two for 35). I had refused to be intimidated by the challenging man in the *toque blanche*. Instead of anxiety I felt pleasure. I enjoyed the feeling of watching the little girls play their game. I felt the sun beating down on my back.

I felt, in a word, whole.

I should tell you that the moment when the inner self said "Move!" had nothing at all to do with willpower. It's not possible to "pick yourself up by the bootstraps," do or die, and take action in the face of overwhelming conflict. If willpower were the answer, I would never have written this book. That forward leap of the inner self came as the result of a long and meaningful *process*, the process of identifying the contradictions within me and then working them through.[8] Will can't be commanded to perform. When you are clear and unconflicted, your will operates quite automatically.

On the other hand, when you're swamped by feelings and attitudes that are mutually opposed, your will shuts down. What that means is that you aren't able to *choose* what you do in life; you act only because you're *driven* to act. You stay in the same unchallenging job not because you like it and choose it, or because, as some women will tell you, "my work is not as important to me as my family." Like the lawyer, Vivian Knowlton, you stay in it because *your need to subordinate yourself is in direct opposition to your need to succeed and you are lying stagnant between the two needs.*

In the realm of love, you do not choose your mate for the joy of sharing yourself with another human being. If you are in conflict, you marry, as Carolyn Burckhardt did, because of a compulsive and indiscriminate need to be loved, wanted, approved of, taken care of.

It is this same need which blinds you to the fact that not everyone in the world is nice and trustworthy—so that you fall apart when someone is mean or hostile.

It is this need which makes you do anything in your power to avoid quarrels, disapproval, glowering looks.

It is this need, finally, which makes you subordinate yourself, take second place, automatically shoulder the blame. From here you are only one short step to the "poor little me" syndrome. Women who are driven by the compulsion to take second place actually end up impairing their capacities. *To some extent, you become what you are driven to become: tentative, insecure, excessively vulnerable.*

Wrenching Away from the Dependency Trap

Not long after abandoning her life as a "dutiful daughter" and fleeing to the unfettered freedoms of Paris, Simone de Beauvoir met, in the fall of 1929, the man who was to be friend, mentor, and lover for the rest of her life: Jean Paul Sartre. They were both in their early twenties, he slightly older than she. In many ways, her quick and solid attachment to this man allowed her to give up her ties to the family that had so constrained her during adolescence. It was a flight into the most exotic intellectual terrain. From the first, the two lovers spent virtually all their time together, read the same books, sought out the same friends, and in general developed their ideas so symbiotically that Simone would use such phrases in her memoir as "we thought" and "our idea."

When I began reading *The Prime of Life* (which picks up De Beauvoir's life where *Memoirs of a Dutiful Daughter* leaves off) I was astonished by the amount of fusion she described in her relationship with Sartre. She seemed so entirely enmeshed in *his* sensibility, it was hard to imagine how she would ever extricate herself sufficiently to pursue the fine intellectual and creative work she would one day accomplish on her own. True, Sartre was a genius; still, this bright, zestful woman was virtually in his thrall. "I admired him for holding his destiny in his own hands, unaided," she wrote. "Far from feeling embarrassed at the thought of his superiority, I derived comfort from it."[4]

She was only twenty-one, and apparently as romantic as anyone that age. Still, it seemed that if she were going to disengage from the destructive pattern that was so clearly establishing itself in her relationship with Sartre, she was going to have to do something—something radical. "My trust in him was so complete," she wrote, "that he supplied me with the sort of absolute, unfailing security that I had once had from my parents, or from God."

Simone and Jean Paul walked the streets of Paris together, talked endlessly, drank aquavit in the bars until two o'clock in the morning. She experienced herself as almost levitating in a delirium of happiness. "My most deep-felt longings were now fulfilled," she wrote. "There was nothing left for me to wish—except that this state of triumphant bliss might continue unwaveringly forever."

The euphoria lasted for over a year—until something disquieting crept in to mar her perfect happiness. She came to suspect that she had relinquished some essential part of herself. Her abandoned response to the onslaught of sensual and intellectual distraction that Paris had to offer was beginning to have a fragmenting effect on her. Her stabs at writing fiction were halfhearted, lacking conviction. "Sometimes I felt I was doing a school assignment, sometimes that I had lapsed into parody," she wrote.

For eighteen months De Beauvoir lived in an acute state of conflict. "Though I still enthusiastically ran after all the good things of this world, I was beginning to think that they kept me from my real vocation: I was well on the road to self-betrayal and self-destruction." The books she had always read so obsessively she now perceived she was reading in a scattered, unfocused way, with no real intellectual goal. She was writing in her journal only sporadically.

Conflict, the desire to have it all ways, held her in its paralyzing web. "*I could not bring myself to give up anything*," she wrote, "*and hence I was incapable of making my choice.*"

Simone began to be plagued by self-doubt. The longer she remained inactive—intellectually and emotionally in thrall to Sartre—the more convinced she became of her mediocrity. "I was, beyond any doubt, abdicating," she wrote later. Existing in an ancillary relationship to Sartre had given her false peace of mind, a kind of blissful, anxiety-free state in which nothing much was expected of her except that she be a sprightly companion.

Inevitably, even her sprightliness began to deteriorate. "You used to be so full of little ideas, Beaver," Sartre said, using the nickname he had for her. (He went on to warn her against becoming "one of those female introverts".)

From the perspective of her mature years, De Beauvoir recognized how perilously easy it had been for her to exist, as a young woman, in subjugation to another. Someone "more fascinating" than she. Someone she could look up to, idolize, and in whose shadow she could feel small and secure.

There was, of course, a price. A small, self-effacing voice began to filter through to the young woman's consciousness: "*I am nothing*," it said. "I had ceased to exist on my own terms," she realized, "and was now a mere parasite."

Though feminists think of her as one of the founding voices of modern feminism, Simone de Beauvoir did not view the solution to her predicament as merely cultural. Though she recognized that even her very way of thinking about the problem had to do with the fact that she was a woman, "it was as an individual," she says, "that I attempted to resolve it."

Abruptly, determinedly, Simone decided to take a year's teaching job—away from Sartre, away from Paris—in the city of Marseille. The solitude, she hoped, would strengthen her "against the temptation I had been dodging for two years: that of giving up."

In Marseille, Simone took up a remarkable, rigorous, and obsessive activity in an attempt to exorcise her urge to be dependent. On her two days off a week she walked—not in a leisurely or casual fashion, but with the blindered perseverance of one who is out to overcome a severe handicap. She would put on an old dress and some espadrilles and take a small basket lunch with her; then she would proceed with her adventure into the unknown, climbing every peak, clambering down every gully, exploring "every valley, gorge and defile."

As her strength and endurance increased, so did her mileage. At first she would walk only five or six hours, but soon she was able to take routes requiring nine or ten. In time she was doing more than twenty-five miles a day. "I visited towns large and small, villages, abbeys, and châteaux. . . . With tenacious perseverance I rediscovered my mission to rescue things from oblivion."

Whereas once, she says, she had been "closely dependent upon other people," relying on them to provide her with rules and objectives, now she was having to make her own way, unaided, from one day to the next. She thumbed rides from truck drivers to get her over the most boring stretches of road fast. She took an active, aggressive stance in relation to what she was about. "When I was clambering over rocks and mountains or sliding down screes, I would work out shortcuts, so that each expedition was a work of art in itself."

During that year three things happened that frightened her. Once a dog followed her on her solitary hike and became maddened by thirst as the day wore on. (Eventually he plunged himself into a brook they came to.) Another time a truck driver with whom she'd hitched a ride suddenly pulled off the main road and headed for the only deserted spot in the entire area. When she recognized what was happening, she devised a fast plan. As soon as the truck slowed down for a grade crossing, Simone opened the door and threatened to jump while the truck was still moving. The man "rather shamefacedly," she wrote, pulled up and let her out.

The third episode involved a series of steep gorges up which she struggled one brilliantly sunlit afternoon. The path had become increasingly difficult, and she thought it would be impossible to go back the same way she had come, so she just kept on. "Finally," she writes, "a sheer wall of rock blocked any further advance, and I had to retrace my steps, from one basin to the next. At last I came to a fault in the rock which I dared not jump across."

Here, no doubt, was a real rite of passage—a situation into which few women would deliberately venture. "There was no sound except for the rustle of a snake slithering among the dry stones. No living soul would ever pass through this defile: suppose I broke a leg or twisted an ankle; what would become of me? I shouted, but got no reply. I went on calling for a quarter of an hour. The silence was appalling."

Simone had created a situation in which she could not give up without running the risk of losing her life. What did she do? The only thing she *could* do. She plucked up her courage and, in the end, "got down safe and sound."

De Beauvoir's friends worried over her and advised her that these solitary treks were dangerous. Particularly they begged her to stop hitchhiking. But she was on a far fiercer mission than anyone realized. With passionate single-mindedness, she was retrieving her own soul.

What does it mean to become one's own person? It means to take on the responsibility for one's own existence. To create one's own life. To devise one's own schedule. Simone de Beauvoir's hikes became both the method and the metaphor of her rebirth as an individual. "Alone I walked the mists that hung over the summit of Sainte-Victoire, and trod along the ridge of the Pilon de Roi, bracing myself against a violent wind which sent my beret spinning down into the valley below. Alone again, I got lost in a mountain ravine on the Luberon range. Such moments, with all their warmth, tenderness, and fury, belong to me and no one else."

By July 14, Bastille Day, when she was ready to return to Paris, she had become, in ways that are central, a different person. She had made friends and evaluated people solely on her own. She had found pleasure in solitude. Assessing the lessons she learned in that remarkable year, she wrote: "I hadn't read much, and my novel was worthless. On the other hand I had worked at my chosen profession without losing heart, and had been enriched by new enthusiasm. I was emerging triumphant from the trials to which I had been subjected; separation and loneliness had not destroyed my peace of mind."

And then the ultimate throwaway line, the line that seems so small, such a given, once one has been through the rigors needed to achieve this balanced state: "*I knew that I could now rely on myself.*"

When we begin to see how we contribute to our own weakness and vulnerability, how we actually nourish and defend our inner dependency, then, slowly, we begin to feel stronger. "The more we face down our conflicts and seek out our own solutions," wrote Karen Horney, "the more inner freedom and strength we will gain." It is when we assume responsibility for our own problems that the center of gravity begins to make that crucial shift from the Other to the Self. At this point, something remarkable happens. More energy becomes available to us. Energy that used to get lost in the Energy Leak, as we exhausted ourselves repressing those aspects of our personalities we felt were unacceptable or frightening. Once we no longer need to defend and protect, that same energy is available for more positive efforts. Gradually we become less inhibited, less plagued by fear and anxiety, less deadened by self-contempt. The old Gender Panic with which we have lived for so long disappears. We are less afraid of others. We are less afraid of ourselves.

Springing Free

Ultimately, the goal is emotional spontaneity—an inner liveliness that pervades everything we do, every work project, every social encounter, every love relationship. It comes from the conviction: "I am the first force in my life." And it leads to what Karen Horney calls *wholeheartedness*—the ability "to be without pretense, to be emotionally sincere, to be able to put the whole of oneself into one's feelings, one's work, one's beliefs."[5]

I have thought about the women I've met who seem to possess wholeheartedness. Some are complex, creative, highly talented types; others lead simpler, less visibly dramatic lives. But whether they are multitalented urban sophisticates or country women up to their elbows in potting glaze, the quality of *thereness*—of having "sprung free"—is undeniable. Their experience of life is qualitatively different from that of those who haven't sprung free: richer, less predictable, less bound by rules and institutional imprints. Even their way of *expressing* their experience is different.

Pearl Primus, the choreographer, told how she meandered toward a doctorate in anthropology simply by *being*:

> "My life has been like traveling up a river. Every now and then I would hear singing around the bend, and so around the bend I would go and become occupied with living. Maybe years would go by and I'd realize, 'Oh, my God, I've got to get this Ph.D.' So in the process of working on the Ph.D. I've lived

many rivers and many peoples. Anthropology has become part of me instead of something superimposed."[6]

A moment occurs—a "psychological moment" which may span weeks or even months, but which is often experienced as a particular moment in time—in which the conditions of personality creating the conflict seem to unmesh, as gears unmesh, and the woman is released from the lockup that kept her immobilized. When this happens, all kinds of things become possible. There may be job changes, geographical moves, new relationships, creative pursuits not previously dreamt of.

Women who have sprung free find themselves, quite suddenly, with the energy to *engage*. They cling tenaciously to life, all the while being free to rise and fall in rhythm with its tumults. There is a new experience of *playfulness*, of being fully alive, in which one is freer than ever before to exercise options, to accept or reject according to the desires of one's truest self.

Powerful emotional experiences await those who are really living out their own scripts. A Chicago woman in her early forties who still lives with and loves her husband is also intensely involved with a man she works with. He too is married, so their time together is limited. They look forward to the business trips they manage to take together several times a year. On one of these, the woman decided after a few days that she wanted to go skiing. The man was not a skier, and in any event had further work to do in Boston. "I decided that I would ski by myself," she told me. "I got on a bus in the middle of the afternoon, and as we wound up into the Vermont mountains, it began to snow. I remember sitting by myself on this Greyhound bus, looking out the window and watching the lights come on in the little towns we passed through. I felt so good, so secure in the knowledge that I could be myself, do what I want—*and also be loved* —I started to cry."

The woman who has sprung free has emotional mobility. She is able to move *toward* the things that are satisfying to her and *away* from those that are not.

She is free, also, to succeed: to set goals and take steps to reach those goals without fear that she will fail. Her confidence derives from a realistic evaluation of both her limits and her abilities. One of the most inspiring examples I know of a woman who was free to succeed is Jean Auel. (Her first novel, *The Clan of the Cave Bear*, became an immediate best-seller.) Here is someone who refused to allow her life to be determined for her by external events. Instead, she took the responsibility for shaping her own life—even though there were others who depended on her.

Jean married when she was eighteen. By the time she was twenty-five, she had had five children. Responsible for her household and at the same time working as a keypunch operator at a Tektronix plant near her home in Portland, Oregon, she also went to night school and earned a Master's degree in business. (She had no Bachelor's degree.) With her M.A. in hand she was able to rise to the position of credit manager at Tektronix, with responsibility for $8 million in accounts receivable. Then, a few months after her fortieth birthday, she quit her job: she had decided she wanted to write a novel.

The project began with an idea she got, late one night, for a story about a young Cro-Magnon girl who finds herself living in a more primitive society of Neanderthals. Jean Auel read more than fifty books, studying the lore of primitive peoples. Then she typed out a first draft—450,000 words. In so doing she learned something: she did not know enough about writing novels. So, characteristically, she proceeded to bone up. She began by reading her daughter's college textbooks on fiction writing. She wrote and rewrote. Then, after a few rejections from publishers, she sent a letter to a New York literary agent she'd met at a Portland writers' workshop. Eight weeks later she signed a $130,000 contract for *The Clan of the Cave Bear*.[7]

Here is a woman who has allowed the winds of change to move through her life. Here is a woman who is not afraid to work, to apply herself in untried areas—the unfamiliar, the strange and new. Here is a woman who believes in herself, and belief in self is the bottom line.

I have learned that freedom and independence can't be wrested from others—from the society at large, or from men—but can only be developed, painstakingly, from within. To achieve it, we will have to give up the dependencies we've used, like crutches, to feel safe. Yet the trade-off is not really so perilous. The woman who believes in herself does not have to fool herself with empty dreams of things that are beyond her capabilities. At the same time, she does not waver in the face of those tasks for which she's competent and prepared. She is realistic, well grounded, and self-loving. She is free, at last, to love others—*because* she loves herself. All of these things, and no less, belong to the woman who has sprung free.

Notes and Sources

Chapter I THE WISH TO BE SAVED

1. People who are dependent often show their aggression by criticizing. Dr. Martin Symonds, a New York psychoanalyst who has done studies of the victims of criminals, is interested in how aggression gets manifested by people who perceive themselves as powerless. He writes (in a paper called "Psychodynamics of Aggression in Women") that criticism becomes a kind of substitute for active power. "It is a very effective method with anxious people with low self-esteem. In expressing their critical standards an illusion is created that if they did 'it,' they would do 'it' better. The classical example is the back-seat driver, who expresses what should be done as if he were in the driver's seat. Actually, most back-seat drivers don't drive at all." (*American Journal of Psychoanalysis*, 1976.)

2. This "fury" she expresses reminds me of women who have described themselves as "fierce but dependent" to New York psychiatrist Ruth Moulton. (Moulton, much of whose work is referred to in this book, is Assistant Clinical Professor of Psychiatry at Columbia University and a Training and Supervising Analyst at the William Alanson White Institute and the Columbia Psychoanalytic Clinic in New York City.) In a paper called "Women with Double Lives," she said these women "demanded inordinate reassurance from men and when it was not forthcoming, they turned against the husbands with a kind of 'malevolent transformation' to use Sullivan's term. The husband who fails them is suddenly seen as 'the bad father.' Whereas early in the marriage the patient and her husband fought against parents and conventions, later the husband becomes the enemy, taking the parents' place." (The subject of this paper is discussed further, along with a full citation, in the Notes and Sources for Chapter IV.)

3. "What is dependence?" asks Judith Bardwick, a psychologist at the University of Michigan. "In the beginning it is the normal infant's way of relating to people. Later, in children and in adults, it seems to be a way of coping with stress, a reaction to frustration, or a protection against future frustration. It can be *affectional*—the grasping and forcing of affectionate or protective behavior from someone else, especially from an adult. Dependent behavior can also be a *coping* behavior—one gets help in order to solve a problem that he cannot solve himself. It can also be *aggressive*—by grabbing attention or affection for oneself someone else is prevented from receiving it. In

all cases, dependence means a lack of independence. Dependence is leaning on someone else to supply support." (Quote taken from Bardwick's book *The Psychology of Women: A Study of Biocultural Conflicts*, 1971.)

4. Quote taken from Alexandra Symonds, a psychoanalyst who is married to Martin Symonds (see Note 1) and who has written many papers on the subject of neurotic dependency in successful career women. This particular remark was made in Dr. Symonds' (published) discussion of another psychiatrist's paper, "Psychoanalytic Reflections on Women's Liberation," in the Spring, 1972, issue of the *Journal of Contemporary Psychoanalysis*. (The paper was by Ruth Moulton.)

Chapter II BACKING DOWN: WOMEN'S RETREAT FROM CHALLENGE

1. This and the subsequent quote are taken from Coburn's article "Self-Sabotage: Women's Fear of Success," in *Mademoiselle* (1979).
2. Quote taken from "Can I Stay at Home Without Losing My Identity?" by Anne T. Fleming, *Vogue* (1978).
3. From *The Psychology of Women: A Study of Biocultural Conflicts* (1971).
4. Quote taken from *Working It Out* (1977), an enlightening and unusually articulate book in which twenty-three women writers, artists, scientists, and scholars talk about their lives and work. (Edited by Sara Ruddick and Pamela Daniels.)
5. Figure from the U.S. Department of Labor.
6. Quote taken from Wright's article "Are Working Women *Really* More Satisfied? Evidence from Several National Surveys," published in the *Journal of Marriage and the Family* (1978).
7. The first material to come from this famous study by Terman and Ogden was published in 1947. Follow-up work on the original sample of gifted children was done over the years. The most recent follow-up study (conducted by P. S. Sears and M. H. Odom and reported in *The Psychology of Sex Differences* by Eleanor Maccoby and Carol Jacklin) found that women in later middle age who were gifted as children feel more bitterness and disappointment about their lives than do men who were similarly gifted in childhood. According to Maccoby and Jacklin, "The men, by and large, have had considerably more 'successful' lives in terms of personal achievements outside the domestic sphere, and the women tend to look back with some regret on what they now see as missed opportunities."

   Maccoby and Jacklin reported on another study, published in 1971, showing that *women decrease in ego sufficiency and complexity between the ages of 18 and 26, whereas men increase in these respects.*

   Sociologist Alice Rossi points out that society "expects men to aspire to jobs of the highest occupational prestige consistent with their abilities; indeed, his job should tax and stretch his ability or it will not be 'challenging' enough. If they do not, if a man settles for a job below his abilities, we tend to consider this a 'social problem,' a 'talent loss.' . . . *By sharp contrast, we not only tolerate but encourage women to work in jobs which are below their abilities, precisely because this does release energies for their cen-*

tral roles in the family." (The quote above is from "The Roots of Ambivalence in American Women," published in an anthology called *Readings on the Psychology of Women,* edited by Judith Bardwick.)

Rossi was the one to coin the term "cakewinners" to describe women who put their income toward family "extras" rather than have as a goal their own financial independence.

8. Quote taken from Symonds' paper "Neurotic Dependency in Successful Women," *Journal of the American Academy of Psychoanalysis* (1976).

9. *Ibid.*

10. "The Liberated Woman: Healthy and Neurotic," *Journal of the American Academy of Psychoanalysis* (1974).

11. This information was based on a study of 32,000 students in 200 schools around the country, conducted in 1973 by the American College Testing Program.

12. The fields (according to the Census Bureau) are education, English and journalism, fine and applied arts, foreign languages and literature, nursing, and library science. A decade earlier (1966), 65 percent of all Bachelor's degrees, 76 percent of all Master's degrees, and 47 percent of all doctorates awarded to women were in these fields. "Put another way," said Frances Cerra, who reported these statistics for *The New York Times,* "*70 percent of the increased number of doctorates awarded to women between 1966 and 1976 were in traditionally female courses of study*" (May 11, 1980).

13. Pearl Kramer was originally quoted in an article in *Columbia,* the magazine of Columbia University, titled, "Women's Education and Careers: Is There Still a Sex Link?" (1980).

14. Quotes taken from "The Problems of Working Women," in *The Wall Street Journal,* September 13, 1978, which also reported the rather remarkable fact that of General Motors' 68,000 skilled-trades workers, a paltry 58 (at that writing) were women.

15. Kathy Keating, who wrote up the survey for *Better Homes and Gardens* in an article called "Are Working Mothers Attempting Too Much?" (October, 1978), noted that nonemployed homemakers "don't necessarily live in a land that is all sunshine and roses." Mainly they worry about the frequency of divorce among their middle-aged friends. But, said Keating, "the concern expressed most frequently and with the most hostility is that the women's rights movement has demeaned the role of the full-time mother."

Apparently these women don't make the connection between being unemployed and dependent (as they are) and their disturbance over the rising divorce rate. Threatened, they direct their anger at the women's movement. (It's worth noting that a survey asking the question "Are Working Mothers Attempting Too Much?" was sufficiently exercising to provoke 30,000 readers to attach letters to the survey form published in *Better Homes.*)

16. An advance into the world after time spent home with the family can be—and usually is—shocking. Women at home rarely recognize how sheltered and untried they are until they attempt "reentry." At home, notes Ruth Moulton, "a woman could remain essentially child-like and dependent, while seeming to take care of her family. Only when she tried to move outward did she discover how phobic, narrow, uninformed, and unprepared she really was." "Women with Double Lives," *Journal of Contemporary Psychoanalysis* (1977).

17. "Pregnancy-to-avoid" is a widely recognized phenomenon. Judith Bardwick notes that when their kids are young, college-educated mothers often complain about how stifled they feel at home and say that they look forward to the day when they can go back to school and "realize their potential." "It's easy to talk," says Bardwick, "but difficult to face potential failure and loss of self-esteem. As their children grow older and the possibility of entering into a profession becomes a reality, their interest declines. The logical and salient mechanism for prohibiting entrance into the occupational world is a new 'accidental' pregnancy" (*The Psychology of Women*).

18. Quote and the one that follows taken from an unpublished paper by Ruth Moulton, "Ambivalence About Motherhood in Career Women."

19. This statistic was quoted by Joyce Miller, president of the Coalition of Labor Union Women, in a *Newsweek* article, "The Super Woman Squeeze" (May 19, 1980).

20. This figure came from the U.S. Census Bureau.

21. These figures were released in the fall of 1980 at a White House Mini-Conference on Older Women, in Des Moines, and reported in *The New York Times* in an article titled " 'If Your Face Isn't Young': Women Confront Problems of Aging" (October 10, 1980).

22. Marjorie Bell Chambers, president of the American Association of University Women, did a study showing, among other things, that the number of displaced homemakers is growing by leaps and bounds. They are single women between the ages of thirty-five and sixty-four who have become responsible for their own support as a result of divorce, separation, or the death of a husband. In 1976, the United States had more than 9.5 million such women—twice the number recorded in 1950. According to Milo Smith, the current number is 25 million. (See "The Displaced Homemaker—Victim of Socioeconomic Change Affecting the American Family" by Marjorie Bell Chambers in *The Journal*, published by the Institute for Socioeconomic Studies. Also, "A Statistical Portrait of Women in the United States" from the Government Printing Office in Washington, D.C.)

23. Alimony has dropped off to such a degree that no woman should consider it something to fall back on if the marriage goes kaput. A 1979 study of 9,000 divorced readers of *McCall's* (published in March of that year) found that only 10 percent were receiving any form of alimony. *McCall's* found that a woman is most likely to be receiving alimony if she and her husband had a joint income of $40,000 or more or if she is over fifty, had been married twenty years or longer, or has three or more children.

24. Quote and statistics taken from "The More Sorrowful Sex," an article in *Psychology Today*, April, 1979.

25. In a test reported by A. A. Benton in the *Journal of Personality* (1973), subjects in opposite-sex pairs were told to bargain with each other and to negotiate a financial contract. The rules of the "task" stipulated that one subject had to win more money than the other. Before the bargaining began, women expected to win less money than men and expected to be less potent and active in the negotiations.

26. Studies showing that women experience higher levels of test anxiety than men have been reported by Bardwick and by Matina Horner. (For Horner, see Notes and Sources for Chapter VI.)

27. Ruth Moulton conducted this study when she began finding that many competent women do not lecture because they're phobic. The observations she made of Columbia postgraduate students were reported in "Some

Effects of the New Feminism," a paper she presented in 1976 to the Joint Meeting of the American Academy of Psychoanalysis and the American Psychiatric Association.

28. First presented on May 4, 1975, Dr. Symonds' talk was subsequently published in the *Journal of the American Academy of Psychoanalysis* (1976) with the title "Neurotic Dependency in Successful Women."

29. Robin Lakoff, "Language and Woman's Place" (1978).

30. Quote taken from "Conversational Politics" (May, 1979).

31. Quote taken from an article called "Women and Success: Why Some Find It So Painful," *The New York Times* (January 28, 1978).

Chapter III   THE FEMININE RESPONSE

1. Anger at men can function as a character defense—one, as Clara Thompson pointed out forty years ago, that carries with it "secondary gains." When there's a general cultural trend toward being angry at an oppressive "male society," the individual woman gets to have "the illusion of going along in the direction of the freedom of her time." This gives her an acceptable out so far as having an intimate relationship with a man is concerned. What she doesn't recognize is that an intimate heterosexual relationship may trigger all the dangerous feelings of earlier childhood dependencies. "Her fight to achieve some sort of superiority over men," says Thompson, "is an attempt to keep the inner psyche from being destroyed." (See Thompson's "Cultural Pressures in the Psychology of Women" in the journal *Psychiatry*, 1942.)

2. The classic explanation of phobia is that it functions as a "displacement mechanism," spreading out anxiety so that the original fear attaches itself to ever more remote and implausible substitutes. Following is a case history of a woman who became phobic about driving when her real fear was of being assertive. The case is taken from *The Theory and Practice of Psychiatry* by Frederick Redlich and Daniel Freeman (New York: Basic Books, 1966).

> The patient, a wan, beautiful and self-effacing professional woman of thirty-two, referred herself for marital problems in which she masochistically endured much from her irresponsible, flamboyant, but passive husband. In her own selfless, quietly efficient way, she was quite domineering, did her work and managed the children, finances, and so forth. In marked contrast to her efficiency, her only apparent "weakness" was a striking and (for suburban life) curiously inconvenient fear of driving a car, a function she equated with power and masculinity. She felt the sports car she urged upon her husband was too bold an auto for her and (although solidly sensible about most matters) she irately asserted that without a mechanic's knowledge of mechanics, she or anyone would be an unsafe driver, endangering herself and her children. She accordingly avoided learning to drive (other than through exasperated, sporadic, and complicated demonstrations from her spouse), and, since she never asked for favors, she either walked or occasionally was offered rides by friends or her husband.

She really thought little of herself as a woman and of women generally and yet, in this one area, exaggerated "womanly helplessness" and in addition ridiculously overestimated the consequences of assertiveness; in this her spoiled husband was only too willing to encourage her by calling reasonable requests "bossiness." Her phobia appeared to be an attempt to protect herself from complaints that she was aggressive and bossy (that is, in the driver's seat), and it expressed her need to be dependent, which she equated with weakness. As she vented guilt about dependency wishes and aggressive strivings and as she began to distinguish between competence and masculinity, the phobia lessened . . . .

3. New and unorthodox theories are emerging on the subject of women's phobias. One such is Dr. Robert Seidenberg's concept of "the trauma of eventlessness." On the basis of information from his patients, he believes that some women become phobic contemplating the sheer eventlessness of their lives. The anxiety arises over the fear that their lives will continue in the same meaningless way indefinitely. These women are afraid of life, but they are even more afraid of the lifelessness of their lives. In them, says Seidenberg, the onset of phobic anxiety is self-preservative, a crying out against the fact that they are *objects in their own lives*. (Seidenberg, a Professor of psychiatry at Upstate Medical Center in Syracuse, New York, has written widely in an attempt to bring about a reevaluation of the forces operating on and within women. Three articles of his, including "The Trauma of Eventlessness," can be found in *Psychoanalysis and Women*, edited by Jean Baker Miller, M.D.)

Chapter IV BECOMING HELPLESS

1. Laura Carper is director of the Mayflower Nursery Playcenter in Detroit. Her article "Sexism in the Nursery," appeared in *Harper's* in April, 1978.
2. It is the mandate of the Girls Clubs of America to offer comprehensive social and educational services to girls and young women, aged six to twenty-one, from low-income families. The organization has focused a lot of attention recently on the fact that girls in our culture are not being helped toward independence any more than they ever were. Edith Phelps's remarks were quoted in an article on "The Plight of U.S. Girls" published in *The New York Times*, January, 1979.
3. Elizabeth Douvan is one of the major contributors of data on the psychological experience of adolescent girls in America. This particular conclusion was based on an in-depth comparison of 1,045 boys aged fourteen through sixteen and 2,005 girls aged eleven through eighteen. The study is described at length in *The Adolescent Experience*, by Douvan and Joseph Adelson, published in 1966. The authors noted that as girls get older they become more sophisticated and rational in their dependence. An eleven-year-old girl will claim to obey parental rules because "rules help kids," whereas an eighteen-year-old young woman has rationalized her need to comply, saying she doesn't want to "worry her parents."
4. Relevant data can be found in the *Journal of Pediatrics*, in an article (1956) by N. Bayley called "Growth Curves of Height and Weight by Age for Boys and Girls, Scaled According to Physical Maturity." (The fact that

infant girls are more verbally, perceptually, and cognitively skilled than infant boys has been long recognized in the field of infant psychology.)

5. Eleanor Maccoby was until recently head of the Psychology Department at Stanford University. One of the chief experts in the field of sex differences, Maccoby has for years run a program of research on child development at Stanford and is particularly esteemed for her work on sex differences in intellectual functioning. Her book *The Development of Sex Differences* has been a major text in psychology departments since it was published in 1966. More recently (1974) she has published *The Psychology of Sex Differences*, coauthored by Carol Nagy Jacklin of Stanford. This is a remarkable reference work that has an annotated bibliography covering more than 1,400 references on psychological differences (aggression, independence, anxiety, ability to do analytic work, etc.) between men and women. Each reference includes the summary and results of a test that's been conducted—thus presenting an amazing range of information between two covers.

6. The fact that boys exhibit more independent behavior than girls, and that the independence gap widens in adolescence, is fully recognized. The *reasons* for this are the subject of current study, and the findings are often controversial. This particular theory on developmental differences between boys and girls in relation to independence has been carefully articulated by Judith Bardwick and Elizabeth Douvan in an essay called, "Ambivalence: The Socialization of Women." It was published in 1971 in *Woman in Sexist Society*, a collection of writings edited by Vivian Gornick and B. K. Moran.

7. Kagan and Moss studied 44 boys and 45 girls from 1929 to 1954. They found dependency remarkably high in females over this whole twenty-five-year period. In fact, the correlation in the dependency behavior of females in childhood, at adolescence, and in early adulthood was higher than for any other behavior dimension they measured. The pattern indicated was predictive. High-dependent girls become high-dependent women, and low-dependent girls become low-dependent women.

8. In the section I've called "Overhelp and the Crippling of Girls," comparative data on how infant boys and infant girls are treated—and responded to—by mothers come from a major overview of studies in the field conducted by Lois Wladis Hoffman of the University of Michigan, titled "Early Childhood Experiences and Women's Achievement Motives," which was published in *Journal of Social Issues* (1972). The study is notable both for its comprehensiveness and for the strength of conviction with which Lois Hoffman makes connections and draws conclusions.

9. In *The Psychology of Women*, Judith Bardwick reported a number of studies relating to girls' lack of confidence. In 1960, Crandall and Robson reported studies of children aged three to five and six to eight. The girls lacked confidence in their work and looked for help and approval from adults. The authors noted that as boys grow older they tend to return to tasks at which they have earlier failed, whereas girls tend to withdraw from the possibility of failing again.

In 1962, Tyler, Rafferty and Tyler reported studies showing that the girls in nursery school who tried to get recognition for achievement were also the girls who made more attempts to get love and affection. Elementary-school girls who tried hardest to achieve were also more eager to gain approval. The correlation between achievement and gaining love and/or approval was not true for boys. Many psychologists have noted that girls are involved in achievement mainly as a way of securing love and approval, whereas boys are involved in achievement—or mastery—mainly for its own sake.

10. Bardwick reported a study by Crandall, Katlovsky, and Preston (1962) showing that first- to third-grade girls lacked confidence and expected to fail, whereas boys expected to succeed. In this study at least, lack of confidence in girls increased with intelligence. Not only were boys more realistic about their expectations for themselves; they had higher standards and a feeling that they, rather than fate or other people, were going to determine whether they were eventually able to succeed.

11. Quote taken from the paper by Lois Hoffman cited above (see Note 8). My italics.

12. Dr. Moulton talked about this "good girl syndrome," and the intrapsychic issues leading to it, in a paper she presented in 1976 to the Joint Meeting of the American Academy of Psychoanalysis and the American Psychiatric Association: "Twenty Years of Progress in Psychoanalysis."

13. Hilde Bruch, M.D., made this statement when interviewed by *People* (June 26, 1978). Fascinating material on mother–daughter relationships and anorexia can be found in Dr. Bruch's text *Eating Disorders* (New York: Basic Books, 1973). She cites a Finnish study showing that mothers of anorexics were inhibited in their sexual response and dissatisfied in their marriages. The mothers earned unusually high scores in intelligence tests, but their education, status, and work were often beneath their capacities. The authors of the study felt that these women, frustrated in the use of their own intellectual abilities and gifts, had become resigned to their fate by the time the anorexic child was born, and had endowed this child with the task of compensating them for their own disappointment. They could accept only a passively receiving child, suffocating all tendencies to independence. The physical adolescence of the girl aroused fear and panic in the mothers as an expression of independence they had not been able to prevent.

14. Martin Seligman, *Helplessness* (1975). Follingstad's quotes were taken from an interview I had with her at the University of South Carolina.

15. A poignant colorlessness, shapelessness, lack of definition is deliberately striven after by girls, while boys pursue an all-out search for commitment and goals (they have to *provide*, after all). Why do girls remain colorless? "They have to remain fluid and malleable in personal identity in order to adapt to the needs of the men they marry," Elizabeth Douvan suggests in "Sex Differences in Adolescent Character Process" (*Merrill-Palmer Quarterly*, 1957). This pattern, she says, "reflects forces that are felt more or less by most girls in our culture." Unfortunately, by the time they reach adulthood, the same fear of defining themselves is considered neurotic.

16. In interviewing women students at the University of Michigan, Judith Bardwick noticed a discrepancy between their postured independence and the way they related to the men with whom they were involved. The women, she says, were highly motivated to *perceive themselves* as independent. "They talk about earning their own living, living alone, and so on. At that point in the interview they usually say that their relationship with their boyfriend or husband is '50–50' and neither dominates. After a while, when they describe the masculinity and successful characteristics of their partners, it usually becomes clear that either the male does dominate in having a final say in decision-making, or the female wishes that he did—so she either perceives him as dominating or puts him in a position of making the final decisions." (From *The Psychology of Women*.)

17. In the early Sixties, at the Institute for the Study of Human Problems at Stanford University, Marjorie M. Lozoff studied 49 "able college women" to see how their relationships with their parents affected their sense of personal autonomy. She found that daughters with career-oriented mothers tend to develop a variety of talents and interests early in life. However, few of the women in her sample *had* mothers who combined career and family. These women, observed Lozoff, were left "struggling with perceived ambitions and talents as alien forces that had to be dealt with in a personally unique and often troubled manner."

Lozoff's paper on this study, "Fathers and Autonomy in Women," was published in *Women and Success* (1974).

18. The artist, Miriam Schapiro (see Chapter II), described the effect on her of this split view (father, effective; mother, ineffective). Like so many women, Miriam tried to resolve the conflict by identifying with her father, also an artist. "Although today I admire my mother for striving to exceed her limitations," she writes, "as a child I was acutely conscious of them. My mother's view of the world was not a 'world' view; she lived 'inside,' at home."

When the Depression forced Miriam's mother to take a job in a department store, it had a constructive effect on her daughter. "Once she had 'real' work—'worldly' work—I began to assign her a space I had previously reserved for my father; however, I still believed that to be out in the world, making your mark on it, you had to be a man." (This quote is taken from *Working It Out*, 1977.)

19. Quote taken from *Working It Out*.

20. Quote taken from a paper by Ruth Moulton called "Women with Double Lives." In it Moulton shows that an unresolved conflict in relation to Daddy leads many women to appeal to the support of men over the entire span of their lives. Professional women who don't receive enough support for their work from their husbands—women, that is, who have an excessive need for support—will turn to other men, often having affairs with men in their fields as a way of gaining the "consensual validation" they require in order to be able to produce.

21. From case studies described in "Women with Double Lives."

22. From *Memoirs of a Dutiful Daughter*, the first in a series of autobiographical books written over the span of De Beauvoir's lifetime.

23. In her above-cited study of "able college women," Marjorie Lozoff ferreted out a group of what she called "supercompetents." (Surely Simone de Beauvoir would have been considered such.) The fathers of the "supercompetents," says Lozoff, "were aloof, self-disciplined, and perfectionistic." Their demand for perfection from their daughters "frequently had a narcissistic tinge to it. The young women seemed hesitant to rebel against their fathers' requests because of concern about the withdrawal of what little love they received."

24. Quotes taken from *Herself* (1972), an autobiographical work by Hortense Calisher.

25. In the living room of her apartment on Central Park West I asked Ruth Moulton if she didn't think a lot of women's mothers were threatened by their daughters' decisions to lead lives that are different from theirs. She told me, "I would say there are many more who are either overtly discouraging or subtly discouraging than there are those who say, 'I'm very pleased for you; I wish I had been able to do what you did.'" Then, with charac-

teristic candor, this remarkable feminist psychoanalyst in her sixties provided me with an example from her own life. "My mother was a musician. I tried to be a pianist but I didn't have the talent, and she was instrumental in getting me to stop taking piano lessons because she felt I wasn't getting anywhere. As soon as I took science courses I got straight A's with no effort. My father was a scientist, so this was obviously the direction to go in. At first my mother didn't object, but then she was threatened by my going to medical school. She had the feeling that either I would be unmarriageable or, if I married, I would have conflict and competition with my husband and wouldn't be able to raise my children properly. She herself had never done anything except some music teaching in her own home at a time when her children were already in school, so it didn't conflict with her time with us, and to her that was compatible. But she couldn't see how I could be a doctor and be with my children; she found it threatening and she discouraged me."

26. Described in a *Psychology Today* article called "The Sexes Under Scrutiny: From Old Biases to New Theories" (November, 1978).

27. In an analysis of the psychological literature on women and self-confidence, Ellen Lenney cites several studies indicating that women flounder when they're not reassured about how well they're doing. ("Women's Self-Confidence in Achievement Settings," *Psychological Bulletin*, 1977.)

28. This study by Schwartz and Clausen was described in the article cited above (Schwartz, S. H., and Clausen, G. T., "Responsibility Norms in Helping in an Emergency," *Journal of Personality and Social Psychology*, 1970).

29. Women tend to be conservative about their judgment in situations that are ambiguous, according to studies reported in *Half the Human Experience: The Psychology of Women* (1976). On the other hand, in situations that seem very certain, "a counterphobic release of boldness seems to occur," allowing these same women to get quite sassy and authoritarian.

30. In her pioneering work *The Development of Sex Differences* (1966), Eleanor Maccoby spends some time discussing studies related to the effects of dependency on intellectual capabilities. "An individual who is dependent and conforming is oriented toward stimuli emanating from other people," she writes. "Perhaps he finds it difficult to ignore these stimuli in favor of internal thought processes. Analytic thinking appears to require more internal "processing; Kagan et al. (1963) have shown it to be associated with longer reaction times than global responding." J. Kagan, H. A. Moss, and I. E. Siegel are the authors of a paper titled "The Psychological Significance of Styles of Conceptualization," which is included in *Basic Cognitive Processes in Children*, edited by J. C. Wright and J. Kagan (Monographs of the Society for Research in Child Development, 1963).

31. These observations were made by R. S. Wyer, M. Henninger, and M. Wolfson in a study, "Informational Determinants of Females' Self-Attributions and Observers' Judgments of Them in an Achievement Situation," in *Journal of Personality and Social Psychology* (1975).

32. Clara Thompson was a psychoanalyst who broke new ground in helping to change the way women were perceived in the psychiatric profession. In *On Women*, a posthumously published book based on her early papers, one finds that the insights she had in the 1940s are distinctly relevant today. She wrote: "Even when a woman has become consciously convinced of her value she still has to contend with the unconscious effects of training, dis-

crimination against her, and traumatic experiences which keep alive the attitude of inferiority."

Dr. Thompson, who was the first president of the Washington-Baltimore Psychoanalytic Institute, first vice-president of the American Association for the Advancement of Psychoanalysis, and first executive director of the William Alanson White Institute in New York, was all too aware of the way in which society encourages the female to be dependent. "She lives in a culture which provides no security for her except a permanent so-called love relationship. It is known that the neurotic need of love is a mechanism for establishing security in a dependency relation. . . . To the extent that a woman has a greater need of love than a man it is also to be interpreted as a device for establishing security in a cultural situation producing dependency. *Being loved not only is part of woman's natural life in the same way as it is part of man's, but it also becomes, of necessity, her profession.*" (Italics mine.)

Chapter V   BLIND DEVOTION

1. Quotes taken from *Husbands and Wives: A Nationwide Survey of Marriage.* Conducted by Crossley Surveys, Inc. of New York, the study included 3,880 men and women.
2. Quotes taken from *New York Times* article titled "Doctors' Wives: Many Report Marriage Is a Disappointment," by Leslie Bennetts (May 7, 1979).
3. For problems of separation-individuation in marriage, read *Marriage and Personal Development* by psychologists Rubin Blanck and Gertrude Blanck (1968). Also "On the Significance of Normal Separation-Individuation Phase," by M. S. Mahler, published in *Drives, Affects and Behavior*, edited by M. Schur (1953).
4. This idea of "reengulfment" is discussed in an article titled "Marriage and the Capacity to Be Alone," by Joan Wexler and John Steidl, in *Psychiatry* (1978). Both Wexler and Steidl are assistant professors of Psychiatry in Social Work at the Yale University Medical School. They say: "Fusion is an attempt to avoid separateness, forgo intuition and mature empathy, and recapture a state of primitive empathy. . . ."
5. *Ibid.*
6. Simone de Beauvoir is chillingly astute on the subject of how far women will go to manipulate a protective environment for themselves. Cf. *The Second Sex*; note, particularly, the section on "Marriage."
7. Quote taken from *Marriage and Personal Development*, cited above.
8. Marcia Perlstein lives and works in Berkeley, California, where I interviewed her.
9. Quote taken from "Psychology of the Female: A New Look," in *Psychoanalysis and Women* (1973) edited by Jean Baker Miller, M.D.
10. Barrie Thorne is a linguistics scholar who teaches at Michigan State University. I interviewed her at Stanford, where she was spending a year as a visiting professor. Barrie made me aware of the work being done on women and language discussed in the text and Notes of Chapter II.

11. The information on good girls and orgasms was reported in *Newsweek*, October 22, 1979. (Refer also to Ruth Moulton's "good girl syndrome" in Chapter II.)

12. See Jessie Bernard, *The Future of Marriage* for a discussion of the excessive amount of "adapting" women do in marriage situations. Bernard cites studies showing that the mental health of married women is worse than that of single women or married or single men.

    A 1960 study of 2,000 married men and women found consistently higher levels of anxiety in married women than in married men, but the authors managed to find a positive way of interpreting these data. The wives' worrying, they said, implied "an investment in life." The nonworrying husbands they construed as lacking "involvement and aspiration." (*Americans View Their Mental Health: A Nationwide Interview Survey* by Gerald Gurin, Joseph Veroff, and Sheila Field.)

13. Quote taken from *The Future of Marriage*.

CHAPTER VI   GENDER PANIC

1. A full description of Fear of Success and the studies Horner conducted is in "The Motive to Avoid Success and Changing Aspirations of College Women," reprinted in *Readings on the Psychology of Women*. The paper was first presented at a symposium, "Women on Campus: 1970," sponsored by the Center for the Continuing Education of Women, Ann Arbor, Michigan. (Note: Matina Horner is currently President of Radcliffe College.)

2. Horner's conclusions about women and success are supported by other studies. Women have lower expectations for success than men do for a wide variety of tasks and age groups (Crandall, 1969). It has been shown that people with high expectations of success tend to do better than those with low expectations, regardless of actual ability (Tyler, 1958). Much of this work was summarized in *Half the Human Experience: The Psychology of Women*. Authors Hyde and Rosenberg say: "Females expect not to do well, which promotes not doing well. When females fail, it reinforces their belief in their own lack of abilities, further lowering their expectation of success and making success less likely. When females succeed, they attribute it to luck, and thus expectations of their own success are not increased."

    One woman whose attitude substantiates this theory is Katharine Graham, publisher of *The Washington Post*. "I still don't believe I have it," she told Wyndham Robertson of *Fortune*, referring to the newspaper. "It's luck. I know it sounds girlish to say that." ("The Ten Highest-Ranking Women in Big Business," April, 1973.)

3. The schools where these remarkably traditional male views were elicited were Brown, Princeton, Wellesley, Dartmouth, Barnard, and Stony Brook. Data came from an extensive survey conducted in 1978 and presented in December of that year at a conference at Brown University called "Women/Men/College: The Educational Implications of Sex Roles in Transition."

4. In the above-cited paper by Horner she notes other studies (Tulkin, 1968, and Jensen, 1970) that indicate a high correlation in Fear of Success be-

tween black men and white women. School performance does not bear much relation to career goals for either group.

5. This information was published in "Psychological Barriers to Success in Women" by Matina S. Horner and Mary R. Walsh and anthologized in Ruth Kundsin's *Women and Success* (1974).

6. Sulka's kids may have more to worry about than their physical support. "If ever there is a schizophrenic mother, it is the one whose aimlessness causes her to cling to her children with the desperation of a drowning person," says Robert Seidenberg. "The child is never allowed to test reality on his own, never learns his own boundaries, often fails to distinguish between the animate and the inanimate. He treats the world as a 'thing,' just as he has been treated by a mother who has no 'thing.' A mother who has something is apt to behave quite differently." (By "thing," Dr. Seidenberg does not mean a penis, as Freud would have it, but an identity of her own that's separate from her relationship to her children, an identity stemming from a relationship with the world outside. See "Is Anatomy Destiny?" in *Psychoanalysis and Women*.)

7. The wrenching separation of divorce often rearouses "basic questions of identity" in women for whom marriage has become the basic reference point, the major definition of self. "For the woman who never really confronted questions of her own identity, who went from the role-identity of daughter to that of wife, divorce may be the first time, in her aloneness and failure, that she confronts the issue of her values, her needs, her goals," writes Bardwick in *The Psychology of Women*.

8. Taken from the Hoffman study described in Notes and Sources, Chapter II.

9. Pioneer women, long touted as our feisty foremothers, were not, it turns out, as independent as they might have been, in the inner, psychological sense. Like modern women, when their men were away they were able to *behave* independently in order to survive, but they didn't particularly like it. They were put off by demands of adult living. That, at least, is what a feminist history scholar, Julie Jeffrey, discovered when she decided to investigate how those pioneer women actually *felt* about their lives. One woman wrote in her diary at night (before blowing out the candle): "Allway beeing accostum to have someone to depende on, it is quite new to attend to business transactions and it pesters me no little." Quoting extensively from letters and diaries, Jeffrey showed that the pioneer women were eager to return to the simple jobs of domesticity as soon as their husbands came home from slaying the Indians. It was domesticity, says Jeffrey, disappointed, "that gave their lives meaning." Jeffrey's book, *Frontier Women*, was published in 1979.

10. Even an achiever like Margaret Mead consciously sought not to appear to "compete" with men and considered herself more feminine than other professional women of her time. In her autobiographical book *Blackberry Winter*, 1973, she reported having just returned from a long trip in the field. Both she and her husband (she wrote) were "starved" for talk. However, when they met with the anthropologist Gregory Bateson, Margaret discreetly dropped back, so that the two men could spend the night talking "without interruption."

11. Discussing this moral conflict in "Is Anatomy Destiny?" (see above), Seidenberg goes on to warn: "In spite of later worldly education . . . these

earlier lessons from kin take priority and can be overcome only by vigorous self-purging efforts."

12. Quotes taken from an article, "When Homemaking Becomes Job No. 2," in *The New York Times* by Leslie Bennetts, July 14, 1979.

13. "Marriage: What Women Expect and What They Get," *McCall's*, January, 1980.

14. Another article in the same *Wall Street Journal* series (1978) quoted Kristin Moore of the Urban Institute, in Washington, D.C.: "The husband may do some of the more interesting or challenging things around the house but women still have to do the large amount of housework." Most jobholding women still put in 80- to 100-hour work weeks when the work they do at home is added to the work they do outside the home.

15. Quotes and statistics from Nadine Brozan's article in *The New York Times* "Men and Housework: Do They or Don't They?" November 1, 1980.

16. This information was produced in the study conducted by Wright referred to in the text and Notes and Sources for Chapter II.

17. *The New York Times* article, titled "A Record $3.2 Million is Pledged by Bantam for New Krantz Novel," was accompanied by a photograph of Ms. Krantz taken by Francesco Scavullo. Mr. Scavullo did not photograph her ironing.

18. Quote taken from *Working It Out*, edited by Ruddich and Daniels (1977).

19. The writer Anne Taylor Fleming reported a startling phenomenon in a *New York Times Magazine* article she called "The Liberated Cook." "After finding jobs and analysts and, in some cases, new husbands, women are back in the kitchen, cooking, seriously cooking with an edge of tenderness. Maybe it's an act of atonement. Maybe it's a hedge against professional disappointment. Maybe cooking is a lot more fun than most of the work women have found to do. To women who have found success less rewarding than they dreamed, offices less hospitable than they imagined, kitchens are suddenly friendly places again, safe places to crawl into after mean days."

And then, the *coup de grâce*: "*The meals these women make and the parties they give earn them easier praise than their jobs. Husbands are appreciative, proud, touched to come upon their wives smelling of yeast and smudged with flour, their curls matted by steam.*" (October 28, 1979)

20. Some women manage the trick of earning an independent income and still retaining a basic dependency by marrying extremely rich and influential men. One such is Helen Gurley Brown, who, as Editor-in-Chief of *Cosmopolitan*, certainly earns enough to call her own shots. However, in relation to her husband of twenty years, film producer David Brown, Helen chooses to play an old female game. Before rushing off to work in the morning she cooks him three-course breakfasts "from scratch"—roast-beef hash, cheese rarebit, cauliflower pancakes. She doesn't sit down to eat with him, she told a reporter for *The New York Times*. "I wait on him hand and foot." Explaining the reciprocity she perceives in the arrangement, she added, "But David does things for me. For example, I can write any check I want and he never questions me." ("To Breakfast or Not to Breakfast?" by Enid Nemy, March 25, 1979)

CHAPTER VII SPRINGING FREE

1. The basis for this final chapter is Karen Horney's theory that conflict—the crashing in upon each other of quite opposite drives—is at the root of neurosis. A trend toward self-effacement and excessive need for love, for example, might be in conflict with an opposite drive to be expansive, competitive, and somewhat detached from the need for love. This, it seems to me, is exactly the situation in which women find themselves today.

It was also, apparently, the situation in which women found themselves in the Thirties and Forties, when Karen Horney was doing so much work to change the psychoanalytic view of women. (She died in 1952.) Horney was the first internationally esteemed psychoanalyst to differ fundamentally with Freud's view of feminine psychology (see Horney's *Feminine Psychology*) and to conceive of a holistic-dynamic view, in which the individual and society, internal and external forces, present and past influences are all mutually interacting and whose effects on the personality—its defenses and symptoms —are not easily teased out.

In a paper called "The Overvaluation of Love" which she published in 1934 (*Psychoanalytic Quarterly*, vol. 3), she began to examine, in the light of her knowledge of her women patients, the problem of modern women in a "patriarchal society." She noticed that many women have a desire to "love a man and be loved" that is compulsive and driven in its extremeness. They are not able to have good and lasting relations with men, are inhibited in their work and impoverished in their interests, and often end up feeling anxious, inadequate, and even ugly. In some cases they develop compulsive drives for achievement which, instead of following up themselves, they project onto their male partners.

In her next paper, "The Neurotic Need for Love (included in *Feminine Psychology*)," Horney went further with these ideas, distinguishing between a healthy or spontaneous need for love and one that's compulsive and self-serving.

Feminists embraced Karen Horney because she countered Freud's theory of penis envy. She also placed a greater emphasis on current life situations and destructive attitudes, to which old infantile drives take a back seat so far as *causing* neurosis is concerned. Ultimately, Horney's theory of neurosis is far more constructive and optimistic than Freud's. We both cause and maintain neurosis within ourselves, and thus within us all there lie the ways and means and strength to expunge it. (See her fourth and culminating book, *Neurosis and Human Growth: The Struggle Toward Self-Realization*, 1950.)

2. Horney shows that various types of "impoverishment" afflict the personality when conflicts go unresolved: a feeling of strain; an impairment of moral integrity (replaced, often, by a "pseudo-morality" which has to do with keeping up unconscious pretenses, such as the pretense of loving, of goodness, or of taking real responsibility); and a feeling of hopelessness. Hopelessness comes from knowing, on some level, that making a change in external circumstances will not really do the trick. Layer upon layer of conflict has been built up, and it seems impossible to extricate oneself. Hopelessness is experi-

enced as an ongoing or chronic pessimism, or depression, or hypersensitivity to disappointment.

3. An almost step-by-step description of what's involved in the process of "working through" neurotic conflict can be found on pages 230 to 233 of Horney's *Our Inner Conflicts* (1945).

4. The story of this part of Simone de Beauvoir's life, including the direct quotes, comes from *The Prime of Life* (1976).

5. Horney, *Our Inner Conflicts.*

6. The quote from Pearl Primus comes from a feature story published in *The New York Times*, March 18, 1979.

7. Gerald Jonas, "Behind the Best Sellers," *The New York Times Book Review*, October 26, 1980.

Bibliography

BOOKS

Bardwick, Judith M. *The Psychology of Women: A Study of Biocultural Conflicts*, New York: Harper and Row, 1971.

——. *Readings on the Psychology of Women*. New York: Harper and Row, 1972.

Bernard, Jessie. *American Family Behavior*. New York: Harper, 1952.

——. *The Future of Marriage*. New York: Macmillan, 1971.

Blanck, Rubin, and Blanck, Gertrude. *Marriage and Personal Development*. New York: Columbia University Press, 1968.

Bruch, Hilde, M.D. *Eating Disorders*. New York: Basic Books, 1973.

Calisher, Hortense. *Herself*. New York: Arbor House, 1972.

Chesler, Phyllis, and Goodman, Emily Jane. *Women, Money and Power*. New York: William Morrow, 1976.

De Beauvoir, Simone. *Memoirs of a Dutiful Daughter*. New York: World Publishing Company, 1959.

——. *The Prime of Life*. New York: Harper and Row, 1976.

——. *The Second Sex*. New York: Alfred A. Knopf, 1953.

Deutsch, Helene. *The Psychology of Women: A Psychoanalytic Interpretation*. New York: Grune and Stratton, 1945.

Douvan, Elizabeth, and Adelson, Joseph. *The Adolescent Experience*. New York: John Wiley and Sons, 1966.

Erikson, Erik H. *Childhood and Society*. New York: Norton, 1950.

Friedan, Betty. *The Feminine Mystique*. New York: Dell, 1977.

——. *It Changed My Life*. New York: Dell, 1977.

Gornick, Vivian, and Moran, Barbara K., eds. *Woman in Sexist Society*. New York: Basic Books, 1971.

Gurin, Gerald; Veroff, Joseph; and Field, Sheila. *Americans View Their Mental Health: A Nationwide Interview Survey*. New York: Basic Books, 1960.

Horney, Karen, in Kelman, Harold, ed. *Feminine Psychology*. New York: Norton, 1967.

——. *Neurosis and Human Growth: The Struggle Toward Self-Realization*. New York: Norton, 1950.

——. *Our Inner Conflicts*. New York: Norton, 1945.

——. *Self-Analysis*. New York: Norton, 1942.

Hyde, Janet Shibley, and Rosenberg, B. G. *Half the Human Experience: The Psychology of Women*. Lexington, Massachusetts: D. C. Heath, 1976.

Jeffrey, Julie. *Frontier Women*. New York: Hill and Wang, 1979.

Kagan, J., and Moss, H. A. *Birth to Maturity*. New York: John Wiley and Sons, 1962.

Maccoby, Eleanor, ed. *The Development of Sex Differences*. Stanford: Stanford University Press, 1966.

—— and Jacklin, Carol Nagy. *The Psychology of Sex Differences*. Stanford: Stanford University Press, 1974.

Mahler, M. S., in Schur, M., ed. *Drives, Affects and Behavior*. New York: International Universities Press, 1953.

Martin, Barclay. *Anxiety and Neurotic Disorders*. New York: John Wiley and Sons, 1971.

Martin, D. *Battered Wives*. San Francisco: Glide Publications, 1976.

Martinson, Floyd Mansfield. *Family in Society*. New York: Dodd, Mead, 1970.

Mead, Margaret. *Blackberry Winter*. New York: Simon and Schuster, 1973.

Miller, Jean Baker, M.D., ed. *Psychoanalysis and Women*. Baltimore: Penguin Books, 1973.

——. *Toward a New Psychology of Women*. Boston: Beacon Press, 1976.

National Manpower Council. *Womanpower*. New York: Columbia University Press, 1957.

Pietropinto, Anthony, and Simenauer, Jacqueline. *Husbands and Wives*. New York: Times Books, 1979.

Plath, Sylvia. *The Bell Jar*. New York: Harper and Row, 1971.

Redlich, Frederick C., and Freedman, Daniel X. *The Theory and Practice of Psychiatry*. New York: Basic Books, 1966.

Rubins, Jack L. *Karen Horney*. New York: The Dial Press, 1978.

Ruddich, Sara, and Daniels, Pamela, eds. *Working It Out*. New York: Pantheon, 1977.

Scarf, Maggie. *Unfinished Business*. New York: Doubleday, 1980.

Seligman, Martin. *Helplessness*. San Francisco: W. H. Freeman and Company, 1975.

Sherman, J. A. *On the Psychology of Women: A Survey of Empirical Studies.* Springfield, Illinois: Charles C. Thomas, 1971.

Slater, Philip. *The Pursuit of Loneliness.* Boston: Beacon Press, 1970.

Spence, Janet, and Helmreich, Robert L. *The Psychological Dimensions of Masculinity and Femininity: Their Correlates and Antecedents.* Houston: University of Texas Press, 1978.

Terman, L. M., and Ogden, Melita H. *The Gifted Child Grows Up.* Stanford: Stanford University Press, 1947.

Thompson, Clara M. *On Women.* New York: Basic Books, 1964.

ARTICLES

Adams, Virginia. "Jane Crow in the Army," *Psychology Today*, October, 1980.

Bardwick, Judith M., and Douvan, Elizabeth. "Ambivalence: The Socialization of Women," in Vivian Gornick and Barbara K. Moran, eds. *Woman in Sexist Society.* New York: Basic Books, 1971.

Bart, Pauline B. "Depression in Middle-Aged Women," in Vivian Gornick and Barbara K. Moran, eds. *Woman in Sexist Society.* New York: Basic Books, 1971.

Bayley, N. "Growth Curves of Height and Weight by Age for Boys and Girls, Scaled According to Physical Maturity," *Journal of Pediatrics*, vol. 48, 1956, pp. 187–194.

Bennetts, Leslie. "Doctors' Wives: Many Report Marriage Is a Disappointment," *New York Times*, May 7, 1979.

———. "When Homemaking Becomes Job No. 2," *New York Times*, July 14, 1979.

Bernard, Jessie. "The Paradox of the Happy Marriage," in Vivian Gornick and Barbara K. Moran, eds. *Woman in Sexist Society.* New York: Basic Books, 1971.

Binger, Carl A. L. "Emotional Disturbance Among College Women," in Graham Baline, ed. *Emotional Problems of the Student.* New York: Doubleday, 1961.

Bird, Caroline. "How They Split the Money," *Woman's Day*, May 22, 1979.

Blackburn, Patricia. "An Anorexic, I Nearly Starved Myself," *Mademoiselle*, October, 1979.

Blackwell, Kate, and Ferguson, Karen. "Pensions: Are There Holes in Your Security Blanket?" *Ms.*, October, 1973.

Bodine, Ann. "Sex Differentiation in Language," presented at Conference on Women and Language, Rutgers University, 1973.

Broverman, Inge K., *et al.* "Sex Role Stereotypes and Clinical Judgments of Mental Health," *Journal of Consulting and Clinical Psychology*, vol. 34, February, 1970.

Brozan, Nadine. "Conference Laments Plight of U.S. Girls," *New York Times*, January 27, 1979.

——. "Men and Housework: Do They or Don't They?" *New York Times*, November 1, 1980.

Carper, Laura. "Sex Roles in the Nursery," *Harper's*, April, 1978, p. 51.

Cerra, Frances. "Study Finds College Women Still Aim for Traditional Jobs," *New York Times*, May 11, 1980.

Chodorow, Nancy. "Family Structure and Feminine Personality," in Rosaldo, Michelle Z., and Lemphere, Louise, eds. *Woman, Culture and Society*, Stanford: Stanford University Press, 1974.

Coburn, Judith. "Self-Sabotage: Why Women Fear Success," *Mademoiselle*, September, 1979.

Cohen, Mabel Blake. "Personal Identity and Sexual Identity," *Psychiatry*, vol. 29, 1966, pp. 1–14.

Crandall, V. C. "Sex Differences in Expectancy of Intellectual and Academic Reinforcement," in C. P. Smith, ed. *Achievement Related Motives in Children*. New York: Russell Sage Foundation, 1969.

Crandall, V. J., and Rabson, A. "Children's Repetition Choices in an Intellectual Achievement Situation, Following Success and Failure," *Journal of Genetic Psychology*, vol. 97, 1960, pp. 161–168.

Deutsch, Helene. "The Genesis of Agoraphobia," *International Journal of Psycho-Analysis*," vol. 10, 1929.

Douvan, Elizabeth. "Sex Differences in Adolescent Character Process," *Merrill-Palmer Quarterly*, vol. 6, 1957, pp. 203–211.

Erikson, Erik H. "Inner and Outer Space: Reflections on Womanhood," *Daedalus*, Spring, 1964.

Fleming, Anne T. "Can I Stay at Home Without Losing My Identity?" *Vogue*, August, 1978.

——. "The Liberated Cook," *The New York Times Magazine*, October 28, 1979.

Flint, Jerry. "Income of Working Wives Forming Buffer to Inflation," *New York Times*, December 8, 1979.

Follingstad, Diane R. "A Reconceptualization of Issues in the Treatment of Abused Women: A Case Study." Unpublished paper.

Frodi, Ann; Macaulay, Jacqueline; and Thorne, Pauline. "Are Women Always Less Aggressive Than Men? A Review of the Experimental Literature," *Psychological Bulletin*, vol. 8, no. 4, 1977.

Futterman, S. "Personality Trends in Wives of Alcoholics," *Journal of Psychiatric Social Work*, vol. 23, 1953, pp. 37–41.

Gittelson, Natalie. "Marriage: What Women Expect and What They Get," *McCall's*, January, 1980.

Glenn, Norval D. "The Contribution of Marriage to the Psychological Well-Being of Males and Females," *Journal of Marriage and the Family*, August, 1975.

Goffman, Erving. "Gender Advertisements," *Studies in the Anthropology of Visual Communication*, vol. 3, 1977, entire issue.

Gornick, Vivian. "Why Women Fear Success," *New York*, December 20, 1971.

Gutman, D. L. "Women and the Conception of Ego Strength," *Merrill-Palmer Quarterly*, 11 (3), 1965.

Hacker, Andrew. "Divorce a la Mode," *The New York Review of Books*, May 3, 1979, p. 23.

Harmants, M. G. "Effects of Anxiety, Motivating Instructions, Success and Failure Reports, and Sex of Subject Upon Level of Aspiration and Performance." Unpublished master's thesis, University of Washington, 1962.

"Helping Women Have Orgasms," *Newsweek*, October 22, 1979.

Hoffman, Lois Wladis. "Early Childhood Experiences and Women's Achievement Motives," *Journal of Social Issues*, vol. 28, no. 2, 1972.

Horner, Matina. "Fail: Bright Women," *Psychology Today*, 3 (6): 36, 1969.

——. "The Motive to Avoid Success and Changing Aspirations of College Women," in Judith Bardwick, ed. *Readings in the Psychology of Women*. New York: Harper and Row, 1972.

——. "Sex Differences in Achievement Motivation and Performance in Competitive and Non-Competitive Situations." Unpublished doctoral dissertation, University of Michigan, 1968.

——. "Toward an Understanding of Achievement Related Conflicts in Women," *Journal of Social Issues*, 1972.

—— and Walsh, M. R. "Psychological Barriers to Success in Women," in Ruth B. Kundsin, ed. *Women and Success*. New York: William Morrow, 1974.

Horney, Karen. "The Neurotic Need for Love," in Harold Kelman, ed. *Feminine Psychology*. New York: Norton, 1967.

——. "The Overvaluation of Love, A Study of a Common Present-Day Feminine Type," *Psychoanalytic Quarterly*, vol. 3, 1934.

House, W. C. "Actual and Perceived Differences in Male and Female Expectancies and Minimal Goal Levels as a Function of Competition," *Journal of Personality*, 1974, pp. 493–509.

—— and Penney, V. "Valence of Expected and Unexpected Outcomes as a Function of Locus of Control and Type of Expectancy," *Journal of Personality and Social Psychology*, vol. 29, 1974, pp. 454–463.

Johnson, F. A., and Johnson, C. L. "Roles Strain in High-Commitment

Career Women," *Journal of the American Academy of Psychoanalysis,* 4 (1), 1976.

Kagan, J.; Moss, H. A.; and Siegel, I. E. "The Psychological Significance of Styles of Conceptualization," in J. C. Wright and J. Kagan, eds. *Basic Cognitive Processes in Children,* Monographs of the Society for Research in Child Development, 28, no. 2, 1963.

Keating, Kathy. "Are Working Mothers Attempting Too Much?" *Better Homes and Gardens,* October, 1978.

Kernberg, O. T. "Barriers to Falling and Remaining in Love," *Journal of the American Psychoanalytical Association,* vol. 22, no. 3, 1974.

Keyserling, Mary Dublin. "New Realities in Women's Work Lives: Some Challenges to Action," in *Today's Girls: Tomorrow's Women,* A National Seminar. New York: Girls Clubs of America, 1978, p. 40.

Klemesrud, Judy. " 'If Your Face Isn't Young': Women Confront Problems of Aging," *New York Times,* October 10, 1980.

Kosner, Alice. "Starting Over: What Divorced Women Discover," *McCall's,* March, 1979.

Kramer, Cheris. "Women's Speech: Separate But Unequal?" *Quarterly Journal of Speech,* February, 1974, pp. 14–24.

——; Thorne, Barrie; and Henley, Nancy. "Perspectives on Language and Communication," *Signs,* Spring, 1978.

Lakoff, Robin. "Language and Women's Place," *Language in Society,* vol. 2, 1973, pp. 45–79.

Langway, Lynn. "The Superwoman Squeeze," *Newsweek,* May 19, 1980.

Lavigne, Meg. "Women's Education and Careers: Is There Still a Sex Link?" *Columbia,* Summer, 1980.

Lenney, Ellen. "Women's Self-Confidence in Achievement Settings," *Psychological Bulletin,* vol. 84, no. 1, January, 1977.

Lozoff, Marjorie M. "Fathers and Autonomy in Women," in Ruth Kundsin, ed. *Women and Success.* New York: William Morrow, 1974.

Lynn, D. B. "The Process of Learning Parental and Sex-Role Identification," *Journal of Marriage and the Family,* 28 (4), 1966.

Maccoby, Eleanor. "Sex Differences in Intellectual Functioning," in Eleanor Maccoby, ed. *The Development of Sex Differences.* Stanford: Stanford University Press, 1966, pp. 25–36, 38–44, 46–55.

——. "Woman's Intellect," in S. M. Farber and R. L. Wilson, eds. *The Potential of Woman.* New York: McGraw-Hill, 1963.

—— and Edith M. Dowley. "Activity Level and Intellectual Functioning in Normal Preschool Children," *Child Development,* vol. 36, no. 3, 1965, pp. 761–770.

McCandless, B. R.; Bilous, C. B.; and Bennett, H. L. "Peer Popularity and Dependence on Adults in Preschool Age Socialization," *Child Development*, vol. 32, 1961.

McClelland, D. C. "Wanted: A New Self-Image for Women," in R. J. Lifton, ed. *The Woman in America*. New York: Houghton Mifflin, 1965, pp. 173–192.

McMahon, I. D. "Relationships Between Causal Attributions and Expectancy of Success," *Journal of Personality and Social Psychology*, vol. 28, 1973, pp. 108–114.

Medwick, Cathleen. "Will I Be Able to Manage Both Marriage and Career?" *Vogue*, August, 1978.

"Money and Working Women," *U.S. News and World Report*, January 15, 1979, p. 71.

Moulton, Ruth. "Ambivalence About Motherhood in Career Women." Unpublished paper.

——. "Some Effects of the New Feminism—on Men and Women," *Journal of American Psychoanalysis*, vol. 134, no. 1, January, 1977, pp. 1–6.

——. "Psychoanalytic Reflections on Women's Liberation," *Journal of Contemporary Psychoanalysis*, vol. 8, no. 2, Spring, 1972, p. 214.

——. "A Survey and Re-evaluation of the Concept of Penis Envy," *Contemporary Psychoanalysis*, vol. 7, 1970, pp. 84–104.

——. "Women with Double Lives," *Journal of Contemporary Psychoanalysis*, vol. 13, January, 1977, p. 64.

Nemy, Enid. "To Breakfast or Not to Breakfast?" *New York Times*, March 25, 1979.

Parlee, Mary Brown. "Conversational Politics," *Psychology Today*, May, 1979.

——. "The Sexes Under Scrutiny: From Old Biases to New Theories," *Psychology Today*, November, 1978, p. 65.

Patterson, M., and Sells, L. "Women Dropouts From Higher Education," in A. S. Rossi and A. Calderwood, eds. *Academic Women on the Move*. New York: Russell Sage Foundation, 1973.

Rossi, Alice S. "The Roots of Ambivalence in American Women," in Judith Bardwick, ed. *Readings in the Psychology of Women*. New York: Harper and Row, 1972.

Robertson, Syndham. "The Ten Highest-Ranking Women in Big Business," *Fortune*, April, 1973.

Rothbart, Mary, and Maccoby, Eleanor. "Parents' Differential Reactions to Sons and Daughters," *Journal of Personality and Social Psychology*, 4 (3), 1966.

Salzman, Leon. "Psychology of the Female: A New Look," in Jean Baker

Miller, ed. *Psychoanalysis and Women*. Baltimore: Penguin Books, 1973.

Scarf, Maggie. "The More Sorrowful Sex," *Psychology Today*, April, 1979.

Schaefer, E. S., and Bayley, Nancy. "Maternal Behavior, Child Behavior, and their Inter-Correlations from Infancy through Adolescence," *Monographs of the Society for Child Research Development*, 28 (3), 1963.

Schapiro, Miriam. "Notes from a Conversation on Art, Feminism and Work," in Sara Ruddich and Pamela Daniels, eds. *Working It Out*. New York: Pantheon, 1977.

Schwartz, S. H., and Clausen, G. T. "Responsibility Norms in Helping in an Emergency," *Journal of Personality and Social Psychology*, vol. 16, 1970, pp. 299–310.

Seidenberg, Robert. "Is Anatomy Destiny?" in Jean Baker Miller, ed. *Psychoanalysis and Women*. Baltimore: Penguin Books, 1973, p. 306.

———. "The Trauma of Eventlessness," *Psychoanalytic Review*, vol. 59, 1972, pp. 95–109.

Simon, Jane. "Love: Addiction or Road to Self-Realization?" *The American Journal of Psychoanalysis*, vol. 35, 1975, pp. 359–364.

Steiger, Jo Ann M. "Career Education: Who Needs It?" in *Today's Girls: Tomorrow's Women, A National Seminar*, New York: Girls Clubs of America, 1978, p. 45.

Stoller, Robert J. "The Bedrock of Masculinity and Femininity: Bisexuality," *Archives of General Psychiatry*, vol. 26, 1972, pp. 207–212.

———. "The Sense of Femaleness," *Psychoanalytic Quarterly*, vol. 37, 1968, pp. 42–55.

Symonds, Alexandra. "The Liberated Woman: Healthy and Neurotic," *American Journal of Psychoanalysis*, 1974.

———. "The Myth of Femininity: A Panel," *American Journal of Psychoanalysis*, vol. 33, no. 1, pp. 42–55.

———. "Neurotic Dependency in Successful Women," *Journal of the American Academy of Psychoanalysis*, April, 1976, pp. 95–103.

———. "Phobias After Marriage: Women's Declaration of Dependence," *American Journal of Psychoanalysis*, November, 1971, p. 31.

Symonds, Martin. "Psychodynamics of Aggression in Women," *American Journal of Psychoanalysis*, vol. 36, 1976.

Thompson, Clara. "Cultural Pressures in the Psychology of Women," *Psychiatry*, vol. 5, 1942, pp. 331–339.

———. "Some Effects of the Derogatory Attitude Toward Female Sexuality," *Psychiatry*, vol. 13, 1950, pp. 349–354.

Thurman, David. "A Backward and Forward Look at Educational Arrangements for Women and Men." Unpublished paper presented at

The Educational Implications of Sex Roles in Transition Conference, Brown University, December, 1978.

Van Gelder, Lawrence. "Time Spent on Housework Declines," *New York Times*, January 10, 1979.

Verheyden-Hilliard, Mary Ellen. "Counseling: Potential Superbomb Against Sexism," *American Education*, April, 1977.

Wells, Patricia. "Food and the Working Wife," *New York Times*, May 23, 1979.

Wenkart, Antonia. "Self-Acceptance," *American Journal of Psychoanalysis*, vol. 15, no. 2, 1955.

Wernimont, Paul F., and Fitzpatrick, Susan. "The Meaning of Money," *Psychiatry*, vol. 56, no. 2, 1972.

Wexler, Joan, and Steidl, John. "Marriage and the Capacity to Be Alone," *Psychiatry*, vol. 41, February, 1978.

Willig, Wanda. "Dreams," *American Journal of Psychoanalysis*, vol. 18, no. 2, 1958.

Willoughby, Raymond R. "The Relationship to Emotionality of Age, Sex, and Conjugal Condition," *American Journal of Sociology*, vol. 43, March, 1938.

"Women and Success: Why Some Find It So Painful," *New York Times*, January 28, 1978.

"Women at Work: Still Fighting Stereotyped Roles?" *U.S. News and World Report*, January 15, 1979, p. 73.

"Working Women: Joys and Sorrows," *Ibid.*, p. 64.

Wright, James D. "Are Working Women *Really* More Satisfied? Evidence from Several National Surveys," *Journal of Marriage and the Family*, May, 1978.

Wyer, R. S., Jr.; Henniger, M.; and Wolfson, M. "Informational Determinants of Females' Self-Attributions and Observers' Judgments of Them in an Achievement Situation," *Journal of Personality and Social Psychology*, vol. 32, 1975, pp. 556–570.

Yollin, Patricia. "When Suddenly a Housewife Isn't," *California Living*, May 7, 1978.

Zimmerman, Don H., and West, Candace. "Sex Roles, Interruptions and Silences in Conversation," in Barrie Thorne and Nancy Henley, eds. *Language and Sex: Difference and Dominance*. Rowley, Massachusetts: Newbury House, 1975.

About the Author

Colette Dowling came to New York in 1958 as a winner of the *Mademoiselle* Guest Editor Contest. She worked on the magazine's staff for four years and shortly thereafter began a free-lance writing career. Since then she has had over a hundred articles published in such magazines as *Harper's*, *The New York Times Magazine*, *Esquire*, *Redbook*, *New York*, and *The Saturday Review*.

In addition to writing books of her own (*The Skin Game* and *How to Love a Member of the Opposite Sex: A Memoir*), she is a co-principal with Lowell Miller of The Print Project, which conceives and packages books that are researched and written by others.

Colette lives and works in Rhinebeck, New York. She has three teen-age children.